365

Favorite Brand Name ™

SLOW COOKER

■ RECIPES & MORE ■

PUBLICATIONS INTERNATIONAL, LTD.

Microwave Cooking: Microwave ovens vary in wattage. Use the cooking times as guidelines and check for doneness before adding more time.

365
Favorite Brand Name ™
SLOW COOKER
▪ RECIPES & MORE ▪

Slow Cooker
Basics

Slow cookers can prepare just about any type of food you can imagine. Hearty soups and stews, creative chicken, pork and beef recipes, exciting party ideas and old-fashioned breads and desserts are all included in this publication. Inviting the family over for a relaxed Sunday afternoon meal? Surprise them with Coq au Vin. Have a case of the winter blues? A comforting beef stew is just the thing. Need an easy dessert? Poached Fruit & Nut Baked Apples fit the bill. By following these easy and enticing recipes, you can prepare wonderful meals without a lot of fuss, bother or time.

Slow cookers were introduced in the 1970's and are finding renewed popularity in the 1990's. Considering the hectic pace of today's lifestyle, it's no wonder so many people have rediscovered this time-saving kitchen helper. Spend a few minutes preparing the ingredients, turn on the slow cooker and relax. Low heat and long cooking times take the stress out of meal preparation. Leave for work or a day of leisure and come home 4, 8 or even 10 hours later to a hot, delicious meal.

ABOUT SLOW COOKERS

The original and best-selling slow cooker is the The Rival Company's CROCK-POT® Slow Cooker. The name "CROCK-POT®" is often used interchangeably with "slow cooker." There are two types of slow cookers. The most popular models, including the CROCK-POT® Slow Cooker,

Slow cookers come in a variety of sizes and styles.

SLOW COOKER BASICS

have heat coils circling the crockery insert, allowing heat to surround the food and cook evenly. The LOW (about 200°F) and HIGH (about 300°F) settings regulate cooking temperatures. One hour on HIGH equals 2 to 2½ hours on LOW. Less common models of slow cookers have heat coils only on the bottom and have an adjustable thermostat. If you own this type, consult your manufacturer's instructions for advice on converting the recipes in this cookbook.

THE BENEFITS
• No need for constant attention or frequent stirring

• No worry about burning or overcooking

• No sink full of pots and pans to scrub at the end of a long day

• Great for parties and buffets

• Keeps your kitchen cool by keeping your oven turned off

• Saves energy—cooking on the low setting uses less energy than most light bulbs

THE BASICS
• As with conventional cooking recipes, slow cooker recipe time ranges are provided to account for variables such as temperature of ingredients before cooking, how full the slow cooker is and even altitude. Once you become familiar with your slow cooker, you'll have a good idea which end of the range to use.

• Manufacturers recommend that slow cookers should be one-half to three-quarters full for best results.

• Keep a lid on it! The slow cooker can take as long as twenty minutes to regain the heat lost when the cover is removed. If the recipe calls for stirring or checking the dish near the end of the cooking time, replace the lid as quickly as you can.

• To clean your slow cooker, follow the manufacturer's instructions. To make cleanup even easier, spray with nonstick cooking spray before adding food.

• Always taste the finished dish before serving to adjust seasonings to your preference. Consider adding a dash of the following: salt, pepper, seasoned salt, seasoned herb blends, lemon juice, soy sauce, Worcestershire sauce, flavored vinegar, freshly ground pepper or minced fresh herbs.

TIPS AND TECHNIQUES
Adapting Recipes: If you'd like to adapt your own favorite recipe to a slow cooker, you'll need to follow a few guidelines. First, try to find a similar slow cooker recipe in this publication or your manufacturer's guide. Note the cooking times, liquid, quantity and size of meat and vegetable pieces. Because the slow cooker captures moisture, you will want to reduce the amount of liquid, often by as much as half. Add dairy products toward the end of the cooking time so they do not curdle. Follow the chart on page 6 to estimate the cooking time you will need.

SLOW COOKER BASICS

TIME GUIDE

If Recipe Says:	Cook on Low:*	or	Cook on High:
15 to 30 minutes	4 to 6 hours		1½ to 2 hours
35 to 45 minutes	6 to 10 hours		3 to 4 hours
50 minutes to 3 hours	8 to 18 hours		4 to 6 hours

*Most uncooked meat and vegetable combinations will require at least 8 hours on LOW
Reprinted with permission from Rival's Crock-Pot® Slow cooker instruction book.

Selecting the Right Meat: A good tip to keep in mind while shopping is that you can, and in fact should, use tougher, inexpensive cuts of meat. Top-quality cuts, such as loin chops or filet mignon, fall apart during long cooking periods and therefore are not great choices to use in the slow cooker. Keep those for roasting, broiling or grilling and save money when you use your slow cooker. You will be amazed to find even the toughest cuts come out fork-tender and flavorful.

Reducing Fat: The slow cooker can help you make lower-fat meals because you won't be cooking in fat as you do when you stir-fry and sauté. And tougher, inexpensive cuts of meat have less fat than prime cuts. Many recipes call for trimming excess fat from meat.

If you do use fatty cuts of meat, such as ribs, consider browning them first on top of the range to cook off excess fat before adding them to the slow cooker.

Chicken skin tends to shrivel and curl in the slow cooker, so most recipes call for skinless chicken. If you use skin-on pieces, brown them before adding them to the slow cooker. If you would rather remove the skin, use the following technique. Freeze the chicken until firm, but not hard. (Do not refreeze thawed chicken.) Grasp the skin with a clean cotton kitchen towel or paper towel and pull away from meat; discard skin. When finished skinning chicken, launder towel before using it again.

You can easily remove most of the fat from accumulated juices, soups and canned broths. The simplest way is to refrigerate the liquid for several hours or overnight. The fat will congeal and float to the top for easy removal. If you plan to use the liquid right away, ladle it into a bowl or measuring cup. Let it stand about 5 minutes so the fat can rise to the surface. Skim with a large spoon. You can also lightly pull a sheet of clean paper towel over the surface, letting the

SLOW COOKER BASICS

grease be absorbed. To degrease canned broth, refrigerate the unopened can. Simply spoon the congealed fat off the surface after opening the can.

Cutting Your Vegetables: Vegetables often take longer to cook than meats. Cut vegetables into small, thin pieces and place them near the bottom or sides of the slow cooker. Pay careful attention to the recipe instructions in order to cut vegetables to the proper size so they will cook in the amount of time given.

Food Safety Tips: If you do any advance preparation, such as trimming meat or cutting vegetables, make sure you then cover and refrigerate the food until you are ready to start cooking. Store uncooked meats and vegetables separately. If you are preparing meat, poultry or fish, remember to wash your cutting board, utensils and hands with soap and hot water before touching other foods.

Once your dish is cooked, don't keep it in the slow cooker too long. Foods need to be kept cooler than 40°F or hotter than 140°F to avoid the growth of harmful bacteria. Remove food to a clean container, cover and refrigerate as soon as possible. *Do not reheat leftovers in the slow cooker.* Use a microwave oven, the range-top or the oven for reheating.

Foil to the Rescue: To easily lift a dish or a meatloaf out of the slow cooker, make foil handles according to the following directions.

Tear off three 18×3-inch styrips of heavy-duty foil. Crisscross strips so they resemble spokes of a wheel. Place your dish or food in center of strips.

Pull foil strips up and over and place into slow cooker. Leave them in while you cook so you can easily lift item out again when ready.

By following these simple techniques and using the exciting recipes in this cookbook, you will soon be preparing wonderful dishes with minimal effort.

Slow Cooker
Super Starters

1 CAPONATA

1 medium eggplant (about 1 pound),
   peeled and cut into ½-inch pieces
1 can (14½ ounces) diced Italian plum
   tomatoes, undrained
1 medium onion, chopped
1 red bell pepper, cut into ½-inch pieces
½ cup prepared medium-hot salsa
¼ cup extra-virgin olive oil
2 tablespoons capers, drained
2 tablespoons balsamic vinegar
3 cloves garlic, minced
1 teaspoon dried oregano leaves
¼ teaspoon salt
⅓ cup packed fresh basil, cut into thin
   strips
   Toasted sliced Italian or French bread

MIX all ingredients except basil and bread in
slow cooker. Cover and cook on LOW 7 to 8
hours or until vegetables are crisp-tender.
Stir in basil. Serve at room temperature on
toasted bread.   *Makes about 5¼ cups*

2 HOT BROCCOLI–
CHEESE DIP

¾ cup butter
3 stalks celery, thinly sliced
1 medium onion, chopped
1 can (4 ounces) sliced mushrooms,
   drained
3 tablespoons flour
1 can (10½ ounces) condensed cream of
   celery soup
1 package (10 ounces) frozen broccoli
   spears or chopped broccoli, thawed
1 garlic cheese roll (5 to 6 ounces), cut up

In small skillet, melt butter and sauté celery,
onion and mushrooms. Stir in flour. Turn
into lightly greased CROCK-POT®; stir in
remaining ingredients. Cover and cook on
High, stirring about every 15 minutes, until
cheese is melted. Turn to Low about 2 to 4
hours or until ready to serve. Serve hot with
corn chips, raw cauliflowerets, carrot strips,
celery chunks and radishes.

   Makes about 1 quart

Caponata

3 CHICKEN WINGS IN HONEY SAUCE

3 pounds chicken wings (16 wings)
  Salt and black pepper to taste
2 cups honey
1 cup soy sauce
½ cup ketchup
¼ cup oil
2 cloves garlic, minced
  Sesame seeds (optional)

Rinse chicken and pat dry. Cut off and discard wing tips. Cut each wing at joint to make two sections. Sprinkle wing parts with salt and pepper. Place wings on broiler pan. Broil 4 to 5 inches from heat 20 minutes, 10 minutes a side or until chicken is brown. Transfer chicken to CROCK-POT®.

For sauce, combine honey, soy sauce, ketchup, oil and garlic in bowl. Pour over chicken wings. Cover and cook on Low 4 to 5 hours or on High 2 to 2½ hours. Garnish with sesame seeds, if desired.

Makes about 32 appetizers

4 MARINERS' FONDUE

2 cans (10¾ ounces each) condensed
  cream of celery soup
2 cups grated sharp processed cheese
1 cup chunked cooked lobster
½ cup chopped cooked shrimp
½ cup chopped cooked crabmeat
¼ cup finely chopped cooked scallops
  Dash paprika
  Dash cayenne pepper
1 loaf French bread, cut into 1-inch cubes

Combine all ingredients except bread cubes in lightly greased CROCK-POT®; stir thoroughly. Cover and cook on High 1 hour or until cheese is melted. Turn to Low for serving. Using fondue forks, dip bread cubes into fondue.   *Makes about 1½ quarts*

Chicken Wings in Honey Sauce

5 BARBECUED MEATBALLS

2 pounds lean ground beef
1⅓ cups ketchup, divided
3 tablespoons seasoned dry bread crumbs
1 egg, slightly beaten
2 tablespoons dried onion flakes
¾ teaspoon garlic salt
½ teaspoon black pepper
1 cup packed brown sugar
1 can (6 ounces) tomato paste
¼ cup reduced-sodium soy sauce
¼ cup cider vinegar
1½ teaspoons hot pepper sauce
   Diced bell peppers (optional)

PREHEAT oven to 350°F. Combine ground beef, ⅓ cup ketchup, bread crumbs, egg, onion flakes, garlic salt and black pepper in medium bowl. Mix lightly but thoroughly; shape into 1-inch meatballs. Place meatballs in two 15×10-inch jelly-roll pans or shallow roasting pans. Bake 18 minutes or until browned. Transfer meatballs to slow cooker.

MIX remaining 1 cup ketchup, sugar, tomato paste, soy sauce, vinegar and hot pepper sauce in medium bowl. Pour over meatballs. Cover and cook on LOW 4 hours. Serve with cocktail picks. Garnish with bell peppers, if desired.   *Makes about 4 dozen meatballs*

VARIATION: For Barbecued Franks, arrange 2 (12-ounce) packages or 3 (8-ounce) packages cocktail franks in slow cooker. Combine 1 cup ketchup with sugar, tomato paste, soy sauce, vinegar and hot pepper sauce; pour over franks. Cook according to directions for Barbecued Meatballs.

6 "HOT" CHEESE AND BACON DIP

16 slices bacon, diced
2 packages (8 ounces each) cream cheese, softened, cut into cubes
4 cups mild shredded Cheddar cheese
1 cup half-and-half
2 teaspoons Worcestershire sauce
1 teaspoon dry minced onion
½ teaspoon dry mustard
½ teaspoon salt
2 to 3 drops hot pepper sauce

Fry bacon in skillet until crisp; drain on paper towels and set aside. Place cream cheese, Cheddar cheese, half-and-half, Worcestershire sauce, minced onion, mustard, salt and hot pepper sauce in CROCK-POT®. Set on Low and allow cheese to melt, stirring occasionally about 1 hour. Taste and adjust seasonings. Stir in bacon and serve directly from CROCK-POT®. Serve with apple or pear slices or French bread slices.

TIP: If serving with fruit slices, dip slices in lemon juice to prevent browning.

Barbecued Meatballs

SLOW COOKER SUPER STARTERS

7 PARTY MIX

3 cups bite-size rice cereal
2 cups O-shaped oat cereal
2 cups bite-size shredded wheat cereal
1 cup peanuts, pecans or cashews
1 cup thin pretzel sticks (optional)
½ cup butter or margarine, melted
4 tablespoons Worcestershire sauce
   Dash hot pepper sauce
½ teaspoon seasoned salt
½ teaspoon garlic salt
½ teaspoon onion salt

Combine cereals, nuts and pretzels in CROCK-POT®. Mix melted butter with remaining ingredients in small bowl; pour over cereal mixture in CROCK-POT® and toss lightly to coat. *Do not cover CROCK-POT®.* Cook on High 2 hours, stirring well every 30 minutes; turn to Low 2 to 6 hours. Store in airtight container.

Makes 10 cups

8 CHICKEN WINGS IN BBQ SAUCE

3 pounds chicken wings (16 wings)
   Salt and black pepper to taste
1½ cups any variety barbecue sauce
¼ cup honey
2 teaspoons prepared mustard or spicy mustard
2 teaspoons Worcestershire sauce
   Hot pepper sauce to taste (optional)

Rinse chicken and pat dry. Cut off and discard wing tips. Cut each wing at joint to make two sections. Sprinkle wing parts with salt and pepper. Place wings on broiler pan. Broil 4 to 5 inches from heat 20 minutes, 10 minutes a side or until chicken is brown. Transfer chicken to CROCK-POT®.

For sauce, combine barbecue sauce, honey, mustard, Worcestershire sauce and hot pepper sauce, if desired, in small mixing bowl. Pour over chicken wings. Cover and cook on Low 4 to 5 hours or on High 2 to 2½ hours. Serve directly from CROCK-POT®.

Makes about 32 appetizers

Party Mix

SLOW COOKER SUPER STARTERS

9 CHILI CON QUESO

1 pound pasteurized process cheese
  spread, cut into cubes
1 can (10 ounces) diced tomatoes and
  green chiles, undrained
1 cup sliced green onions
2 teaspoons ground coriander
2 teaspoons ground cumin
¾ teaspoon hot pepper sauce
  Green onion strips (optional)
  Hot pepper slices (optional)

COMBINE all ingredients except green onion strips and hot pepper slices in slow cooker until well blended. Cover and cook on LOW 2 to 3 hours or until hot.* Garnish with green onion strips and hot pepper slices, if desired.   *Makes 3 cups*

COOK'S NOOK: Serve Chili con Queso with tortilla chips. Or, for something different, cut pita bread into triangles and toast in preheated 400°F oven for 5 minutes or until crisp.

* Chili will be very hot; use caution when serving.

10 CHICKEN WINGS IN TERIYAKI SAUCE

3 pounds chicken wings (16 wings)
1 large onion, chopped
1 cup brown sugar
1 cup soy sauce
¼ cup dry cooking sherry
2 teaspoons ground ginger
2 cloves garlic, minced

Rinse chicken and pat dry. Cut off and discard wing tips. Cut each wing at joint to make two sections. Place wing parts on broiler pan. Broil 4 to 5 inches from heat 20 minutes, 10 minutes a side or until chicken is brown. Transfer chicken to CROCK-POT®.

Mix together onion, brown sugar, soy sauce, cooking sherry, ginger and garlic in bowl. Pour over chicken wings. Cover and cook on Low 5 to 6 hours or on High 2 to 3 hours. Stir chicken wings once to ensure wings are evenly coated with sauce. Serve from CROCK-POT®.

Makes about 32 appetizers

Chili con Queso

SLOW COOKER SUPER STARTERS

11 HAMBURGER DIP

2 pounds lean ground beef
1 cup chopped onion
2 cans (8 ounces each) tomato sauce
2 packages (8 ounces each) cream cheese, softened, cut into cubes
²/₃ cup grated Parmesan cheese
½ cup ketchup
2 cloves garlic, minced *or* ¼ teaspoon garlic powder
2 teaspoons white granulated sugar
1½ teaspoons oregano
1 teaspoon mild chili powder
Salt to taste

In large skillet, brown ground beef with onion; drain fat. Pour browned meat and onion into CROCK-POT®. Add tomato sauce, cream cheese, Parmesan cheese, ketchup, garlic, sugar, oregano, chili powder and salt. Set CROCK-POT® on Low 1½ to 2 hours or until cream cheese has melted and is thoroughly blended. Stir, taste and adjust seasoning if desired. Serve with cubed French bread or tortilla chips.

If spicier dip is desired, use hot chili powder in place of mild chili powder.

12 BBQ MEATBALLS

MEATBALLS
2 pounds ground beef
1 cup onion flavored bread crumbs or plain-flavored crumbs
2 packages onion soup mix
2 teaspoons Worcestershire sauce
1 teaspoon garlic powder
2 eggs

In large bowl, combine all ingredients. Shape into meatballs. Brown in skillet with 1 tablespoon oil. Drain on paper towel.

Makes about 60 meatballs

BBQ SAUCE
2 cans (6 ounces each) tomato paste
2 large onions, chopped
½ cup brown sugar
½ cup sweet pickle relish
½ cup beef broth
2 cloves garlic, minced
¼ cup Worcestershire sauce
¼ cup red wine vinegar
2 teaspoons salt
2 teaspoons dry mustard

Add sauce ingredients to CROCK-POT® and stir well. Place meatballs in CROCK-POT® and cook on Low 5 to 6 hours or on High 2 to 3 hours or until hot. Serve directly from CROCK-POT®.

13 HOT REFRIED BEAN DIP

1 can (16 ounces) refried beans, drained
  and mashed
¼ pound lean ground beef
3 tablespoons bacon fat
1 pound processed American cheese,
  cubed
1 to 3 tablespoons taco sauce
1 tablespoon taco spice
  Garlic salt

In large skillet, brown beans and ground beef in bacon fat. Add to CROCK-POT®. Stir in remaining ingredients. Cover and cook on High 1 to 2 hours or until cheese is melted, stirring occasionally. Turn to Low until ready to serve, up to 6 hours. Serve with warm tortilla chips.   *Makes about 1½ quarts*

14 SPICY FRANKS

1 cup ketchup
¼ cup firmly packed light brown sugar
1 tablespoon red wine vinegar
2 teaspoons soy sauce
2 teaspoons Dijon-style mustard
⅛ teaspoon garlic powder
1 pound frankfurters, cut into 1-inch
    pieces or 1 pound cocktail wieners or
    smoked sausages

Place ketchup, brown sugar, vinegar, soy sauce, mustard and garlic powder in CROCK-POT® Cover and cook on High until blended, 1 to 2 hours. Stir in frankfurters. Cook 1 to 2 hours or until thoroughly heated. Turn to Low to keep warm and serve from CROCK-POT®.

15 ORANGE–CIDER PUNCH

6 cups orange juice
2 cups apple cider or apple juice
1 cup sugar
2 cinnamon sticks
1 whole nutmeg
2 cups vodka (optional)

Mix all ingredients except vodka in CROCK-POT®; stir well. Cover and cook on Low 4 to 10 hours or on High 2 to 3 hours. Just before serving, stir in vodka. Serve hot, in punch cups.
Makes 10 to 15 servings (about 2½ quarts)

16 HOT SPICED CHERRY CIDER

3½ quarts apple cider
2 cinnamon sticks
2 packages (3 ounces each) cherry-
    flavored gelatin

In 4-, 5- or 6-quart CROCK-POT®, mix together apple cider and cinnamon sticks. Heat on High 3 hours. Stir in cherry-flavored gelatin. Keep on High 1 more hour and allow gelatin to dissolve. Turn to Low to keep warm. Serve directly from CROCK-POT®.

SLOW COOKER SUPER STARTERS

17 MULLED WINE

2 bottles (750 ml each) dry red wine, such as Cabernet Sauvignon
1 cup light corn syrup
1 cup water
1 square (8 inches) double-thickness cheesecloth
  Peel of 1 large orange
1 cinnamon stick, broken into halves
8 whole cloves
1 whole nutmeg

COMBINE wine, corn syrup and water in slow cooker. Rinse cheesecloth; squeeze out water. Wrap orange peel, cinnamon stick halves, cloves and nutmeg in cheesecloth. Tie securely with cotton string or strip of cheesecloth. Add to slow cooker. Cover and cook on HIGH 2 to 2½ hours. Discard spice bag; ladle into mugs.   *Makes 12 servings*

18 HOT SPICED WINE

2 bottles dry red wine
3 apples, peeled, cored and thinly sliced
½ cup sugar
1 teaspoon lemon juice
2 cinnamon sticks
3 whole cloves

Combine all ingredients in CROCK-POT®; stir well. Cover and cook on Low 4 to 12 hours or on High 1 to 2 hours. Serve hot, in punch cups or mugs.
      Makes 6 to 8 servings (about 2 quarts)

19 HOT CRANBERRY TEA

1 package (8 ounces) fresh cranberries
3 quarts water, divided
2 cups sugar
1 cup cinnamon red hots
24 whole cloves
3 cinnamon sticks
  Juice from 3 oranges
  Juice from 3 lemons

Boil cranberries in 1 quart of water 10 minutes; set aside. Mix in 4-, 5- or 6-quart CROCK-POT®, 2 quarts water, sugar, red hots, cloves and cinnamon sticks; cover and heat on High approximately 1 hour or until red hots dissolve. Strain cranberry mixture and stir liquid into CROCK-POT®. Mix in juice from oranges and lemons. Cover and heat on High 2 hours, turn to Low to keep warm and serve directly from CROCK-POT®.

Mulled Wine

SLOW COOKER SUPER STARTERS

20 MOCHA SUPREME

2 quarts brewed strong coffee
½ cup instant hot chocolate beverage mix
1 cinnamon stick, broken into halves
1 cup whipping cream
1 tablespoon powdered sugar

PLACE coffee, hot chocolate mix and cinnamon stick halves in slow cooker; stir. Cover and cook on HIGH 2 to 2½ hours or until hot. Remove and discard cinnamon stick halves.

BEAT cream in medium bowl with electric mixer on high speed until soft peaks form. Add powdered sugar; beat until stiff peaks form. Ladle hot beverage into mugs; top with whipped cream.   *Makes 8 servings*

COOK'S NOOK: You can whip cream faster if you first chill the beaters and bowls in the freezer for 15 minutes.

21 WARM FRUIT PUNCH

8 cups water
1 can (12 ounces) frozen cranberry-raspberry juice concentrate, thawed
1 can (12 ounces) frozen orange juice concentrate, thawed
1 can (6 ounces) frozen lemonade concentrate, thawed
½ cup sugar
4 cinnamon sticks
¼ teaspoon whole cloves
¼ teaspoon whole allspice
   Thin orange slice halves, unpeeled, for garnish

In 6-quart CROCK-POT®, combine all ingredients. (The spices can be tied in a cheesecloth and placed in punch, if desired.) Cover and heat on High 3 hours, then turn to Low. Remove spices from CROCK-POT® with small strainer or slotted spoon. Serve directly from CROCK-POT®. Garnish with orange slice halves, if desired.

Mocha Supreme

SLOW COOKER SUPER STARTERS

22 MULLED APPLE CIDER

2 quarts bottled apple cider or juice (not unfiltered)
¼ cup packed brown sugar
1 square (8 inches) double-thickness cheesecloth
8 allspice berries
4 cinnamon sticks, broken into halves
12 whole cloves
1 large orange
Additional cinnamon sticks (optional)

COMBINE apple cider and brown sugar in slow cooker. Rinse cheesecloth; squeeze out water. Wrap allspice berries and cinnamon stick halves in cheesecloth; tie securely with cotton string or strip of cheesecloth. Stick cloves randomly into orange; cut orange into quarters. Place spice bag and orange quarters in cider mixture. Cover and cook on HIGH 2½ to 3 hours. Once cooked, cider may be turned to LOW and kept warm up to 3 additional hours. Discard spice bag and orange; ladle cider into mugs. Garnish with additional cinnamon sticks, if desired.

Makes 10 servings

TIP: To make inserting cloves into the orange a little easier, first pierce the orange skin with the point of wooden skewer. Remove the skewer and insert a clove.

23 HOT CRANBERRY PUNCH

4 cups unsweetened pineapple juice
4 cups cranberry juice
½ cup packed brown sugar
1 cup water
1 teaspoon whole cloves *and* 1 cinnamon stick tied in cheesecloth
1 to 2 cups vodka

Combine all ingredients except vodka in CROCK-POT®. Cover and cook on Low 4 to 10 hours. Add vodka before serving. Serve hot, in punch cups.
Makes 10 to 15 servings (about 2½ quarts)

24 SPICY PEACH PUNCH

1 jar (46 ounces) peach nectar
1 jar (20 ounces) orange juice
2 tablespoons plus ½ cup light brown sugar
1 cinnamon stick
¾ teaspoon whole cloves
1 tablespoon lime juice

Combine peach nectar, orange juice and 2 tablespoons sugar in CROCK-POT®. Tie spices in cheesecloth bag or add loosely to punch. Cover and set on Low 2 hours or on High 1 hour. Stir in ½ cup sugar and lime juice. Allow sugar to dissolve, approximately 30 minutes. Adjust to taste. Turn to Low to keep punch warm. Serve from CROCK-POT®.

Mulled Apple Cider

Slow Cooker
Main Dishes

25 FAVORITE BEEF STEW

3 carrots, cut lengthwise into halves, then cut into 1-inch pieces
3 ribs celery, cut into 1-inch pieces
2 large potatoes, peeled and cut into ½-inch pieces
1½ cups chopped onions
3 cloves garlic, chopped
1 bay leaf
1½ tablespoons Worcestershire sauce
¾ teaspoon dried thyme leaves
¾ teaspoon dried basil leaves
½ teaspoon black pepper
2 pounds lean beef stew meat, cut into 1-inch pieces
1 can (about 14 ounces) diced tomatoes, undrained
1 can (about 14 ounces) reduced-sodium beef broth
¼ cup all-purpose flour
½ cup cold water

LAYER ingredients in slow cooker in the following order: carrots, celery, potatoes, onions, garlic, bay leaf, Worcestershire sauce, thyme, basil, pepper, beef, tomatoes with juice and broth. Cover and cook on LOW 8 to 9 hours.

REMOVE beef and vegetables to large serving bowl; cover and keep warm. Remove and discard bay leaf. Turn slow cooker to HIGH; cover. Mix flour and water in small bowl until smooth. Add ½ cup cooking liquid; mix well. Stir flour mixture into slow cooker. Cover and cook 15 minutes or until thickened. Pour sauce over meat and vegetables. Serve immediately.

Makes 6 to 8 servings

Favorite Beef Stew

SLOW COOKER MAIN DISHES

26 BEEF FAJITAS

1½ pounds beef flank steak
1 cup chopped onion
1 green bell pepper, cut into ½-inch
    pieces
1 jalapeño pepper,* chopped
1 tablespoon cilantro
2 cloves garlic, minced *or* ¼ teaspoon
    garlic powder
1 teaspoon chili powder
1 teaspoon ground cumin
1 teaspoon ground coriander
½ teaspoon salt
1 can (8 ounces) chopped tomatoes
12 (8-inch) flour tortillas
    Toppings: sour cream, guacamole,
    shredded Cheddar cheese, salsa

** If using fresh jalapeño peppers, be very careful
when handling. Wear rubber gloves if possible as
jalapeño peppers contain a volatile oil that will burn
if left in direct contact with the skin. Wash hands
immediately after handling.*

Cut flank steak into 6 portions. In any size
CROCK-POT®, combine meat, onion, green
bell pepper, jalapeño pepper, cilantro, garlic,
chili powder, cumin, coriander and salt. Add
tomatoes. Cover and cook on Low 8 to 10
hours or on High 4 to 5 hours.

Remove meat from CROCK-POT® and shred
with fork. Return meat to CROCK-POT® and
stir. To serve fajitas, spread meat mixture
into flour tortillas and top with above
mentioned toppings, if desired. Roll up
tortillas.　　　　　*Makes 12 servings*

27 HEARTY BEEF RAGOÛT

3 pounds boneless beef chuck, cut into
    1-inch pieces
½ cup all-purpose flour
1 teaspoon salt
¼ teaspoon black pepper
1 package (8 ounces) precooked sausage
    links, cut into 1-inch pieces
2 cups chopped leeks
3 to 4 stalks celery, cut up
3 potatoes, peeled and cubed
1 can (16 ounces) whole tomatoes
1 teaspoon dried oregano leaves
2 cloves garlic, minced
½ cup beef broth
1 teaspoon Kitchen Bouquet
2 tablespoons all-purpose flour
3 tablespoons water

Wipe beef well. Combine ½ cup flour with
salt and pepper. Toss beef cubes with flour
mixture to coat thoroughly; place in CROCK-
POT®. Add remaining ingredients except 2
tablespoons flour and water in order listed;
stir well. Cover and cook on Low 8 to 12
hours or on High 4 to 6 hours.

One hour before serving, turn to High
setting. Make smooth paste with 2
tablespoons flour and water; stir into
CROCK-POT®, mixing well. Cover and cook
until thickened.　　　　　*Makes 8 servings*

Beef Fajita

SLOW COOKER MAIN DISHES

28 TACO BAKE

1 pound ground beef
1 onion, chopped
¾ cup water
1 package (1¼ ounces) taco seasoning
1 can (15 ounces) tomato sauce
1 package (8 ounces) shell macaroni, uncooked
1 can (4 ounces) mild chopped green chilies
2 cups mild shredded Cheddar cheese

In large skillet, brown ground beef and onion; drain fat. Add water, taco seasoning and tomato sauce; mix. Simmer 20 minutes. Transfer to CROCK-POT®. Stir in macaroni and chopped green chilies. Cover and cook on Low 6 to 8 hours or on High 3 to 4 hours. In last 30 minutes of cooking, top with shredded Cheddar cheese.

Makes 6 to 8 servings

29 MACARONI AND BEEF

1½ pounds lean ground beef
2 cups uncooked macaroni
2 cans (10¾ ounces each) condensed tomato soup
1 can (16 ounces) whole-kernel corn, drained
½ medium onion, chopped
1 can (4 ounces) sliced mushrooms, drained
Salt and black pepper

In skillet, brown ground beef; drain well. Put into CROCK-POT®. Cook macaroni according to package directions until barely tender; drain well. Add macaroni and remaining ingredients to CROCK-POT®. Stir just enough to blend. Cover and cook on Low 7 to 9 hours or on High 3 to 4 hours.

Makes 4 to 6 servings

30 SWISS STEAK

2 pounds beef round steak, about 1 inch thick
¼ cup all-purpose flour
1 teaspoon salt
1 stalk celery, chopped
2 carrots, pared and chopped
¼ cup chopped onion
½ teaspoon Worcestershire sauce
1 can (8 ounces) tomato sauce
½ cup grated processed American cheese (optional)

Cut steak into 4 serving pieces. Dredge in flour mixed with salt; place in CROCK-POT®. Add chopped vegetables and Worcestershire sauce. Pour tomato sauce over meat and vegetables. Cover and cook on Low 8 to 10 hours or on High 4 to 5 hours.

Just before serving, sprinkle with grated cheese.

Recipe may be doubled for 5-quart CROCK-POT®. Cook the maximum time.

Makes 4 servings

SLOW COOKER MAIN DISHES

31 STUFFED CABBAGE

12 large cabbage leaves
4 cups water
1 pound lean ground beef or lamb
½ cup cooked rice
½ teaspoon salt
¼ teaspoon dried thyme leaves
¼ teaspoon ground nutmeg
¼ teaspoon ground cinnamon
⅛ teaspoon black pepper
1 can (6 ounces) tomato paste
¾ cup water

Wash cabbage leaves. Boil 4 cups water. Turn heat off. Soak leaves in water 5 minutes. Remove, drain and cool.

Combine remaining ingredients except tomato paste and water. Place 2 tablespoons mixture on each leaf and roll firmly. Stack in CROCK-POT®. Combine tomato paste and water and pour over stuffed cabbage. Cover and cook on Low 8 to 10 hours.

Makes 6 servings

32 GOOD 'N' EASY STEW

3 pounds lean stewing beef, cut into 1½-inch cubes
1 can (10½ ounces) condensed cream of mushroom soup or cream of celery soup
1 can (4 ounces) sliced mushrooms, drained (optional)
½ cup sauterne wine or beef broth
1 envelope (1½ ounces) dry onion soup mix

Combine all ingredients in CROCK-POT®. Cover and cook on Low 10 to 12 hours. If desired, thicken gravy with flour.

Makes 8 servings

33 BEEF ROULADES

1½ pounds beef round steak, ½ inch thick
4 slices bacon
¾ cup diced celery
¾ cup diced onion
½ cup diced green bell pepper
1 can (10 ounces) beef gravy

Cut steak into four serving pieces. Place bacon slice on each piece of meat. Mix celery, onion and green bell pepper in medium bowl; place about ½ cup mixture on each piece of meat. Roll up meat; secure ends with wooden picks.

Wipe beef rolls with paper towels. Place in CROCK-POT®. Pour gravy evenly over steaks to thoroughly moisten. Cover CROCK-POT® and cook on Low 8 to 10 hours or on High 4 to 5 hours. Skim off fat before serving.

Makes 4 servings

34 BEEF HASH

2 to 3 cups cut-up cooked beef
2 packages (10 ounces each) frozen hash brown potatoes, thawed
1 cup gravy or beef broth
1 onion, finely chopped
¼ cup butter or margarine, melted
   Salt and black pepper

Place all ingredients in CROCK-POT®. Cover and cook on Low 6 to 8 hours or on High 2 to 3 hours.

Double recipe for 5-quart CROCK-POT®.

Makes 4 servings

SLOW COOKER MAIN DISHES

35 TEXAS–STYLE BARBECUED BRISKET

1 beef brisket (3 to 4 pounds), cut into
    halves, if necessary, to fit slow cooker
3 tablespoons Worcestershire sauce
1 tablespoon chili powder
1 teaspoon celery salt
1 teaspoon black pepper
1 teaspoon liquid smoke
2 cloves garlic, minced
2 bay leaves
    Barbecue Sauce (recipe follows)

TRIM excess fat from meat and discard.
Place meat in resealable plastic food storage
bag. Combine Worcestershire sauce, chili
powder, celery salt, pepper, liquid smoke,
garlic and bay leaves in small bowl. Spread
mixture on all sides of meat; seal bag.
Refrigerate 24 hours.

PLACE meat and marinade in slow cooker.
Cover and cook on LOW 7 hours.
Meanwhile, prepare Barbecue Sauce.

REMOVE meat from slow cooker and pour
juices into 2-cup measure; let stand 5
minutes. Skim fat from juices. Remove and
discard bay leaves. Stir 1 cup of defatted
juices into Barbecue Sauce. Discard
remaining juices. Return meat and Barbecue
Sauce to slow cooker. Cover and cook 1
hour or until meat is fork-tender. Remove
meat to cutting board. Cut across grain into
1/4-inch-thick slices. Serve 2 to 3 tablespoons
Barbecue Sauce over each serving.

Makes 10 to 12 servings

BARBECUE SAUCE

2 tablespoons vegetable oil
1 medium onion, chopped
2 cloves garlic, minced
1 cup ketchup
1/2 cup molasses
1/4 cup cider vinegar
2 teaspoons chili powder
1/2 teaspoon dry mustard

HEAT oil in medium saucepan over medium
heat. Add onion and garlic; cook until onion
is tender. Add remaining ingredients.
Simmer 5 minutes. *Makes 2 1/2 cups*

36 FIVE–ALARM BEEF CHILI

1/4 cup vegetable oil or olive oil, divided
3 to 4 pounds boneless beef chuck, cut
    into pieces
2 onions, chopped
2 green bell peppers, chopped
1 cup beer
1 can (4 ounces) chopped jalapeño or
    mild chili peppers
1/3 cup chili powder
1 tablespoon dried oregano
2 teaspoons ground cumin
1 teaspoon salt

Heat 2 tablespoons oil in skillet over
medium heat. Add beef and brown all sides.
Transfer to CROCK-POT®. Add remaining 2
tablespoons oil to skillet and sauté onions
and green peppers until soft. Transfer to
CROCK-POT®. In CROCK-POT®, stir in beer,
jalapeños, chili powder, oregano, cumin and
salt. Cover and cook on Low 6 to 8 hours or
on High 3 to 4 hours. Serve.

Makes 6 to 8 servings

Texas-Style Barbecued Brisket

37 YANKEE POT ROAST AND VEGETABLES

1 beef chuck pot roast (2½ pounds)
3 medium baking potatoes (about
    1 pound), unpeeled and cut into
    quarters
2 large carrots, cut into ¾-inch slices
2 ribs celery, cut into ¾-inch slices
1 medium onion, sliced
1 large parsnip, cut into ¾-inch slices
2 bay leaves
1 teaspoon dried rosemary leaves
½ teaspoon dried thyme leaves
½ cup reduced-sodium beef broth

TRIM excess fat from meat and discard. Cut into serving pieces; sprinkle with salt and pepper. Combine vegetables, bay leaves, rosemary and thyme in slow cooker. Place beef over vegetables in slow cooker. Pour broth over beef. Cover and cook on LOW 8½ to 9 hours or until beef is fork-tender. Remove beef to serving platter. Arrange vegetables around beef. Remove and discard bay leaves. *Makes 6 servings*

COOK'S NOOK: To make gravy, ladle the juices into a 2-cup measure; let stand 5 minutes. Skim off and discard fat. Measure remaining juices and heat to boil in small saucepan. For each cup of juice, mix 2 tablespoons of flour with ¼ cup of cold water until smooth. Stir mixture into boiling juices. Stir constantly 1 minute or until thickened.

38 BAVARIAN POT ROAST

3 to 4 pounds beef arm pot roast
1 teaspoon vegetable oil
1 teaspoon salt
½ teaspoon ground ginger
⅛ teaspoon black pepper
3 whole cloves
4 medium apples, cored and quartered
1 small onion, sliced
½ cup apple juice or water
3 to 4 tablespoons all-purpose flour
3 to 4 tablespoons water

Wipe roast well and trim off excess fat. Lightly rub top of meat with oil. Dust with salt, ginger and pepper. Insert cloves in roast. Place apples and onions in CROCK-POT® and top with roast (cut roast in half, if necessary, to fit easily). Pour in apple juice. Cover and cook on Low 10 to 12 hours or on High 5 to 6 hours.

Remove roast and apples to warm platter. Turn CROCK-POT® to High. Make a smooth paste with flour and water; stir into CROCK-POT®. Cover and cook until thickened. Pour over roast. *Makes 6 to 8 servings*

Yankee Pot Roast and Vegetables

SLOW COOKER MAIN DISHES

39 BARBECUED BEEF

   3 pounds boneless chuck roast
1½ cups ketchup
 ¼ cup packed brown sugar
 ¼ cup red wine vinegar
   2 tablespoons Dijon-style mustard
   2 tablespoons Worcestershire sauce
   1 teaspoon liquid smoke flavoring
 ½ teaspoon salt
 ¼ teaspoon black pepper
 ¼ teaspoon garlic powder

Place chuck roast in CROCK-POT®. Combine remaining ingredients in mixing bowl. Pour barbecue sauce mixture over chuck roast. Cover and cook on Low 8 to 10 hours or 4 to 5 hours on High. Remove chuck roast from CROCK-POT®; shred meat with fork. Place shredded meat back in CROCK-POT®. Stir meat to evenly coat with sauce. Spoon meat onto sandwich buns and top with additional barbecue sauce if desired.

Makes 12 servings

40 BEEF STROGANOFF

1½ pounds stew meat, cut into 1-inch cubes
   1 tablespoon cooking oil
   1 jar (4 ounces) sliced mushrooms
   1 tablespoon dried minced onion
   2 cloves garlic, minced *or* ¼ teaspoon
       garlic powder
 ½ teaspoon dried crushed oregano
 ¼ teaspoon salt
 ¼ teaspoon black pepper
 ⅛ teaspoon dried crushed thyme
   1 bay leaf
1½ cups beef broth
 ⅓ cup dry cooking sherry
   1 carton (8 ounces) dairy sour cream
 ½ cup all-purpose flour
 ¼ cup water
   4 cups hot cooked noodles or rice

In large skillet, brown beef in hot oil. Drain off fat.

In CROCK-POT®, combine beef, mushrooms, onions, garlic, oregano, salt, pepper, thyme and bay leaf. Pour in beef broth and cooking sherry. Cover; cook on Low 8 to 10 hours or on High 4 to 5 hours. Discard bay leaf.

If using Low heat, turn to High heat. Mix together sour cream, flour and water. Stir about 1 cup of hot liquid into sour cream mixture. Return to cooker; stir to combine. Cover and cook on High 30 minutes or until thickened and bubbly. Serve over noodles or rice. *Makes 6 servings*

Barbecued Beef

SLOW COOKER MAIN DISHES

41 MINESTRONE HAMBURGER SOUP

1 pound lean ground beef
1 large onion, chopped
2 small potatoes, peeled and cubed
2 carrots, pared and sliced
2 stalks celery, sliced
1 can (28 ounces) whole tomatoes
1 cup shredded cabbage
1 small bay leaf
1 teaspoon salt
¼ teaspoon dried thyme leaves
¼ teaspoon dried basil leaves
¼ teaspoon black pepper
    Grated mozzarella or Parmesan cheese

Place all ingredients except cheese in CROCK-POT®; stir thoroughly. Add enough water to cover all ingredients. Cover and cook on Low 8 to 12 hours or on High 3 to 5 hours. Stir well. Serve sprinkled with cheese. *Makes 6 servings*

42 BEEF STOCK

3 beef soup bones
1 to 2 onions, chopped
1 to 2 carrots, pared and chopped
2 stalks celery, chopped
2 tablespoons dried parsley flakes
2 teaspoons salt
2 peppercorns

Place all ingredients in CROCK-POT®. Add enough water to cover all ingredients. Cover and cook on Low 12 to 24 hours or on High 4 to 6 hours. If cooked on High, the stock will be lighter in color and less concentrated. Strain and refrigerate. Keeps well 4 to 5 days or may be frozen.
Makes 8 cups strained stock

VEAL STOCK: Substitute veal bones for beef bones.

43 FLANK STEAK TERIYAKI

2 pounds beef flank steak
6 slices canned juice-packed pineapple
    (reserve ½ cup juice)
2 tablespoons soy sauce
2 tablespoons brown sugar
1 tablespoon dry sherry
1 teaspoon Worcestershire sauce
½ teaspoon ground ginger
2 chicken boullion cubes
1½ cups boiling water
1 cup uncooked long-grain converted rice

Roll flank steak; tie and cut into 6 individual steaks. In shallow bowl, stir together pineapple juice, soy sauce, sugar, sherry, Worcestershire sauce and ginger. Marinate steaks about 1 hour in soy mixture at room temperature. Dissolve boullion cubes in boiling water; combine with rice and ½ cup of soy mixture in CROCK-POT®. Top each steak with pineapple ring, then place in CROCK-POT®. Cover and cook on Low 8 to 10 hours or on High 3 to 4 hours.
Makes 6 servings

SLOW COOKER MAIN DISHES

44 MEAT LOAF ITALIAN–STYLE

1 can (8 ounces) pizza sauce, divided
1 beaten egg
½ cup chopped onion
½ cup chopped green bell pepper
⅓ cup dry seasoned bread crumbs
½ teaspoon garlic salt
¼ teaspoon black pepper
1½ pounds ground beef
1 cup shredded mozzarella cheese

Reserve ⅓ cup pizza sauce; cover and refrigerate. In bowl, combine remaining pizza sauce and egg. Stir in onion, green bell pepper, bread crumbs, garlic salt and black pepper. Add ground beef and mix well.

Form meat mixture into a loaf and place on 3 strips of foil as described on page 7. Transfer loaf to any size CROCK-POT®. Cover and cook on Low 8 to 10 hours or on High 4 to 6 hours. To ensure doneness, insert meat thermometer into center of loaf; internal temperature should read 170°F.

Spread loaf with reserved ⅓ cup pizza sauce. Sprinkle with mozzarella cheese. Cover and let cook 15 minutes more or until cheese is melted. Using foil strips, lift loaf from CROCK-POT® and transfer to serving plate. Discard foil strips. Serve.

Makes 8 servings

45 AMERICA'S FAVORITE POT ROAST

3 to 4 pounds beef arm or boneless pot roast
¼ cup all-purpose flour
2 teaspoons salt
⅛ teaspoon black pepper
3 potatoes, peeled and quartered
3 carrots, pared, sliced lengthwise and cut into 2-inch pieces
2 small onions, sliced
1 stalk celery, cut into 2-inch pieces
1 jar (2 ounces) mushrooms, drained *or* ¼ cup mushroom gravy
3 tablespoons all-purpose flour
¼ cup water

Trim all excess fat from roast; brown and drain if using chuck or another highly marbled cut. Combine ¼ cup flour, salt and pepper in small bowl. Coat meat with flour mixture. Place all vegetables except mushrooms in CROCK-POT® and top with roast (cut roast in half, if necessary, to fit easily). Spread mushrooms evenly over top of roast. Cover and cook on Low 10 to 12 hours.

If desired, turn to High during last hour to soften vegetables and make a gravy. To thicken gravy, make a smooth paste of 3 tablespoons flour and water; stir into CROCK-POT®. Season to taste before serving. *Makes 4 to 6 servings*

SLOW COOKER MAIN DISHES

46 FEIJOADA COMPLETA

1½ pounds country-style ribs or pork
    spareribs
 1 corned beef (1½ pounds)
½ pound smoked link sausage, such as
    Polish or andouille
½ pound fresh link sausage, such as
    bratwurst or breakfast links
 3 cups water
 1 can (15½ ounces) black beans, rinsed
    and drained
 1 cup chopped onion
 4 cloves garlic, minced
 1 jalapeño pepper, seeded and chopped
    Chili-Lemon Sauce (recipe follows)

TRIM excess fat from ribs. Combine all
ingredients except Chili-Lemon Sauce in
slow cooker; stir to mix well. Cover and
cook on LOW 7 to 8 hours or until meats are
fork-tender. Meanwhile, prepare Chili-
Lemon Sauce.

REMOVE meats to cutting board. Slice
corned beef; place on large serving platter.
Arrange remaining meat around corned beef.
Cover meat and keep warm.

DRAIN liquid from beans, leaving just
enough liquid so beans are moist. Transfer to
serving bowl. Serve with Chili-Lemon Sauce.
Makes 10 to 12 servings

CHILI–LEMON SAUCE
¾ cup lemon juice
 1 small onion, coarsely chopped
 3 jalapeño peppers, seeded and chopped
 3 cloves garlic, cut into halves

PLACE all ingredients in food processor or
blender. Process until smooth. Serve at room
temperature.

47 SPAGHETTI MEAT SAUCE

½ pound sweet or hot Italian link sausage
 1 pound ground chuck
 1 pound round steak or stewing beef, cut
    into 1-inch cubes
 2 cans (16 ounces each) Italian-style
    tomatoes, broken up
 1 can (8 ounces) tomato sauce
 1 can (6 ounces) tomato paste
 2 medium onions, chopped
 1 large green bell pepper, seeded and
    chopped
 2 tablespoons sugar
 1 tablespoon salt
 2 cloves garlic, minced
 2 teaspoons leaf basil
⅛ teaspoon crushed red pepper

Remove sausage from casings; brown in
skillet with ground chuck and round steak.
Break up sausage and ground meat with
wooden spoon or fork as they brown; drain
well. Add to CROCK-POT® with remaining
ingredients; stir well. Cover and cook on
Low 8 to 16 hours or on High 4 to 6 hours.
For thicker sauce, cook on High last 2 hours,
removing cover for last hour.

NOTE: This sauce may be made 1 to 2 days
in advance and refrigerated. It also freezes
well.

Feijoada Completa

SLOW COOKER MAIN DISHES

48 SPARERIBS SIMMERED IN ORANGE SAUCE

4 pounds country-style pork spareribs
2 tablespoons vegetable oil
2 medium white onions, cut into ¼-inch slices
1 to 2 tablespoons dried ancho chilies, seeded and finely chopped
½ teaspoon ground cinnamon
¼ teaspoon ground cloves
1 can (16 ounces) tomatoes, undrained
2 cloves garlic
½ cup orange juice
⅓ cup dry white wine
⅓ cup packed brown sugar
1 teaspoon shredded orange peel
½ teaspoon salt
1 to 2 tablespoons cider vinegar

TRIM excess fat from ribs. Cut into individual riblets. Heat oil in large skillet over medium heat. Add ribs; cook 10 minutes or until browned on all sides. Remove to plate. Remove and discard all but 2 tablespoons drippings from skillet. Add onions, chilies, cinnamon and cloves. Cook and stir 4 minutes or until softened. Transfer onion mixture to slow cooker.

PROCESS tomatoes with juice and garlic in food processor or blender until smooth.

COMBINE tomato mixture, orange juice, wine, sugar, orange peel and salt in slow cooker. Add ribs; stir to coat. Cover and cook on LOW 5 hours or until ribs are fork-tender. Remove ribs to plates. Ladle out liquid to medium bowl. Let stand 5 minutes. Skim and discard fat. Stir in vinegar; serve over ribs. Serve with carrots and garnish with orange wedges, if desired.

Makes 4 to 6 servings

49 PORK, POTATO AND GREEN BEAN STEW

2 cans (14½ ounces each) chicken broth, divided
1 pound boneless pork loin, trimmed of fat and cut into pieces
4 red potatoes, cut into ½-inch cubes
1 onion, chopped
2 garlic cloves, minced
⅓ cup all-purpose flour
2 cups frozen cut green beans
2 teaspoons Worcestershire sauce
½ teaspoon dried thyme leaves
½ teaspoon black pepper

Heat 1 can chicken broth, pork loin, potatoes, onion and garlic in large skillet 5 to 10 minutes over medium heat. Transfer to CROCK-POT®.

Combine ¾ cup chicken broth and flour in small bowl. Set aside.

Add remaining broth, green beans, Worcestershire sauce, thyme and pepper to CROCK-POT®; stir. Cover and cook 8 to 10 hours on Low or 4 to 5 hours on High. If on Low, turn to High last 30 minutes and stir in flour mixture. Cook 30 minutes to thicken. Serve.

Makes 8 servings

Spareribs Simmered in Orange Sauce

SLOW COOKER MAIN DISHES

50 PORK CHOPS WITH JALAPEÑO–PECAN CORNBREAD STUFFING

6 boneless loin pork chops, 1 inch thick (1½ pounds)
¾ cup chopped onion
¾ cup chopped celery
½ cup coarsely chopped pecans
½ medium jalapeño pepper,* seeded and chopped
1 teaspoon rubbed sage
½ teaspoon dried rosemary leaves
⅛ teaspoon black pepper
4 cups unseasoned cornbread stuffing mix
1¼ cups reduced-sodium chicken broth
1 egg, slightly beaten

Jalapeño peppers can sting and irritate the skin; wear rubber gloves when handling peppers and do not touch eyes.

TRIM excess fat from pork and discard. Spray large skillet with nonstick cooking spray; heat over medium heat. Add pork; cook 10 minutes or until browned on all sides. Remove; set aside. Add onion, celery, pecans, jalapeño pepper, sage, rosemary and black pepper to skillet. Cook 5 minutes or until tender; set aside.

COMBINE cornbread stuffing mix, vegetable mixture and broth in medium bowl. Stir in egg. Spoon stuffing mixture into slow cooker. Arrange pork on top. Cover and cook on LOW about 5 hours or until pork is tender and barely pink in center. Serve with vegetable salad, if desired.

Makes 6 servings

NOTE: If you prefer a moister dressing, increase the chicken broth to 1½ cups.

51 FRUIT AND HAM LOAF

¾ cup dried fruit bits
2 tablespoons apple butter
1 pound ground, fully cooked ham
½ pound ground pork
½ cup graham cracker crumbs
¼ cup milk
1 beaten egg
½ teaspoon black pepper
½ cup packed brown sugar
2 tablespoons apple juice
½ teaspoon dry mustard

In small bowl, combine fruit bits and apple butter. In large bowl, combine ham, pork, graham cracker crumbs, milk, egg and pepper.

Crisscross 3 foil strips as described on page 7 (atop a sheet of waxed paper to keep counter clean). In center of foil strips pat half of meat mixture into 7-inch circle. Spread fruit mixture on meat circle to within 1 inch of edges. Top with remaining meat mixture. Press edges of meat to seal well. Bringing up foil strips, lift and transfer to any size CROCK-POT®. Press meat away from sides of CROCK-POT® to avoid excess browning. Cover and cook on Low 8 to 10 hours or on High 4 to 6 hours. Loaf is done when meat thermometer inserted reads 170°F.

In small bowl, combine brown sugar, apple juice and dry mustard. Spread over meat. Cover and cook on Low or High heat 30 minutes more.

Using foil strips, lift ham loaf from CROCK-POT® and transfer to serving plate; discard foil strips. Serve. *Makes 6 to 8 servings*

Pork Chop with Jalapeño-Pecan Cornbread Stuffing

SLOW COOKER MAIN DISHES

52 SAUSAGE–RICE CASSEROLE

1 pound bulk sausage
4 cups water
2 stalks celery, diced
¾ cup raw long-grain converted rice
⅓ cup slivered almonds
1 envelope (1½ ounces) dry chicken
    soup mix
  Salt

In skillet, brown sausage; drain well. Combine all ingredients in lightly greased CROCK-POT®; stir well. Cover and cook on Low 7 to 10 hours or on High 3 to 4 hours or until rice is tender.   *Makes 4 servings*

53 CHOP SUEY

2 to 3 pork shoulder chops, boned, well
    trimmed and diced
2 cups cubed, cooked or raw chicken
1½ cups water chestnuts, thinly sliced
1½ cups bamboo shoots, in julienne strips
1 cup diagonally sliced celery
½ cup chicken broth
2 teaspoons soy sauce
½ teaspoon sugar
  Salt

Combine all ingredients in CROCK-POT®; stir well. Cover and cook on Low 8 to 10 hours or on High 4 to 5 hours. If desired, thicken sauce with cornstarch-water paste just before serving.

Double recipe for 5-quart CROCK-POT®.
          Makes 4 servings

54 GERMAN POTATO SOUP

1 pound potatoes, washed and diced
4 cups beef broth
1 onion, chopped
1 leek, trimmed and diced
2 carrots, peeled and diced
1 cup chopped cabbage
¼ cup chopped parsley
1 bay leaf
2 teaspoons black pepper
1 teaspoon salt
½ teaspoon caraway seeds
¼ teaspoon nutmeg
½ cup sour cream
1 pound bacon, cooked and diced

Combine potatoes, broth, onion, leek, carrots, cabbage and parsley in CROCK-POT®. Stir in seasonings. Cover and cook on Low 8 to 10 hours or on High 4 to 5 hours. Remove and discard bay leaf. Using a slotted spoon remove potatoes and mash. Combine potatoes with sour cream. Return to CROCK-POT® and stir. Stir in bacon pieces. Serve.

For 6-quart CROCK-POT®, use 6 cups of beef broth, 2 leeks, 3 carrots, diced and 2 pounds potatoes. Season as desired.
          Makes 6 to 8 servings

SLOW COOKER MAIN DISHES

55 MEXICAN CARNITAS

1 package (10 ounces) frozen French-style
    green beans, partially thawed
2 tablespoons minced onion
2 tablespoons chopped pimiento
½ teaspoon seasoned salt
⅛ teaspoon pepper
1 pound lean boneless pork, cut into small
    cubes

Place green beans in CROCK-POT®. Top with onion, pimiento, seasoned salt and pepper; add cubed pork. Cover and cook on Low 7 to 9 hours.

Double recipe for 5-quart CROCK-POT®.

Makes 3 to 4 servings

56 HAM TETRAZZINI

1 can (10¾ ounces) condensed cream of
    mushroom soup
1 to 1½ cups cubed cooked ham
½ cup evaporated or scalded milk
½ cup stuffed olives, sliced (optional)
½ cup grated Romano or Parmesan cheese
1½ teaspoons prepared horseradish
1 can (4 ounces) sliced mushrooms,
    drained
¼ cup dry sherry or dry white wine
1 package (5 ounces) spaghetti
2 tablespoons butter, melted

Combine all ingredients except spaghetti and butter in CROCK-POT®; stir well. Cover and cook on Low 6 to 8 hours.

Just before serving, cook spaghetti according to package directions; drain and toss with butter. Stir into CROCK-POT®. Sprinkle additional grated cheese over top.

This recipe may be doubled for 5-quart CROCK-POT®.   *Makes 4 servings*

57 HAM AND CHEESE SUPPER

2 cups ground cooked ham (about
    ½ pound)
½ cup finely crushed cheese crackers
⅓ cup barbecue sauce
1 egg
4 large potatoes, peeled and thinly sliced
1 medium onion, thinly sliced
2 tablespoons butter
2 tablespoons vegetable oil
⅔ cup evaporated milk
1 cup grated mozzarella cheese
1 teaspoon salt
¼ teaspoon paprika
⅛ teaspoon black pepper

Combine ground ham, crushed crackers, barbecue sauce and egg; shape into 6 patties. In large skillet, sauté potato and onion slices in butter and oil over medium heat, turning frequently to prevent browning. Drain and place in CROCK-POT®.

Combine milk, cheese and seasonings; pour over potatoes and onions. Layer ham patties on top. Cover and cook on Low 3 to 5 hours.

Makes 6 servings

SLOW COOKER MAIN DISHES

58 PORK STEW

2 tablespoons vegetable oil, divided
3 pounds fresh lean boneless pork butt,
    cut into 1½-inch cubes
2 medium white onions, thinly sliced
3 cloves garlic, minced
1 teaspoon salt
1 teaspoon ground cumin
¾ teaspoon dried oregano leaves
1 can (8 ounces) tomatillos, drained and
    chopped or 1 cup husked and
    chopped fresh tomatillos
1 can (4 ounces) chopped green chilies,
    drained
½ cup reduced-sodium chicken broth
1 large tomato, peeled and coarsely
    chopped
¼ cup fresh cilantro, chopped or
    ½ teaspoon ground coriander
2 teaspoons lime juice
4 cups hot cooked white rice
½ cup toasted slivered almonds (optional)

HEAT 1 tablespoon oil in large skillet over medium heat. Add pork; cook 10 minutes or until browned on all sides. Remove and set aside. Heat remaining 1 tablespoon oil in skillet. Add onions, garlic, salt, cumin and oregano; cook and stir 2 minutes or until soft.

COMBINE pork, onion mixture and remaining ingredients except rice and almonds in slow cooker; mix well. Cover and cook on LOW 5 hours or until pork is tender and barely pink in center. Serve over rice and sprinkle with almonds, if desired.

Makes 10 servings

59 BAKED HAM WITH MUSTARD GLAZE

3 to 5 pounds precooked ham, drained
10 to 12 whole cloves
½ cup brown sugar
1 tablespoon prepared mustard
2 teaspoons lemon juice
2 tablespoons orange juice
2 tablespoons cornstarch

Score ham in diamond pattern and stud with cloves. Place in CROCK-POT®. Combine brown sugar, mustard and lemon juice; spoon over ham. Cover and cook on High 1 hour, then on Low 6 to 7 hours or until ham is hot.

Remove ham to warm serving platter. Turn CROCK-POT® to High setting. Combine orange juice and cornstarch to form smooth paste. Stir into drippings in CROCK-POT®. Cook stirring occasionally until sauce is thickened. Spoon over ham.

If using 5- or 6-quart CROCK-POT® and cooking larger ham, cook 1 hour on High, then Low 8 to 10 hours.

Makes 12 to 15 servings

Pork Stew

SLOW COOKER MAIN DISHES

60 NAVY BEAN BACON CHOWDER

1½ cups dried navy beans, rinsed
2 cups cold water
6 slices thick-cut bacon
1 medium carrot, cut lengthwise into
    halves, then cut into 1-inch pieces
1 rib celery, chopped
1 medium onion, chopped
1 small turnip, cut into 1-inch pieces
1 teaspoon dried Italian seasoning
⅛ teaspoon black pepper
1 large can (46 ounces) reduced-sodium
    chicken broth
1 cup milk

SOAK beans overnight in cold water.

COOK bacon in medium skillet over medium heat. Drain and crumble. Combine carrot, celery, onion, turnip, Italian seasoning, pepper, beans and bacon in slow cooker; mix slightly. Pour broth over top. Cover and cook on LOW 7½ to 9 hours or until beans are crisp-tender.

LADLE 2 cups of soup mixture into food processor or blender. Process until smooth; return to slow cooker. Add milk; cover and heat on HIGH 10 minutes or until heated through.   *Makes 6 servings*

61 CANDIED POLYNESIAN SPARERIBS

2 pounds lean pork spareribs
⅓ cup soy sauce
1 tablespoon ground ginger
¼ cup cornstarch
1 cup sugar
½ cup cider vinegar
¼ cup water
1 teaspoon salt
½ teaspoon dry mustard
1 small piece gingerroot or crystallized
    ginger (about 1-inch long)

Cut spareribs into individual 3-inch pieces. Mix soy sauce, ground ginger and cornstarch until smooth; brush mixture over spareribs. Place ribs on rack of broiler pan. Bake in preheated 425°F oven 20 minutes to remove fat; drain. Combine remaining ingredients in CROCK-POT®; stir well. Add browned ribs. Cover and cook on Low 8 to 10 hours or on High 4 to 5 hours.

If desired, brown and crisp ribs in broiler for 10 minutes before serving.

Makes 4 servings

Navy Bean Bacon Chowder

SLOW COOKER MAIN DISHES

62 STUFFED PORK CHOPS

4 double pork loin chops, well trimmed
    Salt and black pepper
1 can (12 ounces) whole-kernel corn,
    drained
1 small onion, chopped
1 small green pepper, seeded and chopped
1 cup fresh bread crumbs
1/3 cup uncooked, long-grain converted rice
1/2 teaspoon dried oregano leaves or dried
    sage leaves
1 can (8 ounces) tomato sauce

Cut pocket in each chop, cutting from the edge almost to the bone. Lightly season pockets with salt and pepper. In bowl, combine all ingredients except pork chops and tomato sauce. Pack vegetable mixture into pockets. Secure along fat side with wooden picks.

Pour any remaining vegetable mixture into CROCK-POT®. Moisten top surface of each chop with tomato sauce. Add stuffed pork chops to CROCK-POT®, stacking to fit if necessary. Pour any remaining tomato sauce on top. Cover and cook on Low 8 to 10 hours or on High 4 to 5 hours until done.

To serve, remove pork chops to heatproof platter and mound vegetable-rice mixture in center. *Makes 4 servings*

63 PORK CHOPS AND POTATOES IN MUSTARD SAUCE

6 to 8 pork loin chops
2 tablespoons cooking oil
1 can (10¾ ounces) cream of mushroom
    soup
1/4 cup chicken broth
1/4 cup country Dijon-style mustard
1/2 teaspoon crushed dried thyme leaves
1 clove garlic, minced *or* 1/4 teaspoon
    garlic powder
1/4 teaspoon black pepper
6 medium-sized potatoes, cut into thin
    slices
1 onion, sliced

In large skillet, brown pork chops on both sides in hot oil. Drain fat.

In any size CROCK-POT®, mix cream of mushroom soup, chicken broth, mustard, thyme, garlic and pepper. Add potatoes and onion, stirring to coat. Place browned pork chops on top of potato mixture. Cover and cook on Low 8 to 10 hours or on High 4 to 5 hours. *Makes 6 servings*

Stuffed Pork Chop

SLOW COOKER MAIN DISHES

64 SAVORY PEA SOUP WITH SAUSAGE

8 ounces smoked sausage, cut lengthwise into halves, then cut into ½-inch pieces
2 cans (about 14 ounces each) reduced-sodium chicken broth
1 package (16 ounces) dried split peas, rinsed
3 medium carrots, sliced
2 ribs celery, sliced
1 medium onion, chopped
¾ teaspoon dried marjoram leaves
1 bay leaf

HEAT small skillet over medium heat. Add sausage; cook 5 to 8 minutes or until browned. Drain well. Combine sausage and remaining ingredients in slow cooker. Cover and cook on LOW 4 to 5 hours or until peas are tender. Turn off heat. Remove and discard bay leaf. Cover and let stand 15 minutes to thicken.   *Makes 6 servings*

65 SWEET AND SOUR PORK STEAKS

4 to 6 pork shoulder steaks
1 tablespoon cooking oil
1 can (15 ounces) crushed pineapple
½ cup chopped green bell pepper
½ cup water
⅓ cup brown sugar
2 tablespoons ketchup
1 tablespoon quick-cooking tapioca
3 teaspoons soy sauce
½ teaspoon dry mustard

In large skillet, brown pork steaks on both sides in hot oil. Drain fat. Transfer to any size CROCK-POT®.

In bowl, combine pineapple, green bell pepper, water, sugar, ketchup, tapioca, soy sauce and dry mustard. Pour over pork steaks. Cover and cook on Low 8 to 10 hours or on High 4 to 5 hours. Serve over rice, if desired.   *Makes 4 to 6 servings*

Savory Pea Soup with Sausage

SLOW COOKER MAIN DISHES

66 LAMB IN DILL SAUCE

2 large boiling potatoes, peeled and cut
   into 1-inch cubes
½ cup chopped onion
1½ teaspoons salt
½ teaspoon black pepper
½ teaspoon dried dill weed *or* 4 sprigs
   fresh dill
1 bay leaf
2 pounds lean lamb stew meat, cut into
   1-inch cubes
1 cup plus 3 tablespoons water, divided
2 tablespoons all-purpose flour
1 teaspoon sugar
2 tablespoons lemon juice
   Fresh dill (optional)

LAYER ingredients in slow cooker in the
following order: potatoes, onion, salt,
pepper, dill, bay leaf, lamb and 1 cup water.
Cover and cook on LOW 6 to 8 hours.

REMOVE lamb and potatoes with slotted
spoon; cover and keep warm. Remove and
discard bay leaf. Turn heat to HIGH. Stir
flour and remaining 3 tablespoons water in
small bowl until smooth. Add half of cooking
juices and sugar. Mix well and return to slow
cooker. Cover and cook 15 minutes. Stir in
lemon juice. Return lamb and potatoes to
slow cooker. Cover and cook 10 minutes or
until heated through. Garnish with fresh dill,
if desired.   *Makes 6 servings*

67 LAMB STEW WITH VEGETABLES

3 pounds boneless lamb stewing meat,
   well trimmed
½ cup all-purpose flour
1 teaspoon salt
1 teaspoon sugar
½ teaspoon dried thyme leaves
¼ teaspoon black pepper
¼ teaspoon garlic powder (optional)
1 can (14 ounces) beef broth
3 to 4 potatoes, peeled and cubed
6 to 8 small white onions, chopped
3 large carrots, pared and thinly sliced
1 package (10 ounces) frozen peas

Wipe off any collected juices from lamb.
Combine flour, salt, sugar, thyme, pepper
and garlic powder; toss with lamb to coat
thoroughly. Place all ingredients except peas
in CROCK-POT®; stir well. Cover and cook
on Low 10 to 12 hours. One hour before
serving, turn to High and stir in frozen peas.
Cover and cook until done.
                    Makes 6 to 8 servings

NOTE: Peas may be added at beginning of
cooking, but will darken slightly.

Lamb in Dill Sauce

SLOW COOKER MAIN DISHES

68 LAMB SHANKS WITH SPLIT PEAS

 1 cup dried split green peas
 3 pounds lamb shanks
2½ cups beef broth
 1 large onion, chopped
 2 carrots, pared and sliced
 2 stalks celery, sliced
 Salt and black pepper

To soften peas, cover with 3 times their volume of unsalted water and bring to a boil. Boil 10 minutes, reduce heat, cover and allow to simmer 1½ hours or until peas are tender. Brown lamb shanks under broiler to remove fat; drain well. Mix all ingredients except shanks in CROCK-POT®; stir well. Add shanks, pushing down into liquid. Cover and cook on Low 10 to 12 hours.

Makes 4 to 6 servings

69 LAMB CHOPS WITH ORANGE SAUCE

 8 lamb rib chops
 2 tablespoons vegetable oil
½ cup orange juice
 2 tablespoons honey
 2 tablespoons cornstarch
 2 teaspoons salt
 1 teaspoon grated orange peel

In large skillet, brown lamb chops in oil; drain well. Thoroughly combine orange juice, honey, cornstarch, salt and grated orange peel. Brush browned lamb chops with orange mixture and place in CROCK-POT®. Cover and cook on Low 6 to 8 hours.

If thicker sauce is desired, remove chops before serving and turn CROCK-POT® to High; stir in mixture of 2 tablespoons cornstarch and ¼ cup water. Cook, stirring, until the sauce is transparent.

Makes 4 servings

70 CHICKEN IN WINE

 3 pounds chicken parts, preferably breasts
   and thighs
 Salt and black pepper
 2 tablespoons butter
 1 medium onion, sliced
 1 can (4 ounces) sliced mushrooms,
   drained
½ cup dry sherry
 1 teaspoon Italian seasoning
 Hot cooked rice

Rinse chicken parts and pat dry. Season chicken lightly with salt and pepper. In skillet, melt butter and quickly brown chicken parts; remove with slotted spoon and place in CROCK-POT®. Sauté onion and mushrooms in skillet. Add sherry to skillet and stir, scraping to remove brown particles. Pour contents of skillet into CROCK-POT® over chicken. Sprinkle with Italian seasoning. Cover and cook on Low 8 to 10 hours or on High 3 to 4 hours.

Serve chicken over rice and spoon sauce over top. *Makes 4 to 6 servings*

SLOW COOKER MAIN DISHES

71 CHEESY TURKEY COTTAGE FRIES

3 to 4 cups frozen cottage-style potatoes
2 cups cubed cooked turkey
2 cups frozen cut broccoli, thawed and drained
1 cup pasteurized processed cheese product
1 jar (2 ounces) diced pimiento, drained

Spray inside of CROCK-POT® with cooking spray. Place potatoes in layer in bottom of CROCK-POT®. Stir remaining ingredients together and pour over potatoes. Cook on Low 6 to 8 hours or on High 3 to 4 hours.

Makes 4 (1 cup) servings

72 CHICKEN STUFFING

1 package chicken stuffing mix (12-serving size)
3 cans (10¾ ounces each) cream of chicken soup
3 to 4 cups cooked, cubed chicken
½ cup milk
2 cups shredded mild Cheddar cheese

Prepare stuffing mix according to package directions and place in 5-quart CROCK-POT®. Stir in 2 cans of cream of chicken soup. In mixing bowl, stir together cubed chicken, 1 can cream of chicken soup and milk. Spread over stuffing in CROCK-POT®. Sprinkle cheese over top. Cover and cook on Low 4 to 6 hours or on High 2 to 3 hours.

Makes 8 to 10 servings

73 HOT CHICKEN SALAD

2½ cups diced cooked chicken
1 cup toasted almonds
2 cups diagonally sliced celery
½ cup diced green bell pepper
3 tablespoons lemon juice
1 cup mayonnaise
3 tablespoons grated onion
1 cup cubed processed cheese, divided
1 cup crushed potato chips, divided
½ cup grated Parmesan cheese
Toasted English muffins

Combine all ingredients in CROCK-POT® except half the processed cheese, half the potato chips, half the Parmesan cheese and English muffins. Cover and cook on Low 4 to 6 hours.

Just before serving, sprinkle with remaining processed cheese, potato chips and Parmesan cheese. Serve on toasted English muffins.

Makes 6 to 8 servings

HOT TURKEY SALAD: Substitute diced cooked turkey for the chicken.

SLOW COOKER MAIN DISHES

74 FORTY–CLOVE CHICKEN

1 frying chicken (3 pounds), cut into
    serving pieces
1 to 2 tablespoons olive oil
¼ cup dry white wine
⅛ cup dry vermouth
2 tablespoons chopped fresh parsley *or*
    2 teaspoons dried parsley leaves
2 teaspoons dried basil leaves
1 teaspoon dried oregano leaves
    Pinch of crushed red pepper flakes
40 cloves garlic (about 2 heads), peeled
4 ribs celery, sliced
    Juice and peel of 1 lemon
    Fresh herbs (optional)

REMOVE skin from chicken, if desired. Sprinkle with salt and pepper. Heat oil in large skillet over medium heat. Add chicken; cook 10 minutes or until browned on all sides. Remove to platter.

COMBINE wine, vermouth, parsley, basil, oregano and red pepper flakes in large bowl. Add garlic and celery; coat well. Transfer garlic and celery to slow cooker with slotted spoon. Add chicken to remaining herb mixture; coat well. Place chicken on top of vegetables in slow cooker. Sprinkle lemon juice and peel in slow cooker; add remaining herb mixture. Cover and cook on LOW 6 hours or until chicken is no longer pink in center. Garnish with fresh herbs, if desired.

Makes 4 to 6 servings

75 TURKEY MEATBALLS WITH GRAVY

2 beaten eggs
¾ cup seasoned bread crumbs
½ cup chopped onion
½ cup finely chopped celery
2 tablespoons chopped parsley
½ teaspoon poultry seasoning
¼ teaspoon black pepper
⅛ teaspoon garlic powder
2 pounds ground turkey
1 to 2 teaspoons vegetable oil
1 can (10¾ ounces) undiluted cream of
    mushroom soup
1 cup water
1 envelope (¹⁵⁄₁₆ ounce) turkey gravy mix
½ teaspoon shredded lemon peel
¼ teaspoon crushed dried thyme leaves
1 bay leaf
    Hot cooked mashed potatoes or
    buttered noodles

In large bowl, combine eggs, bread crumbs, onion, celery, parsley, poultry seasoning, pepper and garlic powder. Add ground turkey and mix well. Shape into 1-inch balls.

In large skillet, brown meatballs in oil; drain. Transfer to CROCK-POT®. In bowl, combine soup, water, gravy mix, lemon peel, thyme and bay leaf. Pour over meatballs. Cover and cook on Low 6 to 8 hours or on High 3 to 4 hours. Discard bay leaf. Serve with mashed potatoes or buttered noodles.

Makes 8 servings

Forty-Clove Chicken

SLOW COOKER MAIN DISHES

76 COQ AU VIN

4 slices thick-cut bacon
2 cups frozen pearl onions, thawed
1 cup sliced button mushrooms
1 clove garlic, minced
1 teaspoon dried thyme leaves
⅛ teaspoon black pepper
6 boneless skinless chicken breast halves
    (about 2 pounds)
½ cup dry red wine
¾ cup reduced-sodium chicken broth
¼ cup tomato paste
3 tablespoons all-purpose flour

COOK bacon in medium skillet over medium heat. Drain and crumble. Layer ingredients in slow cooker in the following order: onions, bacon, mushrooms, garlic, thyme, pepper, chicken, wine and broth. Cover and cook on LOW 6 to 8 hours.

REMOVE chicken and vegetables; cover and keep warm. Ladle ½ cup cooking liquid into small bowl; allow to cool slightly. Turn slow cooker to HIGH; cover. Mix reserved liquid, tomato paste and flour until smooth. Return mixture to slow cooker; cover and cook 15 minutes or until thickened. Serve over egg noodles, if desired.   *Makes 6 servings*

77 WHITE CHILI

4 cans (14½ ounces each) chicken broth
1 can (16 ounces) navy beans, drained
1 onion, chopped
2 cloves garlic, minced
1 tablespoon ground white pepper
1 tablespoon dried oregano leaves
1 tablespoon ground cumin
1 teaspoon salt
¼ teaspoon ground cloves
5 cups chopped cooked chicken
2 cans (4 ounces each) chopped green
    chilies
1 cup water
8 flour tortillas
    Monterey Jack cheese
    Salsa
    Sour cream

In CROCK-POT®, combine broth, beans, onion, garlic, white pepper, oregano, cumin, salt, cloves, chicken, green chilies and water. Cover and cook on Low 8 to 10 hours or on High 4 to 5 hours.

To serve, make 4 cuts in each tortilla toward center, but not through and line serving bowls with tortillas, overlapping edges. Spoon in chili. Top with cheese, salsa and sour cream. Serve immediately.
          Makes 8 servings

Coq au Vin

SLOW COOKER MAIN DISHES

78 SOUTHWEST TURKEY TENDERLOIN STEW

1 package (about 1½ pounds) turkey tenderloins, cut into ¾-inch pieces
1 tablespoon chili powder
1 teaspoon ground cumin
¾ teaspoon salt
1 red bell pepper, cut into ¾-inch pieces
1 green bell pepper, cut into ¾-inch pieces
¾ cup chopped red or yellow onion
3 cloves garlic, minced
1 can (15½ ounces) chili beans in spicy sauce, undrained
1 can (14½ ounces) chili-style stewed tomatoes, undrained
¾ cup prepared salsa or picante sauce
Fresh cilantro (optional)

PLACE turkey in slow cooker. Sprinkle chili powder, cumin and salt over turkey; toss to coat. Add red bell pepper, green bell pepper, onion, garlic, beans, tomatoes and salsa. Mix well. Cover and cook on LOW 5 hours or until turkey is no longer pink in center and vegetables are crisp-tender. Ladle into bowls. Garnish with cilantro, if desired.

Makes 6 servings

79 ALMOND CHICKEN

1 can (14 ounces) chicken broth
1 slice bacon, diced
2 tablespoons butter
¾ to 1 pound boned chicken breasts, cut into 1-inch pieces
1½ cups diagonally sliced celery
1 small onion, sliced
1 can (4 ounces) sliced mushrooms, drained
2 tablespoons soy sauce
½ teaspoon salt
Hot cooked rice
⅔ cup slivered almonds, toasted

Pour chicken broth into CROCK-POT®. Cover and turn CROCK-POT® to High.

In large skillet, heat bacon and butter; add chicken pieces and brown quickly on all sides. With slotted spoon, remove browned chicken to CROCK-POT®. Quickly sauté celery, onion and mushrooms in skillet until just slightly limp.

Add contents of skillet to CROCK-POT® with soy sauce and salt; stir well. Cover and cook on Low 6 to 8 hours or on High 3 to 4 hours.

Serve over hot fluffy rice and garnish with toasted almonds.

Makes 4 servings

Southwest Turkey Tenderloin Stew

SLOW COOKER MAIN DISHES

80 THAI TURKEY & NOODLES

1 package (about 1½ pounds) turkey
    tenderloins, cut into ¾-inch pieces
1 red bell pepper, cut into short, thin
    strips
1¼ cups reduced-sodium chicken broth,
    divided
¼ cup reduced-sodium soy sauce
3 cloves garlic, minced
¾ teaspoon crushed red pepper flakes
¼ teaspoon salt
2 tablespoons cornstarch
3 green onions, cut into ½-inch pieces
⅓ cup creamy or chunky peanut butter
    (not natural-style)
12 ounces hot cooked vermicelli pasta
¾ cup peanuts or cashews, chopped
¾ cup cilantro, chopped

PLACE turkey, bell pepper, 1 cup broth, soy
sauce, garlic, red pepper flakes and salt in
slow cooker. Cover and cook on LOW 3
hours.

MIX cornstarch with remaining ¼ cup broth
in small bowl until smooth. Turn slow
cooker to HIGH. Stir in green onions, peanut
butter and cornstarch mixture. Cover and
cook 30 minutes or until sauce is thickened
and turkey is no longer pink in center. Stir
well. Serve over vermicelli. Sprinkle with
peanuts and cilantro.   *Makes 6 servings*

COOK'S NOOK: If you don't have vermicelli
on hand, try substituting ramen noodles.
Discard the flavor packet from ramen soup
mix and drop the noodles into boiling water.
Cook the noodles 2 to 3 minutes or until just
tender. Drain and serve hot.

81 THREE BEAN TURKEY SOUP

1 pound ground turkey
1 cup chopped onion
¾ green bell pepper
2 cloves garlic, minced
1 can (16 ounces) red kidney beans,
    drained
1 can (16 ounces) Great Northern beans
    or pinto beans, drained
1 can (16 ounces) black beans
3 cups water
2 cans (14½ ounces) whole tomatoes,
    undrained and chopped
1 can (8 ounces) tomato sauce
2 cups sliced carrots
2 teaspoons dried oregano leaves
½ teaspoon dried thyme leaves
½ teaspoon chicken-flavored bouillon
    granules
½ teaspoon salt
½ teaspoon black pepper

In large skillet, brown turkey, onion, green
bell pepper and garlic. Drain fat. Transfer to
CROCK-POT®. Add beans, water, tomatoes,
tomato sauce, carrots and seasonings. Stir.
Cover and cook on Low 8 to 10 hours or on
High 4 to 5 hours. Before serving, mash
beans slightly for a thicker soup if desired.
Serve.   *Makes 10 to 12 servings*

Thai Turkey & Noodles

82 GROUND TURKEY TACOS

1 pound ground turkey
1 medium onion, chopped
1 can (4 ounces) sliced mushrooms, drained
1 garlic clove, minced *or* ⅛ teaspoon garlic powder
1 can (6 ounces) tomato paste
½ cup white cooking wine
1 tablespoon chopped parsley
½ teaspoon salt
1 teaspoon pickling spices
4 whole peppercorns
8 taco shells

CREAM SAUCE MADE WITH YOGURT
1 tablespoon margarine or butter
1 tablespoon all-purpose flour
¼ teaspoon salt
⅓ cup milk
1 egg, slightly beaten
½ cup unflavored yogurt
    Dash of ground nutmeg

Brown turkey and onion in skillet over medium heat. In CROCK-POT®, combine turkey, onion, mushrooms, garlic, tomato paste, cooking wine, parsley and salt. Tie pickling spices and peppercorns in cheesecloth bag or tea ball. Add to CROCK-POT®; cover and cook on Low 4 to 5 hours. Remove spice bag. Prepare Cream Sauce as directed. Spoon ¼ cup turkey mixture into each taco shell. Top with Cream Sauce.

CREAM SAUCE MADE WITH YOGURT
In small saucepan, melt margarine or butter; stir in flour and salt. Gradually add milk, stirring continuously. Cook over low heat until thickened. Remove from heat. In small bowl, combine egg, yogurt and nutmeg. Stir into hot mixture. Return to heat and cook over low heat 1 minute, stirring continuously.
Makes 8 tacos

83 "FRIED" CHICKEN

1 (2- to 3-pound) fryer, cut into serving pieces
1 cup all-purpose flour
1 teaspoon salt
1 teaspoon paprika
1 teaspoon dried sage leaves or oregano
¼ teaspoon garlic powder
⅛ teaspoon freshly ground pepper
    Butter or vegetable oil

Rinse chicken pieces and pat dry. Combine flour with remaining ingredients except butter. Toss chicken pieces with flour mixture to coat. In skillet, heat butter to ¼-inch depth and cook chicken over medium-high heat until golden brown. Place browned chicken in CROCK-POT®, adding wings first; add no liquid. Cover and cook on Low 8 to 10 hours or on High 4 to 5 hours.
Makes 4 servings

SLOW COOKER MAIN DISHES

84 BREAKFAST CASSEROLE

1 pound ground turkey sausage
4 tablespoons chopped green onions
2 tablespoons vegetable oil
6 cups cubed French bread
2 cups shredded reduced-fat mild Cheddar cheese
2⅔ cups skim milk
1¼ cups frozen egg substitute, thawed
2 teaspoons prepared mustard
½ teaspoon ground black pepper

In large skillet, brown turkey sausage and green onions in vegetable oil. Drain meat. Coat 4-quart CROCK-POT® with cooking spray and place bread cubes in bottom. Layer sausage mixture and cheese over bread. Combine milk, egg substitute, prepared mustard and pepper. Pour over sausage and cheese. Cover and cook on High 3 to 4 hours.

85 CHICKEN 'N' OLIVES

1 (3-pound) fryer, cut into serving pieces
Salt and black pepper
1 can (8 ounces) tomato sauce
¾ cup beer
½ cup pimiento-stuffed olives
1 large onion, chopped
1 clove garlic, minced
2 bay leaves
Hot cooked rice

Rinse chicken pieces and pat dry. Lightly season with salt and pepper. Combine all ingredients except chicken and rice in CROCK-POT®; stir well. Add chicken pieces; be sure all chicken is coated. Cover and cook on Low 7 to 9 hours. Serve over rice

Makes 4 to 6 servings

86 CHICKEN BREASTS Á L'ORANGE

3 whole chicken breasts, halved
⅔ cup all-purpose flour
1 teaspoon salt
1 teaspoon ground nutmeg
½ teaspoon ground cinnamon
Dash black pepper
Dash garlic powder
2 to 3 sweet potatoes, peeled and cut into ¼-inch slices
1 can (10¾ ounces) condensed cream of celery or cream of chicken soup
1 can (4 ounces) sliced mushrooms, drained
½ cup orange juice
3 tablespoons all-purpose flour
2 teaspoons brown sugar
½ teaspoon grated orange rind
Cooked buttered rice

Rinse chicken breasts and pat dry. Combine ⅔ cup flour with salt, nutmeg, cinnamon, pepper and garlic powder. Thoroughly coat chicken in flour mixture.

Place sweet potato slices in bottom of CROCK-POT®. Place chicken breasts on top.

Combine soup with remaining ingredients except buttered rice; stir well. Pour soup mixture over chicken breasts. Cover and cook on Low 8 to 10 hours or on High 3 to 4 hours or until chicken and vegetables are tender.

Serve chicken and sauce over hot buttered rice. *Makes 6 servings*

SLOW COOKER MAIN DISHES

87 CHICKEN AND VEGETABLE CHOWDER

1 pound boneless skinless chicken breasts, cut into 1-inch pieces
1 can (about 14 ounces) reduced-sodium chicken broth
1 can (10¾ ounces) condensed cream of potato soup
10 ounces frozen broccoli cuts
1 cup sliced carrots
½ cup chopped onion
½ cup whole kernel corn
1 jar (4½ ounces) sliced mushrooms, drained
2 cloves garlic, minced
½ teaspoon dried thyme leaves
⅓ cup half-and-half

COMBINE all ingredients except half-and-half in slow cooker. Cover and cook on LOW 5 hours or until vegetables are tender and chicken is no longer pink in center. Stir in half-and-half. Turn to HIGH. Cover and cook 15 minutes or until heated through.

Makes 6 servings

VARIATION: If desired, ½ cup (2 ounces) shredded Swiss or Cheddar cheese can be added. Add to thickened broth and half-and-half, stirring over LOW heat until melted.

88 TURKEY ENCHILADAS

8 (6-inch) corn tortillas
1 can (10 ounces) enchilada sauce
1 can (15½ ounces) dark red kidney beans
1 cup shredded cooked turkey
1 cup shredded taco-flavored cheese

Make foil handles using technique below, place in CROCK-POT®. Place 1 corn tortilla in bottom of CROCK-POT®. Spoon small amount of enchilada sauce, beans, turkey and cheese over tortilla. Continue layering process until tortillas are gone. Make sure that last layer is cheese layer. Cook on Low 6 to 8 hours or on High 3 to 4 hours. Pull out by foil handles and slice into pie shaped wedges for serving.

FOIL HANDLES: Tear off three 18×2-inch strips of heavy foil or use regular foil folded to double thickness. Crisscross the foil strips in spoke design and place in CROCK-POT® to make lifting of tortilla stack easier.

Chicken and Vegetable Chowder

SLOW COOKER MAIN DISHES

89 TUSCAN PASTA

1 pound boneless skinless chicken breasts,
cut into 1-inch pieces
1 can (15½ ounces) red kidney beans,
rinsed and drained
1 can (15 ounces) tomato sauce
2 cans (14½ ounces each) Italian-style
stewed tomatoes
1 jar (4½ ounces) sliced mushrooms,
drained
1 medium green bell pepper, chopped
½ cup onion, chopped
½ cup celery, chopped
4 cloves garlic, minced
1 cup water
1 teaspoon dried Italian seasoning
6 ounces uncooked thin spaghetti, broken
into halves

PLACE all ingredients except spaghetti in slow cooker. Cover and cook on LOW 4 hours or until vegetables are tender.

TURN to HIGH. Stir in spaghetti; cover. Stir again after 10 minutes. Cover and cook 45 minutes or until pasta is tender. Garnish with basil and bell pepper strips, if desired.

Makes 8 servings

90 TURKEY AND CORN CASSEROLE

1 tablespoon margarine or butter
1 onion, chopped
1 can (16 ounces) cream-style corn
4 large eggs
½ cup evaporated milk
⅓ cup all-purpose flour
Salt to taste
Black pepper to taste
2 cups cooked turkey, chopped
1 cup shredded Cheddar cheese, sharp or
mild

In large skillet, melt margarine over medium heat. Add chopped onion; cook about 5 minutes, stirring often, until softened. Transfer to medium-sized mixing bowl. Whisk creamed corn, eggs, evaporated milk, flour, salt and pepper into onion. Stir in chopped turkey. Transfer to lightly greased CROCK-POT®.

Cover and cook on High 2½ to 3 hours or until knife inserted comes out clean.

Sprinkle top of casserole with cheese; cover and cook until cheese is melted, about 15 minutes. Serve immediately.

Tuscan Pasta

SLOW COOKER MAIN DISHES

91 CHILI TURKEY LOAF

2 pounds ground turkey
1 cup chopped onion
2/3 cup Italian-style seasoned dry bread crumbs
1/2 cup chopped green bell pepper
1/2 cup chili sauce
4 cloves garlic, minced
2 eggs, slightly beaten
2 tablespoons horseradish mustard
1 teaspoon salt
1/2 teaspoon Italian seasoning
1/4 teaspoon black pepper
Prepared salsa (optional)

MAKE foil handles for loaf using technique below. Mix all ingredients except salsa in large bowl. Shape into round loaf and place on top of foil strips. Transfer to bottom of slow cooker using foil handles. Cover and cook on LOW 4½ to 5 hours or until juices run clear and temperature is 170°F. Remove loaf from slow cooker using foil handles. Place on serving plate. Let stand 5 minutes before serving. Cut into wedges and top with salsa, if desired. Serve with steamed carrots, if desired.   *Makes 8 servings*

FOIL HANDLES: Tear off three 18×2-inch strips of heavy foil or use regular foil folded to double thickness. Crisscross the foil strips in spoke design and place in CROCK-POT® to make lifting of turkey loaf easier.

92 CHICKEN PARMESAN

2 cans (10¾ ounces each) cream of mushroom soup, undiluted
1½ cups milk
1 cup white cooking wine
1 cup uncooked converted white rice
1 package onion soup mix
6 chicken breasts, boneless and skinless
6 tablespoons margarine or butter
Salt to taste
Black pepper to taste
Grated Parmesan cheese

Mix cream of mushroom soup, milk, cooking wine, rice and onion soup mix in small mixing bowl. Spray CROCK-POT® with cooking spray. Lay chicken breasts in CROCK-POT®. Place one tablespoon margarine on each chicken breast. Pour soup mixture over chicken breasts. Salt and pepper to taste. Sprinkle with grated Parmesan cheese. Cook on Low 8 to 10 hours or on High 4 to 6 hours.
          Makes 6 servings

Chili Turkey Loaf

SLOW COOKER MAIN DISHES

93 CHICKEN ENCHILADAS

Mexican Gravy (recipe follows)
2 to 3 pounds chopped cooked chicken
1 can (4½ ounces) chopped mild green chilies
1 onion, chopped
8 corn tortillas
1 cup (4 ounces) shredded Monterey Jack cheese
1 cup (4 ounces) shredded mild or sharp Cheddar cheese
1 can (4 ounces) chopped black olives

Prepare Mexican Gravy. In mixing bowl, stir together chicken, chilies, onion and 1 cup Mexican Gravy.

In CROCK-POT®, place foil handles (see page 7). Dip tortilla in Mexican gravy and lay in CROCK-POT®. Spread about 3 tablespoons chicken filling over tortilla and sprinkle with ⅛ of cheeses and olives. Continue layering process until top of CROCK-POT® has been reached. Final layer should be cheese and olive layer. Pour any excess gravy over top of tortilla stack. Cook on Low 4 to 6 hours or on High 1½ to 2½ hours.

MEXICAN GRAVY
¼ cup (½ stick) margarine or butter
½ cup chili powder
⅓ cup all-purpose flour
½ teaspoon garlic salt
¼ teaspoon ground cumin
¼ teaspoon crushed dried oregano
3 cans (15 ounces each) chicken broth
1 can (12 ounces) tomato sauce

Melt margarine in saucepan. In bowl, mix together dry ingredients. Slowly add dry ingredients to margarine, stirring constantly. Mixture will become crumbly. Slowly add chicken broth to margarine mixture, stirring constantly. Stir into tomato sauce.

94 COMPANY CHICKEN CASSEROLE

1 package (8 ounces) noodles
3 cups diced cooked chicken
1½ cups cream-style cottage cheese
1 cup grated sharp processed cheese
1 can (10¾ ounces) condensed cream of chicken soup
½ cup diced celery
½ cup diced green bell pepper
½ cup diced onion
1 can (4 ounces) sliced mushrooms, drained
1 jar (4 ounces) pimiento, diced
½ cup grated Parmesan cheese
½ cup chicken broth
2 tablespoons butter, melted
½ teaspoon dried basil leaves

Cook noodles according to package directions in boiling water until barely tender; drain and rinse thoroughly. In large bowl, combine remaining ingredients with noodles, making certain the noodles are separated and coated with liquid. Pour mixture into greased CROCK-POT®. Cover and cook on Low 6 to 10 hours or on High 3 to 4 hours. *Makes 6 servings*

COMPANY TURKEY CASSEROLE: Substitute diced cooked turkey for chicken.

SLOW COOKER MAIN DISHES

95 CHEESY CHICKEN QUICHE

2 tablespoons corn oil
2 pounds chicken breasts, boneless and skinless
¾ cup all-purpose flour
¾ teaspoon baking powder
½ teaspoon salt
1 cup evaporated milk
2 eggs, beaten
1 cup shredded Cheddar cheese
2 tablespoons chopped onion
2 teaspoons dried parsley flakes

Coat CROCK-POT® with corn oil. Cook chicken on Low 6 to 8 hours or on High 3 to 4 hours or until fork tender. Stir together flour, baking powder, salt, milk and eggs. Fold in cheese, onion and parsley. Pour mixture over chicken and cook 1 hour on High.   *Makes approximately 6 servings*

VARIATION: Cook 1 package (10 ounces) frozen, chopped and thawed broccoli with chicken. Then pour in cheese, flour and egg mixture.

96 CHICKEN DELICIOUS

4 to 6 whole chicken breasts, boned and halved
Lemon juice
Salt and black pepper
Celery salt
Paprika
1 can (10¾ ounces) condensed cream of mushroom soup
1 can (10¾ ounces) condensed cream of celery soup
⅓ cup dry sherry or white wine
Grated Parmesan cheese
Hot cooked rice

Rinse chicken breasts and pat dry. Season with lemon juice, salt, pepper, celery salt and paprika. Place in CROCK-POT®. In medium bowl or pan, mix mushroom and celery soups with sherry. Pour over chicken breasts. Sprinkle with Parmesan cheese. Cover and cook on Low 8 to 10 hours or on High 4 to 5 hours.

Serve chicken and sauce over hot fluffy rice.
     Makes 8 to 12 servings

SLOW COOKER MAIN DISHES

97 JAMBALAYA

2 cups diced boiled ham
2 medium onions, coarsely chopped
2 stalks celery, sliced
½ green bell pepper, seeded and diced
1 can (28 ounces) whole tomatoes
¼ cup tomato paste
3 cloves garlic, minced
1 tablespoon minced parsley
½ teaspoon dried thyme leaves
2 whole cloves
2 tablespoons salad oil
1 cup uncooked long-grain converted rice
1 pound fresh or frozen shrimp, shelled
    and deveined

Thoroughly mix all ingredients except shrimp in CROCK-POT®. Cover and cook on Low 8 to 10 hours.

One hour before serving, turn CROCK-POT® to High. Stir in uncooked shrimp. Cover and cook until shrimp are pink and tender.

Makes 4 to 6 servings

98 SWEET–AND–SOUR SHRIMP

1 package (6 ounces) frozen Chinese pea
    pods, partially thawed
1 can (13 ounces) juice-packed pineapple
    chunks or tidbits (drain and reserve
    ½ juice)
3 tablespoons sugar
2 tablespoons cornstarch
1 chicken bouillon cube
1 cup boiling water
2 teaspoons soy sauce
½ teaspoon ground ginger
2 cans (4½ ounces each) shrimp, rinsed
    and drained
2 tablespoons cider vinegar
    Hot cooked rice

Place pea pods and drained pineapple in CROCK-POT®. In small saucepan, stir together sugar and cornstarch. Dissolve bouillon cube in boiling water and add with juice, soy sauce and ginger to saucepan. Bring to a boil, stirring constantly. Cook sauce about 1 minute or until thickened and transparent. Gently blend sauce into pea pods and pineapple. Cover and cook on Low 5 to 6 hours.

Before serving, add shrimp and vinegar, stirring carefully to avoid breaking up shrimp. Serve over hot rice.

Makes 4 to 5 servings

Jambalaya

SLOW COOKER MAIN DISHES

99 MEDITERRANEAN FISH SOUP

1 medium onion, chopped
½ medium green bell pepper, chopped
2 cloves garlic, minced
1 can (about 14 ounces) whole tomatoes, undrained and coarsely chopped
2 cans (about 14 ounces each) reduced-sodium chicken broth
1 can (8 ounces) tomato sauce
1 jar (2½ ounces) sliced mushrooms
¼ cup ripe olives, sliced
½ cup orange juice
½ cup dry white wine (optional)
2 bay leaves
1 teaspoon dried basil leaves
¼ teaspoon fennel seed, crushed
⅛ teaspoon black pepper
1 pound medium shrimp, peeled

PLACE all ingredients except shrimp in slow cooker. Cover and cook on LOW 4 to 4½ hours or until vegetables are crisp-tender. Stir in shrimp. Cover and cook 15 to 30 minutes or until shrimp are opaque. Remove and discard bay leaves.

Makes 6 servings

COOK'S NOOK: If you prefer a hearty soup, add more fish. Cut 1 pound of whitefish or cod into 1-inch pieces. Add the fish to your slow cooker 45 minutes before serving. Cover and cook on LOW.

100 CIOPPINO

1 pound sea bass, cut into chunks, divided
1 can (4 ounces) sliced mushrooms, undrained
2 carrots, pared and sliced
1 medium onion, chopped
1 small green bell pepper, seeded and chopped
1 clove garlic, minced
1 can (15 ounces) tomato sauce
1 can (14 ounces) beef broth
Salt
⅛ teaspoon seasoned black pepper
½ teaspoon dried oregano leaves
1 can (7 ounces) clams, undrained
½ pound shelled, deveined shrimp
1 small lobster tail (optional)
1 package (6 ounces) frozen crabmeat, thawed and cartilage removed
Minced parsley

Combine half of sea bass in CROCK-POT® with vegetables, garlic, tomato sauce, beef broth and seasonings; stir well. Cover and cook on Low 10 to 12 hours or on High for 2 to 4 hours.

One hour before serving, turn to High and stir in remaining sea bass and seafood. Cover and cook on High 1 hour or until done.

Garnish with minced parsley and serve in soup plates. Accompany with hot Italian bread.

Makes 6 servings

Mediterranean Fish Soup

SLOW COOKER MAIN DISHES

101 VEGGIE MAC AND TUNA

1½ cups (6 ounces) elbow macaroni
3 tablespoons butter or margarine
1 small onion, chopped
½ medium red bell pepper, chopped
½ medium green bell pepper, chopped
¼ cup all-purpose flour
1¾ cups milk
8 ounces cubed light pasteurized process cheese product
½ teaspoon dried marjoram leaves
1 package (10 ounces) frozen peas
1 can (9 ounces) tuna in water, drained

COOK macaroni according to package directions until just tender; drain. Melt butter in medium saucepan over medium heat. Add onion and bell peppers. Cook and stir 5 minutes or until tender. Add flour. Stir constantly over medium heat 2 minutes. Stir in milk and bring to a boil. Boil, stirring constantly, until thickened. Reduce heat to low; add cheese and marjoram. Stir until cheese is melted.

COMBINE macaroni, cheese sauce, peas and tuna in slow cooker. Cover and cook on LOW 2½ hours or until bubbly at edge.

Makes 6 servings

102 EASY SHRIMP CREOLE

2 tablespoons butter or margarine
⅓ cup chopped onion
2 tablespoons buttermilk biscuit mix
1½ cups water
1 can (6 ounces) tomato paste
1 teaspoon salt
Dash black pepper
¼ teaspoon sugar
1 bay leaf
½ cup chopped celery
½ cup chopped green bell pepper
2 pounds frozen shrimp, thawed, shelled and cleaned *or* 3 cans (5 ounces each) shrimp, rinsed and drained
Hot cooked rice

In skillet, melt butter; add onion and cook slightly. Add biscuit mix and stir until well blended. Combine remaining ingredients except shrimp and rice. Add with onion mixture to CROCK-POT®; stir well. Cover and cook on Low 7 to 9 hours.

One hour before serving, turn to High and add shrimp. Remove bay leaf and serve over hot fluffy rice.

Double recipe for 5-quart CROCK-POT®.

Makes 6 servings

Veggie Mac and Tuna

SLOW COOKER MAIN DISHES

103 CLAM CASSEROLE

3 cans (6½ ounces each) minced clams, drained
4 eggs, well beaten
½ cup minced onion
⅓ cup milk
¼ cup butter, melted
¼ cup minced green bell pepper
1 teaspoon salt
18 saltine crackers, coarsely crushed (about 1 cup)

In bowl, mix all ingredients. Pour into well-greased CROCK-POT®. Cover and cook on Low 5 to 6 hours.   *Makes 6 servings*

104 HALIBUT IN CREAMY WINE SAUCE

2 packages (12 ounces each) frozen halibut steaks, thawed
2 tablespoons all-purpose flour
1 tablespoon sugar
¼ teaspoon salt
¼ cup butter
⅓ cup dry white wine
⅔ cup milk or half-and-half
    Lemon wedges

Pat halibut steaks dry; place in CROCK-POT®. Combine flour, sugar and salt.

In saucepan, melt butter; stir in flour mixture. When well blended, add wine and milk; cook over medium heat until thickened, stirring constantly. Allow sauce to boil 1 minute while stirring. Pour sauce over fish. Cover and cook on High 2½ to 3 hours.

Transfer halibut to serving platter; garnish with lemon.   *Makes 6 servings*

105 SWISS–CRAB CASSEROLE

3 tablespoons butter
½ cup chopped celery
½ cup chopped onion
¼ cup chopped green bell pepper (optional)
3 tablespoons all-purpose flour
3 chicken bouillon cubes
2½ cups boiling water
1 cup quick-cooking rice
2 cans (7 ounces each) crabmeat, drained, flaked and cartilage removed
2 cups grated Swiss cheese
1 can (4 ounces) sliced mushrooms, drained
¼ cup sliced pimiento-stuffed olives
¼ cup sliced almonds (optional)
1 cup buttered bread crumbs
½ cup grated Swiss cheese

In skillet, melt butter and lightly sauté celery, onion and green bell pepper. Remove from heat and blend in flour. Dissolve bouillon cubes in boiling water. Add to skillet and bring to a boil, stirring constantly. Cook sauce over medium heat about 2 minutes or until slightly thickened.

Lightly toss remaining ingredients except buttered crumbs and ½ cup grated cheese in CROCK-POT®. Add sauce; stir lightly to blend. Cover and cook on High 3 to 5 hours.

Pour contents of CROCK-POT® into shallow heatproof serving dish. Cover with buttered bread crumbs and sprinkle with ½ cup grated cheese. Set under broiler until cheese is melted and bread crumbs are crunchy brown.   *Makes 4 to 6 servings*

106 FISHERMAN'S CATCH CHOWDER

1 to 1½ pounds fish (use any combination of the following: flounder, ocean perch, pike, rainbow trout, haddock or halibut)
1 can (16 ounces) whole tomatoes, mashed
1 bottle (8 ounces) clam juice
½ cup chopped onion
½ cup chopped celery
½ cup chopped pared carrots
½ cup dry white wine
¼ cup snipped parsley
¼ teaspoon leaf rosemary
1 teaspoon salt
3 tablespoons all-purpose flour
3 tablespoons butter or margarine, melted
⅓ cup light cream

Cut cleaned fish into 1-inch pieces. Combine all ingredients except flour, butter and cream in CROCK-POT®; stir well. Cover and cook on Low 7 to 8 hours or on High 3 to 4 hours.

One hour before serving, combine flour, butter and cream. Stir into fish mixture. Continue to cook until mixture is slightly thickened.

Double recipe for 5-quart CROCK-POT®.

Makes 4 servings

107 HERBED SALMON BAKE

2 chicken bouillon cubes
1 cup boiling water
1 can (16 ounces) salmon, drained and flaked
2 cups seasoned stuffing croutons
1 cup grated Cheddar cheese
2 eggs, beaten
¼ teaspoon dry mustard

Dissolve bouillon cubes in boiling water. Combine all ingredients; mix well. Pour into well-greased CROCK-POT®. Cover and cook on High 2 to 4 hours. *Makes 4 servings*

108 TUNA SALAD CASSEROLE

2 cans (7 ounces each) tuna, drained and flaked
1 can (10¾ ounces) condensed cream of celery soup
3 hard-cooked eggs, chopped
1½ cups diced celery
½ cup mayonnaise
¼ teaspoon black pepper
1½ cups crushed potato chips, divided

Combine all ingredients except ¼ cup of crushed potato chips; stir well. Pour into greased CROCK-POT®. Top with reserved potato chips. Cover and cook on Low 5 to 8 hours. *Makes 4 servings*

SLOW COOKER MAIN DISHES

109 MEDITERRANEAN STEW

1 medium butternut or acorn squash, peeled and cut into 1-inch cubes
2 cups unpeeled eggplant, cut into 1-inch cubes
2 cups sliced zucchini
1 can (15½ ounces) chick-peas (garbanzo beans), rinsed and drained
1 package (10 ounces) frozen cut okra
1 can (8 ounces) tomato sauce
1 cup chopped onion
1 medium tomato, chopped
1 medium carrot, thinly sliced
½ cup reduced-sodium vegetable broth
⅓ cup raisins
1 clove garlic, minced
½ teaspoon ground cumin
½ teaspoon ground turmeric
¼ to ½ teaspoon ground red pepper
¼ teaspoon ground cinnamon
¼ teaspoon paprika
6 to 8 cups hot cooked couscous or rice
Fresh parsley (optional)

COMBINE all ingredients except couscous and parsley in slow cooker; mix well. Cover and cook on LOW 8 to 10 hours or until vegetables are crisp-tender. Serve over couscous. Garnish with parsley, if desired.

Makes 6 servings

110 MONTEREY SPAGHETTI

4 ounces spaghetti, broken into 2-inch pieces
1 egg
1 cup sour cream
¼ cup grated Parmesan cheese
¼ teaspoon garlic powder
3 cups shredded Monterey Jack cheese, divided
1 package (10 ounces) frozen chopped spinach, thawed and drained
1 can (3 ounces) french fried onions, divided

Grease CROCK-POT®. Cook spaghetti in boiling water 5 to 7 minutes. Drain. In small bowl, beat egg. Transfer to CROCK-POT®. Add sour cream, Parmesan cheese and garlic powder. Mix spaghetti, 2 cups Monterey Jack cheese, spinach and half the onions in CROCK-POT®. Cover and cook on Low 6 to 8 hours or on High 3 to 4 hours. In last 30 minutes of cooking, turn to High if cooking on Low and add remainder of Monterey Jack cheese and onions to top of casserole. Serve when cheese is melted.

Makes 6 to 8 servings

Mediterranean Stew

SLOW COOKER MAIN DISHES

111 BEAN AND CORNBREAD CASSEROLE

1 medium onion, chopped
1 medium green bell pepper, chopped
2 cloves garlic minced *or* ¼ teaspoon garlic powder
1 can (16 ounces) red kidney beans, undrained
1 can (16 ounces) pinto beans, undrained
1 can (16 ounces) no-salt-added diced tomatoes, undrained
1 can (8 ounces) no-salt-added tomato sauce
1 teaspoon chili powder
½ teaspoon black pepper
½ teaspoon prepared mustard
⅛ teaspoon hot sauce
1 cup yellow cornmeal
1 cup all-purpose flour
2½ teaspoons baking powder
1 tablespoon sugar
½ teaspoon salt
1¼ cups milk
½ cup egg substitute
3 tablespoons vegetable oil
1 can (8½ ounces) no-salt-added cream-style corn

Lightly grease CROCK-POT®. In skillet over medium heat, cook onion, green pepper and garlic until tender. Transfer to CROCK-POT®. Stir in kidney beans and pinto beans. Add diced tomatoes and juice, tomato sauce, seasonings and hot sauce. Cover and cook on High 1 hour.

In mixing bowl, combine cornmeal, flour, baking powder, sugar and salt. Stir in milk, egg substitute, vegetable oil and cream-style corn. Spoon evenly over bean mixture; may have leftover cornbread depending on size of CROCK-POT® being used (if there is remaining cornbread, spoon into greased muffin tins and bake at 375°F for 30 minutes or until golden brown). Cover and cook on High 1½ to 2 more hours. Serve.

Makes 6 to 8 servings

112 POTATO AND MUSHROOM CHOWDER

½ cup chopped onion
1 cup chopped celery
¼ cup margarine or butter
2 tablespoons all-purpose flour
1 teaspoon salt
½ teaspoon black pepper
2 cups water
2 cups diced peeled potatoes
2 cans (4 ounces each) sliced mushrooms, drained
1 cup chopped carrots
2 cups milk
¼ cup grated Parmesan cheese

In skillet, sauté onion and celery in margarine until onion is translucent. Remove from heat. Add flour, salt and pepper; stir. Place in CROCK-POT®. Add water; stir in potatoes, canned mushrooms and carrots. Cover and cook on Low 6 to 8 hours or on High 3 to 4 hours. If on Low turn to High. Add milk and Parmesan cheese and cook 30 minutes. Serve.

SHORTCUT: Use 2 cups frozen hash browns and 1 cup frozen carrots and cook on High 2 to 3 hours.

Bean and Cornbread Casserole

SLOW COOKER MAIN DISHES

113 LENTIL STEW OVER COUSCOUS

3 cups water
3 cups lentils (1 pound), rinsed
1 can (about 14 ounces) diced tomatoes, undrained
1 can (about 14 ounces) reduced-sodium chicken broth
1 large onion, chopped
1 green bell pepper, chopped
4 ribs celery, chopped
1 medium carrot, cut lengthwise into halves, then cut into 1-inch pieces
2 cloves garlic, chopped
1 teaspoon dried marjoram leaves
¼ teaspoon black pepper
1 tablespoon cider vinegar
1 tablespoon olive oil
4½ to 5 cups hot cooked couscous
   Carrot curls (optional)
   Celery leaves (optional)

COMBINE water, lentils, tomatoes, broth, onion, bell pepper, celery, carrot, garlic, marjoram and black pepper in slow cooker. Stir; cover and cook on LOW 8 to 9 hours.

STIR in vinegar and olive oil. Serve over couscous. Garnish with carrot curls and celery leaves, if desired.

Makes 12 servings

TIP: Lentil stew keeps well in the refrigerator for up to one week. Stew can also be frozen in airtight container in freezer up to three months.

114 VEGETABLE CHILI

1 can (28 ounces) whole tomatoes, undrained
1 can (16 ounces) garbanzo beans, drained
2 zucchini, thinly sliced
1 large onion, chopped
2 carrots, thinly sliced
2 celery ribs, thinly sliced
1 red bell pepper, seeded and chopped
1 green bell pepper, seeded and chopped
⅓ cup chili powder
1 can (4 ounces) chopped green chiles
2 cloves garlic, minced
1 tablespoon dried oregano leaves
2 teaspoons ground cumin
1 teaspoon salt
   Sour cream for garnish

In CROCK-POT®, combine tomatoes, beans, zucchini, onion, carrots, celery, bell peppers, chili powder, green chilies, garlic, oregano, cumin and salt. Cover and cook on Low 6 to 8 hours or High 3 to 4 hours. Cook until vegetables are tender. Serve immediately. Garnish with sour cream if desired.

Makes 6 to 8 servings

Lentil Stew over Couscous

SLOW COOKER MAIN DISHES

115 CORN CHOWDER

¾ **cup chopped onion**
2 **tablespoons margarine or butter**
1 **cup frozen hash brown potatoes**
1 **cup diced, cooked ham**
1 **package (10 ounces) frozen corn**
1 **cup cream-style corn**
1 **can (10¾ ounces) cream of mushroom soup, undiluted**
2½ **cups milk**
Salt
Black pepper
Parsley flakes

Combine onion, margarine, potatoes, ham, corn, cream of mushroom soup and milk in CROCK-POT®. Cover and cook on High 4 to 5 hours. Salt and pepper to taste. Garnish with parsley flakes. Serve.

Makes 8 servings

116 FRESH TOMATO SAUCE

4 **cups peeled, seeded and finely chopped tomatoes**
1 **medium onion, minced**
1 **can (6 ounces) tomato paste**
1½ **teaspoons dried basil leaves**
1 **teaspoon sugar**
3 **cloves garlic, crushed**

Combine all ingredients in lightly oiled CROCK-POT®. Cover and cook on Low 6 to 12 hours or on High 4 hours. If thicker sauce is desired, remove cover and cook on High until sauce is reduced.

This is good used in any recipe calling for tomato sauce.

Double recipe for 5-quart CROCK-POT®.

Makes about 5 cups

117 MARINARA SAUCE

2 **cans (28 ounces each) whole tomatoes**
1 **onion, finely chopped**
2 **carrots, pared and finely chopped**
1 **clove garlic, chopped**
2 **tablespoons vegetable oil**
1½ **teaspoons sugar**
1½ **teaspoons salt**

Place tomatoes in batches in blender container; blend until smooth (or purée tomatoes through a food mill).

In skillet, sauté onion, carrots and garlic in oil just until tender (do not brown). Combine all ingredients in CROCK-POT®; stir well. Cover and cook on Low 6 to 10 hours. Remove cover, stir well and cook on High last hour for thicker marinara sauce.

Makes about 6 cups

SLOW COOKER MAIN DISHES

118 BLACK BEAN AND POTATO SOUP

1 can (16 ounces) black beans, drained
2 potatoes, washed and diced
½ pound cooked ham, cut in pieces
6 cups beef broth
¼ cup dried chopped onions
1 can (4 ounces) chopped jalapeño peppers or mild chili peppers
1 clove garlic, minced
1 teaspoon ground cumin
1 teaspoon ground oregano
1 teaspoon ground thyme
⅛ teaspoon ground cloves
   Garnish: sour cream and chopped tomatoes

In CROCK-POT®, combine beans, potatoes, ham, broth, onions, peppers, garlic, cumin, oregano, thyme and cloves. Cover and cook on Low 8 to 10 hours or on High 4 to 5 hours. Serve. Garnish with sour cream and chopped tomatoes if desired.

Makes 6 to 8 servings

119 VEGETABLE AND PASTA SOUP

2 cans (14½ ounces each) beef broth
1 can (14 ounces) whole tomatoes
2 zucchini, thinly sliced
1½ cups water
1 onion, chopped
2 carrots, peeled and thinly sliced
1 tablespoon plus 4 teaspoons dried parsley flakes
1 tablespoon dried oregano leaves
1½ cups small shell-shaped pasta, uncooked
   Grated Parmesan cheese

In CROCK-POT®, combine beef broth, tomatoes, zucchini, water, onion, carrots, parsley and oregano. Cover and cook on Low 8 to 10 hours or High 4 to 5 hours. Stir in uncooked pasta and cook additional 30 minutes or until pasta is tender. Garnish with grated Parmesan cheese. Serve.

Makes 6 to 8 servings

SLOW COOKER MAIN DISHES

120 ARROZ CON QUESO

1 can (16 ounces) whole tomatoes, mashed
1 can (16 ounces) Mexican-style beans
1½ cups uncooked long-grain converted rice
1 large onion, finely chopped
1 cup cottage cheese
1 can (4 ounces) green chili peppers, drained, seeded and chopped
2 tablespoons vegetable oil
3 cloves garlic, minced
2 cups grated Monterey Jack or processed cheese, divided

Mix all ingredients thoroughly except 1 cup grated cheese. Pour mixture into well-greased CROCK-POT®. Cover and cook on Low 6 to 9 hours.

Just before serving, sprinkle with reserved grated cheese.   *Makes 6 to 8 servings*

121 OLD–FASHIONED ONION SOUP

3 pounds large onions, peeled and thinly sliced
½ cup butter, melted
6 to 8 slices French bread, cubed
4 to 5 cups chicken broth

Place sliced onions in CROCK-POT®; pour in butter and mix to coat onions thoroughly. Stir in cubed bread. Add chicken broth to cover; stir well. Cover and cook on Low 10 to 18 hours or on High 4 to 5 hours, stirring occasionally. Stir well during last hour.

Makes 6 to 8 servings

122 MINESTRONE SOUP

2 packages (16 ounces each) frozen vegetables and pasta in garlic seasoned sauce
4 cups reduced-sodium vegetable juice cocktail
2 cans (15½ ounces each) red kidney beans, rinsed and drained
1 cup beef broth
1 tablespoon minced onion
½ teaspoon dried Italian seasoning
½ teaspoon dried basil leaves
½ teaspoon salt
½ teaspoon black pepper

Combine all ingredients in CROCK-POT®. Cover and cook on Low 4 to 6 hours or High 2 to 3 hours. Serve.   *Makes 8 servings*

123 MACARONI AND CHEESE

3 cups cooked macaroni
1 tablespoon butter or margarine, melted
3 cups shredded sharp processed cheese
2 cups evaporated milk
¼ cup finely chopped green bell pepper
¼ cup chopped onion
1 teaspoon salt
¼ teaspoon black pepper

Toss macaroni with butter or margarine. Add remaining ingredients. Pour into lightly greased CROCK-POT®. Cover and cook on High 2 to 3 hours, stirring once or twice.

Arroz con Queso

SLOW COOKER MAIN DISHES

124 GARDEN VEGETABLE TABBOULEH STEW

1 large onion, chopped
2 medium carrots, cut lengthwise into halves, then cut into 1-inch pieces
1 cup green beans, cut into 1-inch pieces
2 medium green onions, thinly sliced
1 small zucchini (4 ounces), sliced
1 can (15½ ounces) chick-peas (garbanzo beans), rinsed and drained
2 cans (14½ ounces each) diced tomatoes, undrained
¼ teaspoon salt
⅛ teaspoon black pepper
1 box (6 to 7 ounces) tabbouleh mix
1½ cups water
¼ cup olive oil
    Sour cream (optional)
    Fresh mint (optional)

LAYER ingredients in slow cooker in the following order: onion, carrots, green beans, green onions, zucchini, chick-peas, tomatoes with juice, salt and pepper. Sprinkle tabbouleh mix over vegetables. Pour water and olive oil evenly over top. Cover and cook on LOW 6 to 8 hours or until vegetables are crisp-tender. Serve in bowls and garnish with sour cream and fresh mint, if desired.   *Makes 4 servings*

125 VEGETABLE CHEESE SOUP

1 can (16 ounces) cream-style corn
1 cup chopped, peeled potatoes
1 cup chopped carrots
½ cup chopped onion
1 teaspoon celery seed
½ teaspoon black pepper
2 cans (14½ ounces each) vegetable broth or chicken broth
1 jar (16 ounces) processed cheese

In CROCK-POT®, combine corn, potatoes, carrots, onion, celery seed and pepper. Add broth. Cover and cook on Low 8 to 10 hours or on High 4 to 5 hours. If using Low, turn to High. Stir cheese into CROCK-POT®. Cover and cook 30 to 60 minutes or until cheese is melted and blended. Serve.
            Makes 4 to 6 servings

TIME–SAVING TIP: Omit the potatoes and chopped carrots. Stir in 1 (10-ounce) bag frozen mixed vegetables. Cover and cook on High 2 to 3 hours and then stir in cheese and continue to cook on High until well blended.

Garden Vegetable Tabbouleh Stew

SLOW COOKER MAIN DISHES

126 MINESTRONE ALLA MILANESE

2 cans (about 14 ounces each) reduced-sodium beef broth
1 can (14½ ounces) diced tomatoes, undrained
1 cup diced potato
1 cup coarsely chopped green cabbage
1 cup coarsely chopped carrots
1 cup sliced zucchini
¾ cup chopped onion
¾ cup sliced fresh green beans
¾ cup coarsely chopped celery
¾ cup water
2 tablespoons olive oil
1 clove garlic, minced
½ teaspoon dried basil leaves
¼ teaspoon dried rosemary leaves
1 bay leaf
1 can (15½ ounces) cannellini beans, rinsed and drained
Grated Parmesan cheese (optional)

COMBINE all ingredients except cannellini beans in slow cooker; mix well. Cover and cook on LOW 5 to 6 hours. Add cannellini beans. Cover and cook on LOW 1 hour or until vegetables are crisp-tender. Remove and discard bay leaf. Garnish with cheese, if desired. *Makes 8 to 10 servings*

127 CREAMY VEGETABLE SOUP

1 large onion, chopped
¼ cup margarine or butter, melted
3 medium sweet potatoes, peeled and chopped
3 zucchini, chopped
1 to 2 cups chopped broccoli
3 cans (14½ ounces each) chicken broth
2 medium potatoes, peeled and shredded
½ teaspoon celery seed
2 teaspoons salt
1 teaspoon ground cumin
1 teaspoon black pepper
2 cups milk

In CROCK-POT®, stir together onion, margarine, sweet potatoes, zucchini and broccoli. Pour in chicken broth and stir. Add potatoes and seasonings. Stir. Cover and cook on Low 8 to 10 hours or on High 4 to 5 hours. Add milk and cook 30 minutes to 1 hour. Serve. *Makes 12 servings*

Minestrone alla Milanese

SLOW COOKER MAIN DISHES

128 BEAN RAGOÛT WITH CILANTRO–CORNMEAL DUMPLINGS

2 cans (14½ ounces each) tomatoes, chopped and juice reserved
1½ cups chopped red bell pepper
1 large onion, chopped
1 can (15½ ounces) pinto or kidney beans, rinsed and drained
1 can (15½ ounces) black beans, rinsed and drained
2 small zucchini, sliced
½ cup chopped green bell pepper
½ cup chopped celery
1 poblano chili pepper,* seeded and chopped
2 cloves garlic, minced
3 tablespoons chili powder
2 teaspoons ground cumin
1 teaspoon dried oregano leaves
½ teaspoon salt, divided
⅛ teaspoon black pepper
¼ cup all-purpose flour
¼ cup yellow cornmeal
½ teaspoon baking powder
1 tablespoon vegetable shortening
2 tablespoons shredded Cheddar cheese
2 teaspoons minced fresh cilantro
¼ cup milk

Chili peppers can sting and irritate the skin; wear rubber gloves when handling peppers and do not touch eyes.

COMBINE tomatoes with juice, red bell pepper, onion, beans, zucchini, green bell pepper, celery, poblano pepper, garlic, chili powder, cumin, oregano, ¼ teaspoon salt and black pepper in slow cooker; mix well. Cover and cook on LOW 7 to 8 hours.

PREPARE dumplings 1 hour before serving. Mix flour, cornmeal, baking powder and remaining ¼ teaspoon salt in medium bowl. Cut in shortening with pastry blender or two knives until mixture resembles coarse crumbs. Stir in cheese and cilantro. Pour milk into flour mixture. Blend just until dry ingredients are moistened. Turn slow cooker to HIGH. Drop dumplings by level tablespoonfuls (larger dumplings will not cook properly) on top of ragoût. Cover and cook 1 hour or until toothpick inserted in dumpling comes out clean.

Makes 6 servings

129 TWO–BEAN CORN CHILI

1 can (16 ounces) black-eyed peas
1 can (16 ounces) navy beans
1 onion, chopped
1 cup water
1 cup fresh, frozen or canned corn
1 cup diced tomatoes
½ cup tomato paste
½ cup chopped scallions
¼ cup diced canned jalapeño peppers
2 teaspoons chili powder
1 teaspoon prepared mustard
½ teaspoon ground cumin
¼ teaspoon dried oregano

Combine above ingredients in CROCK-POT®. Cover and cook on Low 8 to 10 hours or on High 4 to 5 hours. Serve.

Makes 6 to 8 servings

Bean Ragoût with Cilantro-Cornmeal Dumplings

Slow Cooker
Side Dishes

130 BEAN POT MEDLEY

1 can (15½ ounces) black beans, rinsed and drained
1 can (15½ ounces) red beans, rinsed and drained
1 can (15½ ounces) Great Northern beans, rinsed and drained
1 can (15½ ounces) black-eyed peas, rinsed and drained
1 can (8½ ounces) baby lima beans, rinsed and drained
1½ cups ketchup
1 cup chopped onion
1 cup chopped red bell pepper
1 cup chopped green bell pepper
½ cup packed brown sugar
½ cup water
2 to 3 teaspoons cider vinegar
1 teaspoon dry mustard
2 bay leaves
⅛ teaspoon black pepper

COMBINE all ingredients in slow cooker; stir. Cover and cook on LOW 6 to 7 hours or until onion and peppers are tender. Remove and discard bay leaves.

Makes 8 servings

131 ASPARAGUS CASSEROLE

2 packages (10 ounces each) frozen asparagus spears, thawed
2 cups crushed saltine crackers
1 can (10¾ ounces) condensed cream of celery soup
1 can (10¾ ounces) condensed cream of chicken soup
1 cup cubed processed American cheese
1 egg
½ cup slivered almonds

In large bowl, combine all ingredients; stir well. Pour into lightly greased CROCK-POT®. Cover and cook on High 3 to 3½ hours.

After cooking, dish may be held on Low up to 2 hours before serving.

Makes 4 to 6 servings

NOTE: 2 cans (14½ ounces each) asparagus pieces, drained, may be substituted for frozen asparagus.

Bean Pot Medley

SLOW COOKER SIDE DISHES

132 SWEET POTATO CASSEROLE

2 cans (18 ounces each) sweet potatoes, drained and mashed
⅓ cup margarine or butter, melted
2 tablespoons granulated sugar
2 tablespoons brown sugar
1 tablespoon orange juice
2 eggs, beaten
½ cup milk
⅓ cup chopped pecans
⅓ cup brown sugar
2 tablespoons all-purpose flour
2 tablespoons margarine or butter, melted

Lightly grease CROCK-POT®. Mix sweet potatoes, ⅓ cup margarine, 2 tablespoons granulated sugar and 2 tablespoons brown sugar in large bowl. Beat in orange juice, eggs and milk. Transfer to CROCK-POT®.

Combine pecans, ⅓ cup brown sugar, flour and 2 tablespoons margarine. Spread over sweet potatoes.

Cover and cook on High 3 to 4 hours. Serve.
Makes 6 to 8 servings

133 SCALLOPED POTATOES

1 package (16 ounces) frozen hash brown potatoes
1 can (10¾ ounces) cream of mushroom soup
1½ cups milk
1 cup shredded Cheddar cheese
1 small green bell pepper, cut into small pieces
½ cup margarine or butter, melted
¼ cup dried chopped onion
2 tablespoons chopped pimiento
⅛ teaspoon black pepper
1 cup cheese cracker crumbs, divided

Lightly grease CROCK-POT®. Stir together hash brown potatoes, cream of mushroom soup, milk, cheese, green bell pepper, margarine, onion, pimiento, black pepper and ½ cup cracker crumbs. Transfer to CROCK-POT®. Top with remaining cracker crumbs. Cover and cook on High 3 to 4 hours. Serve. *Makes 6 to 8 servings*

Sweet Potato Casserole

SLOW COOKER SIDE DISHES

134 ORANGE–SPICE GLAZED CARROTS

  1 package (32 ounces) baby carrots
  ½ cup packed brown sugar
  ½ cup orange juice
  3 tablespoons butter or margarine
  ¾ teaspoon ground cinnamon
  ¼ teaspoon ground nutmeg
  2 tablespoons cornstarch
  ¼ cup water

COMBINE all ingredients except cornstarch and water in slow cooker. Cover and cook on LOW 3½ to 4 hours or until carrots are crisp-tender. Spoon carrots into serving bowl. Remove juices to small saucepan. Heat to a boil. Mix cornstarch and water in small bowl until blended. Stir into saucepan. Boil 1 minute or until thickened; stir constantly. Pour over carrots.

Makes 6 servings

135 LIMA BEAN CASSEROLE

  2 cans (10¾ ounces each) condensed
     cream of celery soup
  3 packages (10 ounces each) frozen baby
     lima beans, thawed
  2 small onions, thinly sliced
  2 cans (4 ounces each) sliced mushrooms,
     undrained
  1 jar (2 ounces) chopped pimientos,
     drained
  2 teaspoons salt
  ⅛ teaspoon black pepper
  ½ teaspoon dill seed
  ½ cup heavy cream
  1 cup grated Parmesan cheese

Combine all ingredients except heavy cream and Parmesan cheese in CROCK-POT®; stir well. Cover and cook on Low 10 to 12 hours. Add cream just before serving; stir well. Sprinkle Parmesan cheese on top.

Makes 8 to 10 servings

Orange-Spice Glazed Carrots

SLOW COOKER SIDE DISHES

136 LOUISE'S BROCCOLI CASSEROLE

2 packages (10 ounces each) frozen
    broccoli spears, thawed and cut up
1 can (10¾ ounces) condensed cream of
    celery soup
1¼ cups grated sharp Cheddar cheese,
    divided
¼ cup minced green onions
1 cup crushed saltine crackers or potato
    chips

In large bowl, combine broccoli, celery
soup, 1 cup cheese and onions. Pour into
lightly greased CROCK-POT®. Sprinkle top
with crushed crackers, then with remaining
cheese. Cover and cook on Low 5 to 6 hours
or on High 2½ to 3 hours.

Makes 4 to 6 servings

NOTE: If desired, casserole may be spooned
into a baking dish and garnished with
additional grated cheese and broken potato
chips; bake 5 to 10 minutes in 400°F oven.

137 SPINACH NOODLE CASSEROLE

1 package (8 ounces) spinach noodles
2 tablespoons vegetable oil or melted
    butter
1½ cups (12 ounces) sour cream
⅓ cup all-purpose flour
1½ cups small-curd cream-style cottage
    cheese
4 green onions with tops, finely minced
2 teaspoons Worcestershire sauce
    Dash hot pepper sauce
2 teaspoons garlic salt

Cook noodles according to package
directions until barely tender. Rinse in cold
water and drain. Toss with oil. In large bowl,
mix sour cream and flour. Stir in remaining
ingredients. Add noodles and stir well to
coat. Pour into well-greased CROCK-POT®.
Cover and cook on High 1½ to 2½ hours. If
desired, serve with additional sour cream.

Makes 8 servings

Louise's Broccoli Casserole

SLOW COOKER SIDE DISHES

138 BEAN CASSEROLE

3 cans (16 ounces each) pork and beans, drained
1 can (16 ounces) pork and beans, undrained
1 cup shredded sharp Cheddar cheese
¾ cup chopped onion
1 tablespoon plus 1 teaspoon chili powder
4 tablespoons Worcestershire sauce
4 tablespoons brown sugar
2 tablespoons white vinegar
1 tablespoon prepared mustard
8 slices bacon, fried and crumbled

Lightly grease CROCK-POT®. Combine beans, cheese, onion, chili powder, Worcestershire sauce, brown sugar, vinegar and mustard in CROCK-POT®. Top with bacon. Cover and cook on Low 6 to 8 hours or on High 3 to 4 hours. Serve.

Makes 8 to 10 servings

139 CREAM CHEESE POTATOES

2 tablespoons minced or chopped dried onion
2 cloves garlic, minced *or* ¼ teaspoon garlic powder
1 teaspoon salt
¼ teaspoon black pepper
8 medium potatoes, scrubbed and sliced (about 2 pounds)
1 package (8 ounces) cream cheese, cut into cubes

Lightly grease CROCK-POT®. In small bowl, combine onion, garlic, salt and pepper. Layer ¼ of sliced potatoes in bottom of CROCK-POT®. Sprinkle with ¼ seasonings. Layer with ⅓ cream cheese cubes. Continue layering process, ending with layer of potatoes then sprinkle with seasonings. Cover and cook on High 3 to 4 hours. In last hour of cooking, stir potatoes to distribute cream cheese. Serve when potatoes are tender. *Makes 4 to 6 servings*

NOTE: If desired, potatoes can be slightly mashed prior to serving.

TIME–SAVING TIPS: 1. Cook potatoes in boiling water for about 30 minutes or until tender and then cut into strips. Mixture should be cooked on Low 6 to 8 hours or on High 2 hours or until potatoes are tender.

2. Substitute 32 ounces frozen hashbrowns for potatoes and prepare as directed. Cook on Low 4 to 6 hours or on High 2 hours.

SLOW COOKER SIDE DISHES

140 OLD-FASHIONED BAKED BEANS

1 pound dried navy beans
1 medium onion, finely chopped
½ cup ketchup
½ cup packed brown sugar
½ cup dark corn syrup
1 teaspoon paprika
½ teaspoon dried basil leaves
   Salt
1 pound smoked ham, bacon or salt pork, diced

Completely soften beans as directed below. Drain and combine beans and remaining ingredients in large bowl. Pour into CROCK-POT®. Cover and cook on Low 6 to 12 hours or on High 3 to 4 hours.

Makes 8 servings

A BIT ABOUT BEANS: Cooking with dried beans can be tricky, even in a CROCK-POT®. The minerals in the water and variations in voltage affect different types of beans in different ways. For best results, keep these points in mind:

• Dried beans, especially red kidney beans, should be boiled before adding to a recipe. Cover the beans with 3 times their volume of unsalted water and bring to a boil. Boil 10 minutes and reduce heat.

• Beans must be softened completely before combining with sugar and/or acidic foods. (Note: sugar and acid have a hardening effect on beans and will prevent softening.) After boiling beans 10 minutes, reduce heat, cover and allow to simmer 1½ hours or until beans are tender. Soaking in water, if desired, should be completed before boiling. Discard water after soaking or boiling.

141 SPICY WESTERN BEANS

⅓ cup lentils
1⅓ cups water
4 bacon strips, fried, diced and grease reserved
1 onion, chopped
2 tablespoons ketchup
1 teaspoon garlic powder
¾ teaspoon chili powder
½ teaspoon ground cumin
¼ teaspoon dried red pepper flakes
   Bay leaf
1 can (14 ounces) whole tomatoes, undrained, chopped
1 can (16 ounces) pinto beans, undrained
1 can (16 ounces) red kidney beans, undrained

Boil lentils in water 20 to 30 minutes. Drain. In bacon grease, cook onion until transparent. Combine lentils, bacon, onion, ketchup, garlic powder, chili powder, cumin, red pepper flakes, bay leaf, tomatoes and beans in CROCK-POT®. Cook on High 3 to 4 hours. Remove bay leaf. Serve.

Makes 8 to 10 servings

SLOW COOKER SIDE DISHES

142 GREEN BEANS WITH SAVORY MUSHROOM SAUCE

2 packages (10 ounces each) frozen French-style green beans, thawed
1 can (10¾ ounces) condensed cream of mushroom soup, undiluted
¼ cup dry vermouth or dry white wine
4 ounces (1½ cups) fresh mushrooms, sliced
½ teaspoon salt
½ teaspoon dried thyme leaves
¼ teaspoon black pepper
1 cup crushed prepared croutons or canned fried onion rings

COMBINE all ingredients except croutons in slow cooker. Mix until well blended. Cover and cook on LOW 3 to 4 hours or until beans are crisp-tender. Sprinkle with croutons. Serve warm.   *Makes 6 to 8 servings*

143 CHEESY POTATO CASSEROLE

7 medium potatoes (about 2 pounds)
1 can (10¾ ounces) cream of chicken soup
1 carton (8 ounces) sour cream
1 small onion, chopped *or* 1 tablespoon minced onion
¼ cup butter or margarine, melted
1 teaspoon salt
2 cups shredded Cheddar cheese
1½ to 2 cups herb-seasoning stuffing mix
3 tablespoons butter or margarine, melted

Peel and cut potatoes into ¼-inch strips; set aside.

Combine cream of chicken soup, sour cream, onion, ¼ cup melted butter and salt in a bowl.

Lightly butter inside of 5-quart CROCK-POT® and place potatoes inside. Mix 2 cups shredded Cheddar cheese with potatoes. Pour soup mixture into potatoes; mix well. Cover top of potato mixture with stuffing mix and drizzle with 3 tablespoons butter. Cover; cook on Low 8 to 10 hours until potatoes are tender or on High 5 to 6 hours.

TIME–SAVING TIPS: 1. Cook potatoes in boiling water about 30 minutes or until tender and then cut into strips. Mixture should be cooked on Low 6 to 8 hours or on High about 2 hours or until potatoes are tender.

2. Substitute 32 ounces of frozen hashbrowns for potatoes and prepare as directed. Cook on Low 4 to 6 hours or on High 2 hours.

Green Beans with Savory Mushroom Sauce

SLOW COOKER SIDE DISHES

144 RUSSIAN BORSCHT

4 cups thinly sliced green cabbage
1½ pounds fresh beets, shredded
5 small carrots, peeled, cut lengthwise into halves, then cut into 1-inch pieces
1 parsnip, peeled, cut lengthwise into halves, then cut into 1-inch pieces
1 cup chopped onion
4 cloves garlic, minced
1 pound lean beef stew meat, cut into ½-inch cubes
1 can (14½ ounces) diced tomatoes, undrained
3 cans (14½ ounces each) reduced-sodium beef broth
¼ cup lemon juice
1 tablespoon sugar
1 teaspoon black pepper
Sour cream (optional)
Fresh parsley (optional)

LAYER ingredients in slow cooker in the following order: cabbage, beets, carrots, parsnip, onion, garlic, beef, tomatoes with juice, broth, lemon juice, sugar and pepper. Cover and cook on LOW 7 to 9 hours or until vegetables are crisp-tender. Season with additional lemon juice and sugar, if desired. Dollop with sour cream and garnish with parsley, if desired. *Makes 12 servings*

145 CORN PUDDING

1 package (8 ounces) cream cheese, softened
2 eggs, beaten
⅓ cup sugar
1 package (8½ ounces) corn bread muffin mix
1 can (16 ounces) cream-style corn
2⅓ cups fresh or frozen sweet corn
1 cup milk
2 tablespoons margarine or butter, melted
1 teaspoon salt
¼ teaspoon ground nutmeg

Lightly grease CROCK-POT®. In mixing bowl, blend cream cheese, eggs and sugar. Add remaining ingredients and mix well. Transfer to CROCK-POT®. Cover and cook on High 3 to 4 hours. Serve.
Makes 10 to 12 servings

Russian Borscht

SLOW COOKER SIDE DISHES

146 ESCALLOPED CORN

2 tablespoons butter or margarine
½ cup chopped onion
3 tablespoons all-purpose flour
1 cup milk
4 cups frozen corn, thawed, divided
½ teaspoon salt
½ teaspoon dried thyme leaves
¼ teaspoon black pepper
⅛ teaspoon ground nutmeg
   Fresh thyme (optional)

HEAT butter in small saucepan over medium heat. Add onion; cook and stir 5 minutes or until tender. Add flour. Cook over medium heat 1 minute, stirring constantly. Stir in milk and heat to a boil. Boil 1 minute or until thickened, stirring constantly.

PROCESS half the corn in food processor or blender until coarsely chopped. Combine milk mixture, processed and whole corn, salt, dried thyme, pepper and nutmeg in slow cooker. Cover and cook on LOW 3½ to 4 hours or until mixture is bubbly around edge. Garnish with fresh thyme, if desired.

Makes 6 servings

NOTE: If desired, add ½ cup (2 ounces) shredded Cheddar cheese and 2 tablespoons grated Parmesan cheese before serving; stir until melted. Garnish with additional shredded Cheddar cheese, if desired.

147 SWEET–AND–SOUR GREEN BEANS

2 packages (10 ounces each) frozen French-style green beans, partially thawed
4 slices bacon, diced
1 small onion, diced
1 tablespoon all-purpose flour
¼ cup water
¼ cup cider vinegar
2 tablespoons sugar
1 tablespoon chopped pimiento
½ teaspoon salt
   Dash black pepper

Break apart green beans and place in CROCK-POT®. In skillet, fry bacon until crisp; remove bacon to absorbent towels to drain. Pour off all but 2 tablespoons bacon drippings from skillet; sauté onion in bacon drippings (do not brown). Dissolve flour in water; stir into bacon drippings and cook until slightly thickened. Combine bacon and remaining ingredients; stir into thickened onion mixture. Pour over green beans and stir well. Cover and cook on High 1 hour, then turn to Low 7 to 9 hours.

Makes 6 to 8 servings

Escalloped Corn

SLOW COOKER SIDE DISHES

148 BROWN–AND–WHITE RICE

8 slices bacon, diced
½ cup uncooked brown rice
3 cups beef broth
1 cup uncooked long-grain converted rice
1 can (4 ounces) sliced mushrooms, drained
4 green onions with tops, sliced
⅓ cup slivered almonds, toasted
3 tablespoons grated Parmesan cheese

In skillet, fry bacon until partially crisp but still limp. Stir in brown rice and cook over medium heat until rice is light golden brown. Add bacon and browned rice to CROCK-POT® with beef broth, converted rice, mushrooms and green onions; stir well. Cover and cook on Low 6 to 8 hours or on High 2½ to 3½ hours. Before serving; stir well and add salt if needed. Garnish with almonds and cheese.

Makes 6 to 8 servings

149 CORNMEAL MUSH

2 to 4 tablespoons butter or margarine, melted, divided
¼ teaspoon paprika
Dash cayenne pepper
6 cups boiling water
2 cups cornmeal (preferably water ground)
1 teaspoon salt

Use 1 tablespoon butter to lightly grease walls of CROCK-POT®. Add paprika and cayenne pepper. Turn to High. Add water, cornmeal, salt and remaining butter to CROCK-POT®; stir well. Cover and cook on Low 6 to 9 hours or on High 2 to 3 hours, stirring occasionally.

Makes 8 to 10 servings

FRIED CORNMEAL MUSH: Pour hot cornmeal into 2 lightly greased loaf pans. Chill overnight. To serve, cut into ¾-inch slices and fry in butter until browned.

SLOW COOKER SIDE DISHES

150 RED RICE

5 slices bacon
1 large onion, chopped
2 cans (16 ounces each) chopped, peeled tomatoes, undrained
1 cup converted long-grain rice, uncooked
1 cup finely chopped cooked ham
½ teaspoon salt
¼ teaspoon black pepper
⅛ teaspoon hot sauce

Fry bacon in skillet. Remove bacon and crumble. Cook onion in bacon drippings over medium-high heat until tender. Combine bacon, onion, tomatoes with juice, rice, ham and seasonings in CROCK-POT®. Cover and cook on Low 6 to 8 hours or on High 3 to 4 hours. Serve.

If hotter rice is desired, add more hot sauce to taste. *Makes 6 to 8 servings*

151 WILD RICE CASSEROLE

2 medium onions, finely chopped
3 stalks celery, thinly sliced
2 packages (7 ounces each) wild rice and long-grain converted rice mix
2½ cups water
1 can (10¾ ounces) condensed cream of mushroom soup
½ cup butter or margarine, melted
½ pound processed American cheese, cubed
1 can (4 ounces) sliced mushrooms, drained

Combine all ingredients in CROCK-POT®; stir thoroughly. Cover and cook on Low 6 to 10 hours or on High 2 to 3½ hours.

Makes 6 to 8 servings

SLOW COOKER SIDE DISHES

152 RISI BISI

1½ cups converted long-grain white rice
¾ cup chopped onion
2 cloves garlic, minced
2 cans (about 14 ounces each) reduced-
    sodium chicken broth
⅓ cup water
¾ teaspoon Italian seasoning
½ teaspoon dried basil leaves
½ cup frozen peas, thawed
¼ cup grated Parmesan cheese
¼ cup toasted pine nuts (optional)

COMBINE rice, onion and garlic in slow cooker. Heat broth and water in small saucepan to a boil. Stir boiling liquid, Italian seasoning and basil into rice mixture. Cover and cook on LOW 2 to 3 hours or until liquid is absorbed. Add peas. Cover and cook 1 hour. Stir in cheese. Spoon rice into serving bowl. Sprinkle with pine nuts, if desired.

Makes 6 servings

153 HUNGARIAN NOODLE SIDE DISH

3 chicken bouillon cubes
¼ cup boiling water
1 can (10¾ ounces) cream of mushroom
    soup
½ cup chopped onion
2 tablespoons Worcestershire sauce
1 tablespoon poppy seeds
¼ teaspoon garlic powder
¼ teaspoon hot pepper sauce
2 cups cottage cheese
2 cups sour cream
1 package (16 ounces) wide egg noodles,
    cooked and drained
¼ cup shredded Parmesan cheese
    Paprika

Lightly grease CROCK-POT®. In large bowl, dissolve bouillon in water. Add the next six ingredients. Stir in cottage cheese, sour cream and noodles. Transfer to CROCK-POT®. Sprinkle with Parmesan cheese and paprika. Cover and cook on High 3 to 4 hours. Serve immediately.

Makes 8 to 10 servings

Risi Bisi

SLOW COOKER SIDE DISHES

154 RUSTIC POTATOES AU GRATIN

½ cup milk
1 can (10¾ ounces) condensed Cheddar
   cheese soup, undiluted
1 package (8 ounces) cream cheese,
   softened
1 clove garlic, minced
¼ teaspoon ground nutmeg
⅛ teaspoon black pepper
2 pounds baking potatoes,* cut into
   ¼-inch slices
1 small onion, thinly sliced
   Paprika (optional)

Potatoes may be peeled, if desired.

HEAT milk in small saucepan over medium heat until small bubbles form around edge of pan. Remove from heat. Add soup, cheese, garlic, nutmeg and pepper. Stir until smooth. Layer ¼ of potatoes and onion in bottom of slow cooker. Top with ¼ of soup mixture. Repeat layers 3 times, using remaining ingredients. Cover and cook on LOW 6½ to 7 hours or until potatoes are tender and most of liquid is absorbed. Sprinkle with paprika, if desired.   *Makes 6 servings*

155 SPICY RICE CASSEROLE

4 cups boiling water
4 beef bouillon cubes
2 pounds mild bulk pork sausage
2 teaspoons ground cumin
1 teaspoon garlic powder
4 medium onions, chopped
4 medium green bell peppers, chopped
3 jalapeño peppers, seeded and minced
2 packages (6¼ ounces each) converted
   long-grain and wild rice mix

Pour boiling water into CROCK-POT® that has been set to High. Stir in bouillon cubes. Brown sausage, cumin and garlic powder in skillet. Drain. Add onions and green bell peppers; sauté until tender (15 to 20 minutes). Transfer to CROCK-POT®. Stir in jalapeño peppers and rice.

Cover and cook on High 1 hour, then turn to Low and cook 1 to 2 more hours. Serve.
          Makes 10 to 12 servings

NOTE: If a spicier rice casserole is desired, add seasoning mix that is included with rice.

Rustic Potatoes au Gratin

Slow Cooker
Breads & Treats

156 BOSTON BROWN BREAD

3 (16-ounce) cleaned and emptied
  vegetable cans
½ cup rye flour
½ cup yellow cornmeal
½ cup whole wheat flour
3 tablespoons sugar
1 teaspoon baking soda
¾ teaspoon salt
½ cup chopped walnuts
½ cup raisins
1 cup buttermilk*
⅓ cup molasses

* Soured fresh milk may be substituted. To sour, place 1 tablespoon lemon juice plus enough milk to equal 1 cup in 2-cup measure. Stir; let stand 5 minutes before using.

SPRAY vegetable cans and 1 side of three 6-inch-square pieces of aluminum foil with nonstick cooking spray; set aside. Combine rye flour, cornmeal, whole wheat flour, sugar, baking soda and salt in large bowl.

Stir in walnuts and raisins. Whisk buttermilk and molasses in medium bowl until blended. Add buttermilk mixture to dry ingredients; stir until well mixed. Spoon mixture evenly into prepared cans. Place 1 piece of foil, greased side down, on top of each can. Secure foil with rubber bands or cotton string.

PLACE filled cans in slow cooker. Pour boiling water into slow cooker to come halfway up sides of cans. (Make sure foil tops do not touch boiling water.) Cover and cook on LOW 4 hours or until skewer inserted in centers comes out clean. To remove bread, lay cans on side; roll and tap gently on all sides until bread releases. Cool completely on wire racks.

Makes 3 loaves

Boston Brown Bread

SLOW COOKER BREADS & TREATS

157 WHOLE WHEAT BANANA BREAD

²/₃ cup margarine or butter
1 cup sugar
2 eggs
1 cup mashed bananas (2 to 3 bananas)
1 cup whole wheat flour
1 cup all-purpose flour
¼ cup wheat germ
1 teaspoon baking soda
½ teaspoon salt
½ cup chopped pecans or walnuts

Grease and flour inside of Bread 'n Cake Bake Pan.

Cream margarine with electric mixer. Blend in sugar. Add eggs and mashed bananas. Beat until smooth.

In small bowl, combine flours, wheat germ, baking soda, salt and pecans. Add to creamed mixture. Pour into prepared Bread 'n Cake Bake Pan. Place lid on pan. Put Bread 'n Cake Bake Pan in CROCK-POT®. Cover CROCK-POT®. Cook on High 3 to 4 hours. Check after 3 hours for doneness. Bread is done when it is pulling away from sides of Bread 'n Cake Bake Pan.

When bread is done remove Bread 'n Cake Bake Pan from CROCK-POT®. Let bread cool then invert bread on plate and invert again for serving.   *Makes 1 loaf*

158 WHITE BREAD

1 package active dry yeast
1 teaspoon sugar
¼ cup warm water
1 egg
¼ cup vegetable oil
1 cup lukewarm water
1 teaspoon salt
¼ cup sugar
3½ to 4 cups all-purpose flour, divided

In large bowl, dissolve yeast and 1 teaspoon sugar in ¼ cup warm water. Allow to stand until it bubbles and foams. Add egg, oil, lukewarm water, salt, ¼ cup sugar and 2 cups flour. Beat with electric mixer 2 minutes. With wooden spoon, stir in remaining 1½ to 2 cups flour until dough leaves side of bowl. Place dough in well-greased Bread 'n Cake Bake Pan; cover. Place pan in 3½- or 5-quart CROCK-POT®. Cover and bake on High 2 to 3 hours or until edges are browned.

Remove pan and uncover. Let stand 5 minutes. Unmold on cake rack.

Makes 1 loaf

SLOW COOKER BREADS & TREATS

159 ORANGE DATE–NUT BREAD

1 cup snipped dates
4 teaspoons finely shredded orange peel
²⁄₃ cup boiling water
¹⁄₃ cup orange juice
³⁄₄ cup sugar
2 tablespoons shortening
1 egg, slightly beaten
1 teaspoon vanilla
2 cups all-purpose flour
1 teaspoon baking powder
½ teaspoon baking soda
¼ teaspoon salt
½ cup chopped nuts, such as pecans, walnuts, etc.

Grease and flour inside of Bread 'n Cake Bake Pan.

In large bowl, combine snipped dates and orange peel. Stir in boiling water and orange juice. Add sugar, shortening, egg and vanilla, stirring just until mixed.

In medium bowl, combine flour, baking powder, baking soda and salt. Add flour mixture to date mixture. Pour into prepared Bread 'n Cake Bake Pan. Place cover on Bread 'n Cake Bake Pan.

Place Bread 'n Cake Bake Pan in CROCK-POT®. Cover CROCK-POT® and bake on High 1½ to 2 hours. Check bread after 1½ hours for doneness. Bread is done when sides start pulling away from pan. *Makes 1 loaf*

160 HONEY WHEAT BREAD

2 cups warm reconstituted dry milk*
2 tablespoons vegetable oil
¼ cup honey
³⁄₄ teaspoon salt
1 package active dry yeast
3 cups whole wheat flour, divided
³⁄₄ to 1 cup all-purpose flour, divided

* Fresh milk may be used if scalded.

Combine warm (not hot) milk, oil, honey, salt, yeast and half the flour. With electric mixer, beat well about 2 minutes. Add remaining flour; mix well. Place dough in well-greased Bread 'n Cake Bake Pan; cover. Let stand 5 minutes. Place pan in 3½- or 5-quart CROCK-POT®. Cover and bake on High 2 to 3 hours.

Remove pan and uncover. Let stand 5 minutes. Unmold and serve warm.

Makes 1 loaf

SLOW COOKER BREADS & TREATS

161 ENGLISH BREAD PUDDING

16 slices day-old, firm-textured white bread
    (1 small loaf)
1¾ cups milk
  1 package (8 ounces) mixed dried fruit,
    cut into small pieces
  ½ cup chopped nuts
  1 medium apple, cored and chopped
  ¼ cup butter or margarine, melted
  ⅓ cup packed brown sugar
  1 egg, slightly beaten
  1 teaspoon ground cinnamon
  ¼ teaspoon ground nutmeg
  ¼ teaspoon ground cloves

TEAR bread, with crusts, into 1- to 2-inch pieces. Place in slow cooker. Pour milk over bread; let soak 30 minutes. Stir in dried fruit, nuts and apple. Combine remaining ingredients in small bowl. Pour over bread mixture. Stir well to blend. Cover and cook on LOW 3½ to 4 hours or until skewer inserted in center comes out clean.

Makes 6 to 8 servings

COOK'S NOOK: Chopping dried fruits can be difficult. To make the job easier, cut the fruit with kitchen scissors. You can also spray your scissors or chef's knife with nonstick cooking spray before you begin chopping so that the fruit won't stick to the blade.

162 STRAWBERRY CHEESECAKE

CRUST
1¼ cups graham cracker crumbs
  ¼ cup margarine or butter, melted

CHEESECAKE
  2 packages (8 ounces each) plus
    1 (3-ounce) package cream cheese,
    softened
  ½ cup sugar
  2 to 3 tablespoons all-purpose flour
  3 eggs
  ½ cup strawberry preserves
  1 pint fresh strawberries

Preheat oven to 350°F. Grease and flour inside of Bread 'n Cake Bake Pan.

Mix together graham cracker crumbs and melted margarine. Press into Bread 'n Cake Bake Pan. Do not cover with lid. Bake in oven 5 to 7 minutes. Set aside.

With electric mixer, cream softened cream cheese until smooth; mix in sugar and flour. Add eggs, one at a time, beating until fluffy. Fold in strawberry preserves. Pour over baked crust in Bread 'n Cake Bake Pan. Place lid on pan. Place Bread 'n Cake Bake Pan in CROCK-POT® and cover. Cook on High 2½ to 3 hours. Remove lid when cheesecake is set. Remove pan from CROCK-POT®. Allow to cool. Cover and refrigerate 8 hours. Remove and unmold onto plate; invert cheesecake onto serving platter. Top slices with fresh strawberries for serving.

English Bread Pudding

SLOW COOKER BREADS & TREATS

163 POACHED PEARS WITH RASPBERRY SAUCE

4 cups cran-raspberry juice cocktail
2 cups Rhine or Riesling wine
¼ cup sugar
2 cinnamon sticks, broken into halves
4 to 5 firm Bosc or Anjou pears, peeled, cored and seeded
1 package (10 ounces) frozen raspberries in syrup, thawed
Fresh berries (optional)

COMBINE juice, wine, sugar and cinnamon stick halves in slow cooker. Submerge pears in mixture. Cover and cook on LOW 3½ to 4 hours or until pears are tender. Remove and discard cinnamon sticks.

PROCESS raspberries in food processor or blender until smooth; strain out seeds. Spoon raspberry sauce onto serving plates; place pear on top of sauce. Garnish with fresh berries, if desired.

Makes 4 to 5 servings

164 CHOCOLATE NUT CAKE

⅔ cup margarine or butter
1½ cups sugar
4 eggs
1 cup prepared instant mashed potatoes
2 cups all-purpose flour
⅔ cup unsweetened cocoa
2 teaspoons baking powder
1 teaspoon salt
½ teaspoon ground cinnamon
½ cup milk
½ cup chopped pecans

Grease and flour inside of Bread 'n Cake Bake Pan.

Cream margarine with electric mixer. Beat in sugar and eggs until smooth. Mix in cooled potatoes.

In small bowl, combine flour, cocoa, baking powder, salt and cinnamon. Add to creamed mixture alternately with milk. Fold in nuts. Pour into prepared Bread 'n Cake Bake Pan. Place lid on pan. Set Bread 'n Cake Bake Pan inside CROCK-POT®. Cover CROCK-POT® and cook on High 3 to 4 hours or until toothpick inserted comes out clean. Check doneness after 3 hours. When cake is done remove pan from CROCK-POT® and let cool 5 to 10 minutes. Invert cake onto plate and invert again onto serving platter. Serve.

Poached Pears with Raspberry Sauce

SLOW COOKER BREADS & TREATS

165 BLACK FOREST CHEESECAKE

¾ **cup chocolate graham cracker cookies, crushed**
3 **packages (8 ounces each) fat-free cream cheese, softened**
1½ **cups sugar**
¾ **cup egg substitute**
1 **cup semisweet chocolate morsels, melted**
¼ **cup unsweetened cocoa powder**
1½ **teaspoons vanilla**
1 **carton (8 ounces) lite sour cream**
1 **can (21 ounces) cherry pie filling**
¾ **cup reduced-calorie frozen whipped topping, thawed**

Grease and flour Bread 'n Cake Bake Pan. Spread crushed cookies in bottom of pan; set aside.

Beat cream cheese with an electric mixer until fluffy. Gradually add sugar; beat well. Add egg substitute slowly, mixing well. Add melted chocolate, cocoa, vanilla and sour cream until well blended. Pour into prepared Bread 'n Cake Bake Pan. Place lid on pan. Place in CROCK-POT®. Cover CROCK-POT® and cook on High 4 hours. Remove from CROCK-POT® and remove Bread 'n Cake Bake lid. Run knife around edge of pan to release sides. Let cool completely.

Place lid back on Bread 'n Cake Bake Pan and refrigerate cheesecake at least 8 hours. Remove cheesecake from refrigerator, invert pan and run bottom of Bread 'n Cake Bake Pan briefly under warm water. On plate, invert Bread 'n Cake Bake Pan and remove cheesecake. Invert cheesecake right side up onto serving platter. Spread cheesecake with cherry pie filling. Spread with thawed frozen whipped topping or top each slice with a dollop of whipped topping. Slice and serve.

166 SPICED APPLE & CRANBERRY COMPOTE

1 **package (6 ounces) dried apples**
½ **cup (2 ounces) dried cranberries**
2½ **cups cranberry juice cocktail**
½ **cup Rhine wine or apple juice**
½ **cup honey**
2 **cinnamon sticks, broken into halves**
   Frozen yogurt or ice cream (optional)
   Additional cinnamon sticks (optional)

MIX apples, cranberries, juice, wine, honey and cinnamon stick halves in slow cooker. Cover and cook on LOW 4 to 5 hours or until liquid is absorbed and fruit is tender. Remove and discard cinnamon stick halves. Ladle compote into bowls. Serve warm, at room temperature or chilled with scoop of frozen yogurt or ice cream and garnish with additional cinnamon sticks, if desired.

Makes 6 servings

Spiced Apple & Cranberry Compote

SLOW COOKER BREADS & TREATS

167 FRUIT & NUT BAKED APPLES

4 large baking apples, such as Rome
  Beauty or Jonathan
1 tablespoon lemon juice
⅓ cup chopped dried apricots
⅓ cup chopped walnuts or pecans
3 tablespoons packed brown sugar
½ teaspoon ground cinnamon
2 tablespoons melted butter or margarine

SCOOP out center of each apple, leaving
1½-inch-wide cavity about ½ inch from
bottom. Peel top of apple down about 1 inch.
Brush peeled edges evenly with lemon juice.
Mix apricots, walnuts, brown sugar and
cinnamon in small bowl. Add butter; mix
well. Spoon mixture evenly into apple
cavities.

POUR ½ cup water in bottom of slow
cooker. Place 2 apples in bottom of cooker.
Arrange remaining 2 apples above but not
directly on top of bottom apples. Cover and
cook on LOW 3 to 4 hours or until apples are
tender. Serve warm or at room temperature
with caramel ice cream topping, if desired.

Makes 4 servings

COOK'S NOOK: Have you ever wondered
why you need to brush lemon juice around
the top of an apple? Citrus fruits contain an
acid that keeps apples, potatoes and other
white vegetables from discoloring once they
are cut or peeled.

168 SOUR CREAM CHOCOLATE CHIP CAKE

½ cup margarine or butter
1 cup sugar
2 eggs
1 cup sour cream
1 teaspoon vanilla
2½ cups all-purpose flour
1 teaspoon baking soda
1 teaspoon baking powder
½ teaspoon salt
1 cup chocolate chips

Grease and flour inside of Bread 'n Cake
Bake Pan.

In mixing bowl, cream margarine and sugar
with electric mixer. Add eggs and beat well.
Mix in sour cream and vanilla.

In small bowl, combine flour, baking soda,
baking powder and salt. Add to creamed
mixture. Stir in chocolate chips by hand.
Pour into prepared Bread 'n Cake Bake Pan.
Place lid on pan. Place Bread 'n Cake Bake
Pan in CROCK-POT®. Cover CROCK-POT®
and cook on High 4 hours or until toothpick
inserted in center of cake comes out clean.

Fruit & Nut Baked Apples

SLOW COOKER BREADS & TREATS

169 STEAMED SOUTHERN SWEET POTATO CUSTARD

1 can (16 ounces) cut sweet potatoes, drained
1 can (12 ounces) evaporated milk, divided
½ cup packed brown sugar
2 eggs, slightly beaten
1 teaspoon ground cinnamon
½ teaspoon ground ginger
¼ teaspoon salt
Whipped cream (optional)
Ground nutmeg (optional)

PROCESS sweet potatoes with about ¼ cup milk in food processor or blender until smooth. Add remaining milk, brown sugar, eggs, cinnamon, ginger and salt; process until well mixed. Pour into ungreased 1-quart soufflé dish. Cover tightly with foil. Crumple large sheet (about 15×12 inches) of foil; place in bottom of slow cooker. Pour 2 cups water over foil. Make foil handles* and place soufflé dish on top of foil strips.

TRANSFER dish to slow cooker using foil handles; lay foil strips over top of dish. Cover and cook on HIGH 2½ to 3 hours or until skewer inserted in center comes out clean. Using foil strips, lift dish from slow cooker and transfer to wire rack. Uncover; let stand 30 minutes. Garnish with whipped cream and nutmeg, if desired.

Makes 4 servings

* To make foil handles, tear off three 18×3-inch strips of heavy-duty foil. Crisscross the strips so they resemble the spokes of a wheel. Place the dish or food in the center of the strips. Pull the foil strips up and over and place into the slow cooker. Leave them in while you cook so you can easily lift the item out again when ready.

170 TRIPLE CHOCOLATE SURPRISE

1 package chocolate cake mix
1 carton (8 ounces) sour cream
1 package instant chocolate pudding mix
1 cup chocolate chip morsels
¾ cup oil
4 eggs
1 cup water

Spray CROCK-POT® with non-stick cooking spray or lightly grease.

Mix cake mix, sour cream, pudding mix, chocolate chips, oil, eggs and water in bowl by hand. Pour into CROCK-POT®. Cover and cook on Low 6 to 8 hours or on High 3 to 4 hours. Serve hot or warm with ice cream or whipped cream topping.

171 PEACH CRISP

⅔ cup old-fashioned oats
⅓ cup all-purpose baking mix
½ teaspoon ground cinnamon
½ cup sugar
½ cup packed brown sugar
4 cups sliced peaches

Lightly grease inside of CROCK-POT® or spray with non-stick cooking spray.

Mix dry ingredients together in large bowl. Stir in peaches until well blended. Pour into CROCK-POT®. Cover and cook on Low 4 to 6 hours.

Steamed Southern Sweet Potato Custard

Simmering

Savory Soups

172 CHICKEN SOUP AU PISTOU

Olive oil-flavored nonstick cooking
  spray
½ pound boneless skinless chicken breasts,
  cut into ½-inch pieces
1 large onion, diced
3 cans (about 14 ounces each) chicken
  broth
1 can (15 ounces) whole tomatoes,
  undrained
1 can (14 ounces) Great Northern beans,
  rinsed and drained
2 medium carrots, sliced
1 large potato, diced
¼ teaspoon salt
¼ teaspoon black pepper
1 cup frozen Italian green beans
¼ cup pesto
  Grated Parmesan cheese (optional)

SPRAY large saucepan with cooking spray;
heat over medium-high heat until hot. Add
chicken; cook and stir about 5 minutes or
until chicken is browned. Add onion; cook
and stir 2 minutes.

ADD chicken broth, tomatoes with juice,
beans, carrots, potato, salt and pepper. Bring
to a boil, stirring to break up tomatoes.
Reduce heat to low. Cover and simmer 15
minutes, stirring occasionally. Add green
beans; cook about 5 minutes more or until
vegetables are tender.

LADLE soup into bowls. Top each with 1
teaspoon pesto and sprinkle with Parmesan
cheese, if desired.

Makes about 12 cups or 8 servings

Chicken Soup au Pistou

SIMMERING SAVORY SOUPS

173 CREAM OF CHICKEN AND WILD RICE SOUP

5 cups canned chicken broth, divided
½ cup uncooked wild rice, cooked and drained
¼ cup butter
1 large carrot, sliced
1 medium onion, chopped
2 ribs celery, chopped
¼ pound fresh mushrooms, diced
2 tablespoons all-purpose flour
¼ teaspoon salt
¼ teaspoon white pepper
1½ cups chopped cooked chicken
¼ cup dry sherry

1. Combine 2½ cups chicken broth and rice in 2-quart saucepan. Bring to a boil over medium-high heat. Reduce heat to low; simmer, covered, 1 hour or until rice is tender. Drain; set aside.

2. Melt butter in 3-quart saucepan over medium heat. Add carrot; cook and stir 3 minutes. Add onion, celery and mushrooms; cook and stir 3 to 4 minutes until vegetables are tender. Remove from heat. Whisk in flour, salt and pepper until smooth.

3. Gradually stir in remaining 2½ cups chicken broth. Bring to a boil over medium heat; cook and stir 1 minute or until thickened.

4. Stir in chicken and sherry. Reduce heat to low; simmer, uncovered, 3 minutes or until heated through.

5. Spoon ¼ cup cooked rice into each serving bowl. Ladle soup over rice.

Makes 4 to 6 servings

174 HEARTY CHICKEN VEGETABLE SOUP

2 cups BIRDS EYE® frozen Sliced Carrots
1 box (9 ounces) BIRDS EYE® frozen Cut Green Beans
¼ cup water
2 cans (10¾ ounces each) cream of chicken soup
2 cups milk or water
1 cup cooked chicken, cut into ½-inch chunks
⅓ cup chopped green onions and onion tops (optional)

• Combine carrots, beans and ¼ cup water in saucepan. Cook over medium heat 6 to 8 minutes.

• Add soup, milk and chicken; mix well. Cook 4 to 5 minutes or until heated through.

• Garnish individual servings with green onions. *Makes 6 servings*

Prep Time: 3 minutes
Cook Time: 10 to 12 minutes

Cream of Chicken and Wild Rice Soup

SIMMERING SAVORY SOUPS

175 BOUNTY SOUP

½ pound yellow crookneck squash
2 cups frozen mixed vegetables
1 teaspoon dried parsley flakes
⅛ teaspoon dried rosemary
⅛ teaspoon dried thyme leaves
⅛ teaspoon salt
⅛ teaspoon black pepper
2 teaspoons vegetable oil
3 boneless skinless chicken breast halves
  (about ¾ pound), chopped
1 can (about 14 ounces) fat-free reduced-
  sodium chicken broth
1 can (about 14 ounces) stewed tomatoes,
  undrained

1. Cut wide part of squash in half lengthwise; lay flat and cut crosswise into ¼-inch slices. Place squash, mixed vegetables, parsley, rosemary, thyme, salt and pepper in medium bowl.

2. Heat oil in large saucepan over medium-high heat. Add chicken; stir-fry 2 minutes. Stir in vegetables and seasonings. Add broth and tomatoes with liquid, breaking large tomatoes apart. Cover; bring to a boil. Reduce heat to low. Cover; cook 5 minutes or until vegetables are tender.

Makes 4 servings

SERVING SUGGESTION: Serve soup with grilled mozzarella cheese sandwiches.

Prep and Cook Time: 30 minutes

176 CREAMY DIJON TURKEY SOUP

1 cup chopped celery
1 cup thinly sliced onions
3 tablespoons margarine
1 large garlic clove, minced
3 tablespoons all-purpose flour
½ teaspoon salt
¼ teaspoon white pepper
4 cups skim milk
¼ cup Dijon mustard
2 teaspoons reduced sodium chicken
  bouillon granules
2 cups cubed cooked turkey (½- to ¾-inch
  cubes)
French bread (optional)

1. In 3-quart saucepan, over medium-high heat, sauté celery and onions in margarine 5 to 6 minutes or until celery is tender and onions are golden brown. Add garlic and sauté 1 to 2 minutes. Stir in flour, salt and pepper; cook 1 to 2 minutes. Remove pan from heat and slowly add milk, stirring constantly.

2. Return pan to medium-high heat. Stir in mustard and bouillon; cook and stir 5 to 8 minutes or until mixture is thickened and bubbly. Stir in turkey and heat 1 to 2 minutes. Serve with sliced French bread.

Makes 6 servings

*Favorite recipe from **National Turkey Federation***

Bounty Soup

SIMMERING SAVORY SOUPS

177 SOUTH–OF–THE–BORDER CHICKEN SOUP

3 tablespoons vegetable oil
3 corn tortillas, cut into 1/2-inch strips
1/3 cup chopped onion
1/3 cup chopped green and red bell peppers
1 clove garlic, minced
1/4 cup all-purpose flour
2 (13 3/4-ounce) cans chicken broth
2 cups cooked chicken, cubed
1 (15-ounce) can VEG-ALL® Mixed
  Vegetables, undrained
1 teaspoon chili powder

1. Heat oil in large skillet; add tortilla strips and fry, stirring constantly, until golden. Drain on paper towel-lined plate.

2. Add onion and bell peppers to skillet; cook and stir until soft.

3. Add garlic and stir in flour; gradually stir in chicken broth.

4. Add remaining ingredients except tortilla strips; cook until thickened. Sprinkle with tortilla strips before serving.

Makes 4 to 6 servings

178 CHICKEN–IN–EVERY–POT SOUP

1 cup potatoes, cut into 1/2-inch cubes
4 cups chicken stock or broth
1/4 cup dry sherry
1 teaspoon salt or to taste
1/8 teaspoon freshly ground pepper
1 cup onions, halved and thinly sliced
1 cup carrots, cut into 2×1/4-inch sticks
1 cup celery, cut into 2×1/4-inch sticks
1 cup fresh or frozen green beans, cut into
  2-inch pieces
2 cups cooked PERDUE® Chicken, cut into
  2×1/4-inch julienne strips *or* 1 package
  (10 ounces) PERDUE® SHORT CUTS®
  Fresh Original Roasted Carved
  Chicken Breasts
1 cup zucchini, cut into 2×1/4-inch sticks

In medium-sized saucepan over medium-high heat, bring potatoes with enough salted water to cover to boil. Cook 5 minutes; drain, rinse and set aside. In large saucepan, heat stock and sherry to boiling. Season with salt and pepper. Add onions, carrots and celery; simmer 5 minutes. Stir in green beans and chicken; heat soup to boiling. Add zucchini and potatoes; simmer 1 minute longer. *Makes 4 to 6 servings*

CHICKEN MINESTRONE: Add 2 cups cooked, drained fusilli or other pasta, 1 cup chopped stewed tomatoes in their juice and 1/2 cup cooked kidney beans when adding zucchini and potatoes. Stir in 1/2 cup grated Parmesan cheese just before serving.

South-of-the-Border Chicken Soup

SIMMERING SAVORY SOUPS

179 CHICKEN VEGETABLE SOUP

1 bag SUCCESS® Rice
5 cups chicken broth
1½ cups chopped uncooked chicken
1 cup sliced celery
1 cup sliced carrots
½ cup chopped onion
¼ cup chopped fresh parsley
½ teaspoon black pepper
½ teaspoon dried thyme leaves, crushed
1 bay leaf
1 tablespoon lime juice

Prepare rice according to package directions.

Combine broth, chicken, celery, carrots, onion, parsley, pepper, thyme and bay leaf in large saucepan or Dutch oven. Bring to a boil over medium-high heat, stirring once or twice. Reduce heat to low; simmer 10 to 15 minutes or until chicken is no longer pink in center. Remove bay leaf; discard. Stir in rice and lime juice. Garnish, if desired.

Makes 4 servings

180 CHICKEN CILANTRO BISQUE

2½ cups chicken broth
6 ounces boneless, skinless chicken breast meat, cut into chunks
½ cup fresh cilantro leaves
½ cup (about 4) sliced green onions
¼ cup sliced celery
1 large clove garlic, finely chopped
½ teaspoon ground cumin
⅓ cup all-purpose flour
1½ cups (12-fluid-ounce can) CARNATION® Evaporated Skimmed Milk
Salt and freshly ground black pepper, to taste
Garnish: chopped tomatoes, onions and bell peppers

COMBINE broth, chicken, cilantro, green onions, celery, garlic and cumin in large saucepan. Bring to a boil. Reduce heat to low; cover. Cook for 15 minutes. Pour into blender container; add flour. Cover; blend on low speed until smooth.

POUR mixture back into saucepan. Cook over medium heat, stirring constantly, 8 to 10 minutes or until mixture comes to a boil and is thickened. Remove from heat. Gradually stir in evaporated milk; reheat just to serving temperature (do not boil). Season with salt and pepper; garnish if desired.

Makes about 4 servings

Chicken Vegetable Soup

SIMMERING SAVORY SOUPS

181 HOT AND SOUR SOUP

3 cans (about 14 ounces each) chicken
  broth
8 ounces boneless skinless chicken
  breasts, cut into ¼-inch-thick strips
1 cup shredded carrots
1 cup thinly sliced mushrooms
½ cup bamboo shoots, cut into matchstick-
  size strips
2 tablespoons rice vinegar or white wine
  vinegar
½ to ¾ teaspoon white pepper
¼ to ½ teaspoon hot pepper sauce
2 tablespoons cornstarch
2 tablespoons soy sauce
1 tablespoon dry sherry
2 medium green onions, sliced
1 egg, slightly beaten

COMBINE chicken broth, chicken, carrots, mushrooms, bamboo shoots, vinegar, pepper and hot pepper sauce in large saucepan. Bring to a boil over medium-high heat; reduce heat to low. Cover and simmer about 5 minutes or until chicken is no longer pink in center.

STIR together cornstarch, soy sauce and sherry in small bowl until smooth. Add to chicken broth mixture. Cook and stir until mixture comes to a boil. Stir in green onions and egg. Cook about 1 minute, stirring in one direction, until egg is cooked. Ladle soup into bowls.   *Makes about 7 cups or
                            6 side-dish servings*

182 CHICKEN TORTILLA SOUP

6 broiler-fryer chicken thighs, boned,
  skinned, cut into 1-inch pieces
2 tablespoons plus 2 teaspoons vegetable
  oil, divided
4 corn tortillas, halved, cut into ¼-inch
  strips
1 cup chopped onions
2 cloves garlic, minced
2 cans (14½ ounces each) chicken broth,
  fat removed
1 can (10 ounces) diced tomatoes with
  green chilies
½ cup water
1 cup frozen whole kernel corn
¼ cup chopped cilantro
1 tablespoon fresh lime juice
1 teaspoon ground cumin

In Dutch oven, place 2 tablespoons oil and heat to medium-high temperature. Add tortilla strips; cook 3 to 4 minutes or until crisp. Remove with slotted spoon; drain on paper towels. In same Dutch oven, add remaining 2 teaspoons oil and heat to medium-high temperature. Add chicken, onions and garlic; cook, stirring, 5 to 7 minutes or until chicken is lightly browned. Add broth, tomatoes and water; heat to boiling. Reduce heat to medium-low; cover and cook 10 minutes. Add corn, cilantro, lime juice and cumin; cook 5 minutes. Spoon into bowls; top with tortilla strips.

Makes 4 servings

*Favorite recipe from **Delmarva Poultry Industry, Inc.***

Hot and Sour Soup

SIMMERING SAVORY SOUPS

183 MEXICAN TORTILLA SOUP

Nonstick cooking spray
2 pounds boneless skinless chicken
    breasts, cut into ½-inch strips
4 cups diced carrots
2 cups sliced celery
1 cup chopped green bell pepper
1 cup chopped onion
4 cloves garlic, minced
1 teaspoon dried oregano leaves
½ teaspoon ground cumin
1 jalapeño pepper, sliced and seeded*
8 cups fat-free reduced-sodium chicken
    broth
1 large tomato, seeded and chopped
4 to 5 tablespoons lime juice
2 (6-inch) corn tortillas, cut into ¼-inch
    strips
    Salt (optional)
3 tablespoons finely chopped fresh
    cilantro

Jalapeño peppers can sting and irritate the skin; wear rubber gloves when handling peppers and do not touch eyes.

1. Preheat oven to 350°F. Spray large nonstick saucepan with cooking spray; heat over medium heat until hot. Add chicken; cook and stir about 10 minutes or until browned and no longer pink in center. Add carrots, celery, bell pepper, onion, garlic, oregano, cumin and jalapeño pepper; cook and stir over medium heat 5 minutes.

2. Stir in chicken broth, tomato and lime juice; heat to a boil. Reduce heat to low; cover and simmer 15 to 20 minutes.

3. Meanwhile, spray tortilla strips lightly with cooking spray; sprinkle very lightly with salt, if desired. Place on baking sheet. Bake about 10 minutes or until browned and crisp, stirring occasionally.

4. Stir cilantro into soup. Ladle soup into bowls; top with tortilla strips.

Makes 8 servings

Mexican Tortilla Soup

SIMMERING SAVORY SOUPS

184 CHICKEN VEGETABLE SOUP

1 pound boneless skinless chicken breasts, cut into 1-inch pieces
1 cup chopped onion
2 cloves garlic, minced
2 tablespoons FLEISCHMANN'S® Original Spread (70% Corn Oil)
1 (10-ounce) package frozen sliced carrots
4 cups low sodium vegetable juice cocktail
4 cups water
1½ cups uncooked large bow-tie macaroni
1 tablespoon Italian seasoning
1 (10-ounce) package frozen chopped spinach
60 HARVEST CRISPS® 5-Grain Crackers

In large saucepan, over medium-high heat, cook chicken, onion and garlic in spread until onion is tender. Add carrots, vegetable juice, water, macaroni and Italian seasoning. Heat to a boil. Cover; reduce heat to low. Simmer 20 minutes. Stir in spinach; cook 5 minutes more. Serve 1 cup soup with 6 crackers.   *Makes 10 servings*

185 STIR–FRY BEEF & VEGETABLE SOUP

1 pound boneless beef steak, such as sirloin or round steak
2 teaspoons dark sesame oil, divided
3 cans (about 14 ounces each) reduced-sodium beef broth
1 package (16 ounces) frozen stir-fry vegetables
3 green onions, thinly sliced
¼ cup stir-fry sauce

1. Slice beef across grain into ⅛-inch-thick strips; cut strips into bite-size pieces.

2. Heat Dutch oven over high heat. Add 1 teaspoon oil and tilt pan to coat bottom. Add half the beef in single layer; cook 1 minute, without stirring, until slightly browned on bottom. Turn and brown other side about 1 minute. Remove beef from pan with slotted spoon; set aside. Repeat with remaining 1 teaspoon oil and beef; set aside.

3. Add broth to Dutch oven; cover and bring to a boil over high heat. Add vegetables; reduce heat to medium-high and simmer 3 to 5 minutes or until heated through. Add beef, green onions and stir-fry sauce; simmer 1 minute more.   *Makes 6 servings*

SERVING SUGGESTION: Make a quick sesame bread to serve with soup. Brush refrigerated dinner roll dough with water, then dip in sesame seeds before baking.

Prep and cook time: 22 minutes

Stir-Fry Beef & Vegetable Soup

SIMMERING SAVORY SOUPS

186 SOUTHWESTERN SOUP

1 bag (16 ounces) BIRDS EYE® frozen
  Corn
2 cans (15 ounces each) chili
1 cup hot water
½ cup chopped green bell pepper

• Combine all ingredients in saucepan.

• Cook over medium heat 10 to 12 minutes.

Makes 4 to 6 servings

Prep Time: 1 to 2 minutes
Cook Time: 10 to 12 minutes

187 BEEF BARLEY SOUP

½ pound ground beef
2½ cups cold water
  1 (14½-ounce) can stewed tomatoes,
    cut up
¾ cup carrot slices
¾ cup mushroom slices
½ cup quick barley, uncooked
2 garlic cloves, minced
1 teaspoon dried oregano leaves, crushed
½ pound VELVEETA® Pasteurized Process
    Cheese Spread, cubed
  Salt and pepper

Brown meat in large saucepan; drain. Stir in water, tomatoes, carrots, mushrooms, barley, garlic and oregano.

Bring to boil. Reduce heat to low; cover. Simmer 10 minutes or until barley is tender.

Add process cheese spread; stir until melted. Season with salt and pepper to taste.

Makes 6 (1-cup) servings

Prep time: 35 minutes

188 MEXICAN VEGETABLE BEEF SOUP

1 pound ground beef
½ cup chopped onion
1 package (1.0 ounce) LAWRY'S® Taco
    Spices & Seasonings
1 can (28 ounces) whole tomatoes, cut up
1 package (16 ounces) frozen mixed
    vegetables, thawed
1 can (15¼ ounces) kidney beans,
    undrained
1 can (14½ ounces) beef broth
  Corn chips
  Shredded Cheddar cheese

In Dutch oven, brown ground beef and onion, stirring until beef is crumbly and onion is tender; drain fat. Add Taco Spices & Seasonings, tomatoes, vegetables, beans and broth. Bring to a boil over medium-high heat; reduce heat to low and cook, uncovered, 5 minutes, stirring occasionally.

Makes 6 servings

SERVING SUGGESTION: Top each serving with corn chips and shredded cheddar cheese.

HINT: For extra flavor, add chopped cilantro to beef mixture.

Southwestern Soup

154

SIMMERING SAVORY SOUPS

189 SHORT RIB SOUP (KALBITANG)

2 pounds beef short ribs or flanken-style ribs
2 quarts water
2 tablespoons dried cloud ear or other Oriental mushrooms
2 cloves garlic, peeled
½ cup thinly sliced green onions
3 tablespoons soy sauce
2 tablespoons Sesame Salt (recipe follows)
½ teaspoon sesame oil
¼ teaspoon red pepper flakes
1 egg, lightly beaten
1 bunch chives

1. Score both sides of short ribs in diamond pattern with tip of sharp knife.

2. Bring ribs and water to boil in stockpot or 5-quart Dutch oven over high heat. Reduce heat to medium; frequently skim foam that rises to surface until broth is clear. Reduce heat to medium-low; cook, uncovered, about 1½ hours or until meat is tender. Remove ribs from broth; let cool slightly.

3. Place mushrooms in bowl; cover with hot water. Let stand 30 minutes or until caps are soft.

4. Drain mushrooms; squeeze out excess water. Remove and discard stems. Cut caps into thin slices.

5. Cut garlic lengthwise into thin slices with paring knife. Stack several slices; cut into slivers. Cut enough slivers to measure 1 tablespoon.

6. To degrease broth, let stand 5 minutes to allow fat to rise. Quickly pull paper towel across surface of broth, allowing towel to absorb fat. Repeat with clean paper towels as many times as necessary to remove all fat.

(Or, if time allows, refrigerate broth for several hours or overnight and remove fat that rises to surface.)

7. Place ribs on cutting board. Cut meat from bones with utility knife; discard bones and gristle. Cut meat into bite-size pieces.

8. Combine beef, mushrooms, green onions, soy sauce, Sesame Salt, garlic, sesame oil and red pepper flakes in medium bowl. Add beef mixture to degreased beef broth; cook 15 minutes over medium-low heat.

9. Meanwhile, spray 7-inch omelet pan or small skillet with nonstick cooking spray. Pour egg into pan; cook over medium-high heat until set on both sides. Let cool.

10. Cut circles from omelet with round cookie cutter. Cut crescent shapes from circles with edge of round cookie cutter.

11. Ladle soup into individual serving bowls; garnish with omelet crescents and chives.

Makes 4 servings

SESAME SALT
½ cup sesame seeds
¼ teaspoon salt

1. To toast sesame seeds, heat seeds in large skillet over medium-low heat, stirring or shaking pan frequently until seeds begin to pop and turn golden, about 4 to 6 minutes. Set aside to cool.

2. Crush toasted sesame seeds and salt with mortar and pestle or process in clean coffee or spice grinder. Refrigerate in covered glass jar for use in additional Korean recipes.

Makes ½ cup

Short Rib Soup (Kalbitang)

190 SWEET POTATO AND HAM SOUP

1 tablespoon butter or margarine
1 small leek, sliced
1 clove garlic, minced
½ pound ham, cut into ½-inch cubes
2 medium sweet potatoes, peeled and cut into ¾-inch cubes
4 cups reduced-sodium chicken broth
½ teaspoon dried thyme leaves
2 ounces fresh spinach, rinsed, stemmed and coarsely chopped

Melt butter in large saucepan over medium heat. Add leek and garlic. Cook and stir until leek is tender.

Add ham, sweet potatoes, chicken broth and thyme to saucepan. Bring to a boil over high heat. Reduce heat to medium-low; cook 10 minutes or until sweet potatoes are tender.

Stir spinach into soup. Simmer, uncovered, 2 minutes more or until spinach is wilted. Serve immediately.   *Makes 6 servings*

191 SPAM™ WESTERN BEAN SOUP

1 cup chopped onion
1 tablespoon vegetable oil
3 (10½-ounce) cans condensed chicken broth
1 (14½-ounce) can tomatoes, cut up
1 cup sliced carrots
⅓ cup chili sauce
3 tablespoons packed brown sugar
3 tablespoons cider vinegar
2 teaspoons Worcestershire sauce
2 teaspoons prepared mustard
2 (15½-ounce) cans pinto beans, rinsed and drained
1 (12-ounce) can SPAM® Luncheon Meat, cubed
2 tablespoons chopped fresh parsley

In 5-quart saucepan, sauté onion in oil until golden. Stir in chicken broth, tomatoes, carrots, chili sauce, brown sugar, vinegar, Worcestershire sauce and mustard. Mash half the beans with fork; add mashed beans and whole beans to soup. Blend well. Bring to a boil. Cover. Reduce heat and simmer 30 minutes or until carrots are tender. Stir in Spam® and parsley. Simmer 2 minutes.
                    Makes 6 servings

Sweet Potato and Ham Soup

SIMMERING SAVORY SOUPS

192 HOPPIN' JOHN SOUP

4 strips uncooked bacon, chopped
1 large onion, chopped
2 cloves garlic, minced
2 cans (15 ounces each) black-eye peas, undrained
1 can (14½ ounces) reduced-sodium chicken broth
3 to 4 tablespoons FRANK'S® Original REDHOT® Cayenne Pepper Sauce
1 teaspoon dried thyme leaves
1 bay leaf
2 cups cooked long grain rice (¾ cup uncooked rice)
2 tablespoons minced fresh parsley

1. Cook bacon, onion and garlic in large saucepan over medium-high heat 5 minutes or until vegetables are tender.

2. Add peas with liquid, broth, ½ cup water, RedHot® sauce, thyme and bay leaf. Bring to a boil. Reduce heat to low; cook, covered, 15 minutes, stirring occasionally. Remove and discard bay leaf.

3. Combine rice and parsley in medium bowl. Spoon rice evenly into 6 serving bowls. Ladle soup over rice.

Makes 6 servings

NOTE: For an attractive presentation, pack rice mixture into small ramekin dishes. Unmold into soup bowls. Ladle soup around rice.

Prep Time: 15 minutes
Cook Time: 20 minutes

193 SASSY SAUSAGE AND BLACK BEAN SOUP

1 tablespoon vegetable oil
1 medium onion, chopped
2 cloves garlic, minced
1 can (16 ounces) black beans, rinsed and drained
1 can (14½ ounces) stewed tomatoes, undrained
1 can (10½ ounces) kosher condensed beef broth
½ cup prepared chunky salsa
½ cup water
1 package (12 ounces) HEBREW NATIONAL® Beef Hot Sausage
¼ cup chopped cilantro
Lime wedges, for garnish

Heat oil in large saucepan over medium heat. Add onion and garlic; cook 8 minutes or until tender. Stir in beans, tomatoes with liquid, broth, salsa and water. Bring to a boil over high heat.

Cut sausage into ½-inch pieces; stir into soup. Reduce heat. Cover; simmer 15 minutes, stirring occasionally. Ladle into soup bowls; sprinkle with cilantro. Garnish with lime wedges, if desired.

Makes 4 to 5 servings

Hoppin' John Soup

SIMMERING SAVORY SOUPS

194 GINGER WONTON SOUP

4 ounces lean ground pork
½ cup reduced-fat ricotta cheese
½ tablespoon minced fresh cilantro
½ teaspoon ground black pepper
⅛ teaspoon Chinese 5-spice powder
20 fresh or frozen, thawed wonton skins
1 teaspoon vegetable oil
⅓ cup chopped red bell pepper
1 teaspoon grated fresh ginger
2 cans (about 14 ounces each) fat-free reduced-sodium chicken broth
2 teaspoons reduced-sodium soy sauce
4 ounces fresh pea pods
1 can (8¾ ounces) baby corn, rinsed and drained
2 green onions, thinly sliced

1. Cook pork in small nonstick skillet over medium-high heat 4 minutes or until no longer pink. Cool slightly; stir in ricotta cheese, cilantro, black pepper and 5-spice powder.

2. Place 1 teaspoon filling in center of each wonton skin. Fold top corner of wonton over filling. Lightly brush remaining corners with water. Fold left and right corners over filling. Tightly roll filled end toward remaining corner in jelly-roll fashion. Moisten edges with water to seal. Cover and set aside.

3. Heat oil in large saucepan. Add bell pepper and ginger; cook 1 minute. Add chicken broth and soy sauce; bring to a boil. Add pea pods, baby corn and wontons. Reduce heat to medium-low and simmer 4 to 5 minutes or until wontons are tender. Sprinkle with green onions.

Makes 4 (1½-cup) servings

195 "CREAMY" WILD RICE SOUP

6 tablespoons butter
⅓ cup minced onion
½ cup all-purpose flour
3 cups chicken broth
2 cups cooked wild rice
4 ounces sliced mushrooms
½ cup finely chopped ham
½ cup finely grated carrots
3 tablespoons slivered almonds
½ teaspoon salt
1 cup half-and-half
2 tablespoons dry sherry wine
Minced parsley or chives

Melt butter; cook and stir onion until tender. Blend in flour; gradually add broth. Cook, stirring constantly, until mixture comes to a boil. Boil 1 minute. Stir in wild rice, mushrooms, ham, carrots, almonds and salt; simmer about 5 minutes. Blend in half-and-half and sherry. Garnish with minced parsley or chives. *Makes 6 servings*

Favorite recipe from **Minnesota Cultivated Wild Rice Council**

Ginger Wonton Soup

196 LONG SOUP

¼ of small head of cabbage (4 to 6 ounces)
1½ tablespoons vegetable oil
8 ounces boneless lean pork, cut into thin strips
6 cups chicken broth
2 tablespoons soy sauce
½ teaspoon minced fresh ginger
8 green onions with tops, diagonally cut into ½-inch slices
4 ounces Chinese-style thin egg noodles

1. Remove core from cabbage; discard. Shred cabbage.

2. Heat oil in wok or large skillet over medium-high heat. Add cabbage and pork; stir-fry until pork is no longer pink in center, about 5 minutes.

3. Add chicken broth, soy sauce and ginger. Bring to a boil. Reduce heat to low; simmer 10 minutes, stirring occasionally. Stir in onions. Add noodles. Cook just until noodles are tender, 2 to 4 minutes.

Makes 4 servings

197 HEARTY CHORIZO AND BEAN SOUP

1 pound CORTE'S SPECIALS®,* sliced or crumbled
1 large onion, chopped
3 carrots, diced
1 cup chopped celery
2 cups cooked kidney beans, cooking water reserved (1 cup)
2 tomatoes, peeled and diced
3 cups water or stock
1 tablespoon crushed dried chilies
1 teaspoon Worcestershire sauce
1 teaspoon distilled white vinegar
Sour cream

* The Spanish sausage, chorizo, is available in the meat section of the supermarket.

Cook and stir chorizo over medium heat in Dutch oven or large saucepan. Pour off excess fat. Add onion, carrots and celery; cook and stir 2 to 3 minutes.

Add beans, 1 cup cooking water from beans, tomatoes, water, chilies, Worcestershire sauce and vinegar; simmer 30 minutes.

Serve soup in individual bowls garnished with dollop of sour cream.

Makes 4 to 6 servings

Long Soup

SIMMERING SAVORY SOUPS

198 COUNTRY BEAN SOUP

1¼ cups dried navy beans or lima beans, rinsed and drained
4 ounces salt pork or fully cooked ham, chopped
¼ cup chopped onion
½ teaspoon dried oregano leaves
¼ teaspoon salt
¼ teaspoon ground ginger
¼ teaspoon dried sage
¼ teaspoon ground black pepper
2 cups skim milk
2 tablespoons butter

1. Place navy beans in large saucepan; add enough water to cover beans. Bring to a boil; reduce heat and simmer 2 minutes. Remove from heat; cover and let stand 1 hour. (Or, cover beans with water and soak overnight.)

2. Drain beans and return to saucepan. Stir in 2½ cups water, salt pork, onion, oregano, salt, ginger, sage and pepper. Bring to a boil; reduce heat. Cover and simmer 2 to 2½ hours or until beans are tender. (If necessary, add more water during cooking.) Add milk and butter, stirring until mixture is heated through and butter is melted. Season with additional salt and pepper, if desired.

Makes 6 servings

199 MEDITERRANEAN FISH SOUP

4 ounces uncooked pastina or other small pasta
Nonstick cooking spray
¾ cup chopped onion
2 cloves garlic, minced
1 teaspoon fennel seeds
1 can (about 14 ounces) no-salt-added stewed tomatoes
1 can (about 14 ounces) fat-free reduced-sodium chicken broth
1 tablespoon minced fresh parsley
½ teaspoon ground black pepper
¼ teaspoon ground turmeric
8 ounces firm, white-fleshed fish, cut into 1-inch pieces
3 ounces small shrimp, peeled and deveined

1. Cook pasta according to package directions, omitting salt. Drain and set aside.

2. Spray large nonstick saucepan with cooking spray. Add onion, garlic and fennel seeds; cook over medium heat 3 minutes or until onion is soft.

3. Stir in tomatoes, chicken broth, parsley, pepper and turmeric. Bring to a boil; reduce heat and simmer 10 minutes. Add fish and cook 1 minute. Add shrimp and cook until shrimp just begins to turn pink and opaque.

4. Divide pasta among bowls; ladle soup over pasta. *Makes 4 (1½-cup) servings*

Country Bean Soup

SIMMERING SAVORY SOUPS

200 FISHERMAN'S SOUP

⅛ teaspoon dried thyme, crushed
½ pound halibut or other firm white fish
2 tablespoons vegetable oil, divided
1 medium onion, chopped
1 clove garlic, crushed
3 tablespoons all-purpose flour
2 cans (14 ounces each) low-salt chicken broth
1 can (15¼ ounces) DEL MONTE® *FreshCut*™ Brand Golden Sweet Whole Kernel Corn, No Salt Added, undrained
1 can (14½ ounces) DEL MONTE® *FreshCut*™ Whole New Potatoes, drained and chopped

1. Sprinkle thyme over both sides of fish. In large saucepan, cook fish in 1 tablespoon hot oil over medium-high heat until fish flakes easily when tested with a fork. Remove fish from saucepan; set aside.

2. Heat remaining 1 tablespoon oil in same saucepan over medium heat. Add onion and garlic; cook until onion is tender. Stir in flour; cook 1 minute. Stir in broth; cook until thickened, stirring occasionally. Stir in corn and potatoes.

3. Discard skin and bones from fish; cut fish into bite-sized pieces.

4. Add fish to soup just before serving; heat through. Stir in chopped parsley or sliced green onions, if desired.

Makes 4 to 6 servings

Prep Time: 5 minutes
Cook Time: 12 minutes

201 BLACK BEAN BISQUE WITH CRAB

3 cups low sodium chicken broth, defatted
1 jar (12.5 ounces) GUILTLESS GOURMET® Black Bean Dip (mild or spicy)
1 can (6 ounces) crabmeat, drained
2 tablespoons brandy (optional)
6 tablespoons low-fat sour cream
  Chopped fresh chives (optional)

MICROWAVE DIRECTIONS: Combine broth and bean dip in 2-quart glass measure or microwave-safe casserole. Cover with vented plastic wrap or lid; microwave on HIGH (100% power) 6 minutes or until soup starts to bubble.

Stir in crabmeat and brandy, if desired; microwave on MEDIUM (50% power) 2 minutes or to desired serving temperature. To serve, ladle bisque into 8 individual ramekins or soup bowls, dividing evenly. Swirl 1 tablespoon sour cream into each serving. Garnish with chives, if desired.

Makes 8 servings

STOVE–TOP DIRECTIONS: Combine broth and bean dip in 2-quart saucepan; bring to a boil over medium heat. Stir in crabmeat and brandy, if desired; cook 2 minutes or to desired serving temperature. Serve as directed.

Fisherman's Soup

202 SHRIMP, MUSHROOM AND OMELET SOUP

10 to 12 dried shiitake mushrooms (about
    1 ounce)
3 eggs
1 tablespoon chopped fresh chives or
    minced green onion tops
2 teaspoons vegetable oil
3 cans (about 14 ounces each) reduced
    sodium chicken broth
2 tablespoons oyster sauce
12 ounces raw medium shrimp, peeled and
    deveined
3 cups lightly packed fresh spinach leaves,
    washed and stemmed
1 tablespoon lime juice
    Red pepper flakes
    Cilantro sprigs and lime peel for garnish

1. Place mushrooms in bowl; cover with hot water. Let stand 30 minutes or until caps are soft.

2. Meanwhile, beat eggs and chives in small bowl with wire whisk until blended.

3. Heat 10- to 12-inch nonstick skillet over medium-high heat until very hot. Add oil and swirl to coat surface. Pour egg mixture into pan. Reduce heat to medium; cover and cook, without stirring, 2 minutes or until set on bottom. Slide spatula under omelet; lift omelet and tilt pan to allow uncooked egg to flow under. Repeat at several places around omelet.

4. Slide omelet onto flat plate. Hold another plate over omelet and turn omelet over. Slide omelet back into pan to cook other side about 20 seconds. Slide back onto plate.

5. When cool enough to handle, roll up omelet. Slice into $\frac{1}{4}$-inch-wide strips with utility knife.

6. Drain mushrooms; squeeze out excess water. Remove and discard stems. Slice caps into thin strips.

7. Combine mushrooms, chicken broth and oyster sauce in large saucepan. Cover and bring to a boil over high heat. Reduce heat to low; cook 5 minutes. Increase heat to medium-high; add shrimp and cook 2 minutes or until shrimp turn pink and opaque. Add omelet strips and spinach; remove from heat. Cover and let stand 1 to 2 minutes or until spinach wilts slightly. Stir in lime juice. Ladle soup into bowls. Sprinkle with red pepper flakes; garnish, if desired.

Makes 6 servings

Shrimp, Mushroom and Omelet Soup

SIMMERING SAVORY SOUPS

203 SPICY CRAB SOUP

1 pound crabmeat,* cooked, flaked and
    cartilage removed
1 can (28 ounces) crushed tomatoes in
    tomato purée, undrained
2 cups water
1 can (10¾ ounces) fat-free reduced-
    sodium chicken broth
¾ cup chopped celery
¾ cup diced onion
1 teaspoon seafood seasoning
¼ teaspoon lemon-pepper
1 package (10 ounces) frozen corn,
    thawed
1 package (10 ounces) frozen peas,
    thawed

Purchase flake-style or a mixture of flake and chunk crabmeat if purchasing blue crab or surimi blended seafood.

Combine tomatoes with purée, water, broth, celery, onion, seafood seasoning and lemon-pepper in 6-quart saucepan. Bring to a boil over high heat. Reduce heat to low. Cover and simmer 20 to 30 minutes. Add corn and peas; simmer 10 minutes more. Add crabmeat; simmer until heated through.

Makes 6 servings

*Favorite recipe from **National Fisheries Institute***

204 PATRICK'S IRISH LAMB SOUP

1½ pounds fresh lean American lamb
    boneless shoulder, cut into ¾-inch
    cubes
1 tablespoon olive oil
1 medium onion, coarsely chopped
1 bottle (12 ounces) beer *or* ¾ cup water
1 teaspoon seasoned pepper
2 cans (14½ ounces each) beef or chicken
    broth
1 package (0.87 ounce) brown gravy mix
3 cups cubed new potatoes
2 cups thinly sliced carrots
2 cups shredded green cabbage
    Chopped parsley for garnish

Heat oil in 3-quart saucepan over medium-high heat. Cook and stir lamb and onion in oil until lamb is brown and onion is soft. Stir in beer and pepper. Bring to a boil over high heat. Reduce heat to low. Cover and simmer 30 minutes.

Stir in broth and gravy mix. Add potatoes and carrots; cover and simmer 15 to 20 minutes until lamb and vegetables are fork-tender. Stir in cabbage; cook just until cabbage turns bright green. Garnish with chopped parsley.
Makes 8 servings

*Favorite recipe from **American Lamb Council***

SIMMERING SAVORY SOUPS

205 POTATO–CHEESE CALICO SOUP

1 pound potatoes, peeled and thinly sliced
1 cup sliced onion
2½ cups chicken broth
½ cup low-fat milk
1 cup sliced mushrooms
½ cup diced red bell pepper
½ cup sliced green onions
1 cup (4 ounces) finely shredded
   Wisconsin Asiago Cheese
Salt and black pepper (optional)
2 tablespoons chopped fresh parsley

In 3-quart saucepan, combine potatoes,
1 cup onion and broth. Bring to a boil.
Reduce heat to low. Cover; cook until
potatoes are tender, about 10 minutes.
Transfer to blender container; blend until
smooth. Return to saucepan. Stir in milk,
mushrooms, bell pepper and green onions.
Bring to a simmer over medium-low heat.
Add cheese, a few tablespoons at a time,
stirring to melt. Season with salt and black
pepper. Sprinkle with parsley.

Makes 6 servings (6 cups)

*Favorite recipe from **Wisconsin Milk Marketing
Board***

206 BLACK BEAN SOUP

¼ cup mild salsa
1 can (16 ounces) black beans
2 cups water
1 cup cherry tomatoes, tops removed
1½ teaspoons ground cumin
1 teaspoon sugar

Strain salsa, discarding chunks. Drain and
rinse black beans; reserve 1 tablespoon
beans. Place remaining beans with all
ingredients in food processor or blender;
process until smooth. Stir in reserved black
beans and refrigerate until ready to serve.

Makes 4 servings

*Favorite recipe from **The Sugar Association, Inc.***

SIMMERING SAVORY SOUPS

207 HEARTY MINESTRONE SOUP

- 2 cans (10¾ ounces each) condensed Italian tomato soup
- 3 cups water
- 3 cups cooked vegetables, such as zucchini, peas, corn or beans
- 2 cups cooked ditalini pasta
- 1⅓ cups (2.8-ounce can) FRENCH'S® French Fried Onions

Combine soup and water in large saucepan. Add vegetables and pasta. Bring to a boil. Reduce heat. Cook until heated through, stirring often.

Place French Fried Onions in microwavable dish. Microwave on HIGH 1 minute or until onions are golden.

Ladle soup into individual bowls. Sprinkle with French Fried Onions.

Makes 6 servings

Prep Time: 10 minutes
Cook Time: 5 minutes

208 COLD CUCUMBER SOUP

- 1 cucumber, peeled
- 1 cup low-fat buttermilk
- 2 tablespoons red onion, finely chopped
- 1 teaspoon dried mint leaves, crushed
- 1 teaspoon sugar
  Dash hot sauce

Blend all ingredients thoroughly in food processor. Serve immediately or chill before serving. *Makes 2 servings*

Favorite recipe from **The Sugar Association, Inc.**

209 LENTIL SOUP

- 1 tablespoon FILIPPO BERIO® Olive Oil
- 1 medium onion, diced
- 4 cups beef broth
- 1 cup dried lentils, rinsed and drained
- ¼ cup tomato sauce
- 1 teaspoon dried Italian herb seasoning
  Salt and freshly ground black pepper

In large saucepan, heat olive oil over medium heat until hot. Add onion; cook and stir 5 minutes or until softened. Add beef broth; bring mixture to a boil. Stir in lentils, tomato sauce and Italian seasoning. Cover; reduce heat to low and simmer 45 minutes or until lentils are tender. Season to taste with salt and pepper. Serve hot.

Makes 6 servings

Hearty Minestrone Soup

SIMMERING SAVORY SOUPS

210 CHILLED POTATO CUCUMBER SOUP WITH ROASTED RED PEPPER SWIRL

1 large cucumber
1½ cups canned vegetable broth
1 cup chopped leeks
1 cup red potatoes, cubed and peeled
1 cup water
1 teaspoon ground cumin
1 cup buttermilk
½ teaspoon salt
¼ teaspoon ground white pepper
    Red Pepper Swirl (recipe follows)
    Fresh chives for garnish

1. To prepare cucumber, peel with vegetable peeler. Trim ends and discard. Cut cucumber lengthwise into halves. Scoop out seeds, using small spoon; discard seeds. Cut halves into quarters; cut crosswise into ½-inch pieces.

2. Combine cucumber, broth, leeks, potatoes, water and cumin in large saucepan. Bring to a boil over high heat. Reduce heat to low. Cover and simmer 20 minutes or until vegetables are tender. Cool.

3. Process cucumber mixture in food processor in batches until smooth. Pour into large bowl. Stir in buttermilk, salt and pepper. Cover; refrigerate until cold.

4. Just before serving, prepare Roasted Red Pepper Swirl.

5. Ladle soup into bowls; spoon Roasted Red Pepper Swirl into soup and swirl with knife. Garnish, if desired.

Makes 6 servings

ROASTED RED PEPPER SWIRL
    Nonstick cooking spray
3 cups diced red bell peppers
1 small dried hot red chili, seeded and torn
½ cup boiling water
1 clove garlic, sliced
2 teaspoons white wine vinegar

1. Preheat oven to 400°F. Spray nonstick baking sheet with cooking spray. Place bell peppers and chili on prepared baking sheet. Bake 30 minutes or until bell pepper is browned on edges, stirring after 15 minutes.

2. Process peppers, boiling water, garlic and vinegar in food processor until smooth, scraping side of bowl occasionally.

Makes ¾ cup

Chilled Potato Cucumber Soup with Roasted Red Pepper Swirl

SIMMERING SAVORY SOUPS

211 HEARTY TORTILLA CHIP SOUP

1 cup chopped onion
¾ cup finely chopped carrots
1 clove garlic, minced
6 ounces GUILTLESS GOURMET®
    Unsalted Baked Tortilla Chips, divided
3 cans (14½ ounces each) low sodium
    chicken broth, defatted
2 cups water
½ cup each GUILTLESS GOURMET®
    Roasted Red Pepper and Green
    Tomatillo Salsas
1 can (6 ounces) low sodium tomato paste
1 cup (4 ounces) shredded low fat
    Monterey Jack cheese

MICROWAVE DIRECTIONS: Combine onion, carrots and garlic in 3-quart microwave-safe casserole. Cover with vented plastic wrap or lid; microwave on HIGH (100% power) 7 minutes or until vegetables are tender. Finely crush half the tortilla chips. Add crushed chips, broth, water, salsas and tomato paste; stir well. Cover; microwave on HIGH 6 minutes or until soup bubbles. Microwave on MEDIUM (50% power) 5 minutes. To serve, divide remaining tortilla chips and half the cheese among 6 individual soup bowls. Ladle soup over cheese and chips, dividing evenly. Sprinkle with remaining cheese.

Makes 8 servings

STOVE–TOP DIRECTIONS: Bring 2 tablespoons broth to a boil in 3-quart saucepan over medium-high heat. Add onion, carrots and garlic; cook and stir about 5 minutes until vegetables are tender. Finely crush half the tortilla chips. Add crushed chips, remaining broth, water, salsas and tomato paste; stir well. Cook over medium heat until soup comes to a boil. Reduce heat to low; simmer 5 minutes. Serve as directed.

Hearty Tortilla Chip Soup

SIMMERING SAVORY SOUPS

212 TOMATO FRENCH ONION SOUP

4 medium onions, chopped
2 tablespoons butter or margarine
1 can (14½ ounces) DEL MONTE®
   FreshCut™ Brand Diced Tomatoes
1 can (10½ ounces) condensed beef
   consommé
¼ cup dry sherry
4 French bread slices, toasted
1½ cups (6 ounces) shredded Swiss cheese
¼ cup (1 ounce) grated Parmesan cheese

1. Cook onions in butter in large saucepan about 10 minutes. Add undrained tomatoes, reserved liquid, 2 cups water, consommé and sherry to saucepan. Bring to boil, skimming off foam.

2. Reduce heat to medium-low; simmer 10 minutes. Place soup in four broilerproof bowls; top with bread and cheeses. Broil until cheeses are melted and golden.

Makes 4 servings

If broilerproof bowls are not available, place soup in ovenproof bowls and bake at 350°F, 10 minutes.

Prep & Cook Time: 35 minutes

213 CHILLED AVOCADO SOUP

1 tablespoon FILIPPO BERIO® Olive Oil
1 bunch green onions, trimmed and sliced
1 tablespoon all-purpose flour
2 cups chicken broth
2 ripe large avocados, halved, pitted and
   peeled
2 cups milk
½ cup plain low fat yogurt
2 teaspoons lemon juice
   Salt and white pepper

In large saucepan or Dutch oven, heat olive oil over medium heat until hot. Add green onions; cook and stir 2 minutes. Add flour; stir until mixture is smooth. Cook 1 minute. Gradually whisk in chicken broth. Cover; reduce heat to low and simmer 10 minutes. Cool slightly. Meanwhile, coarsely chop avocados.

In blender container or food processor, combine avocados and chicken broth mixture; process until smooth. Transfer to large bowl. Add milk, yogurt and lemon juice. Blend with wire whisk or electric mixer at medium speed until smooth. Season to taste with salt and pepper. Cover; refrigerate at least 2 hours before serving. Serve cold. *Makes 4 to 6 servings*

Tomato French Onion Soup

SIMMERING SAVORY SOUPS

214 CREAM OF PUMPKIN CURRY SOUP

3 tablespoons butter
1 cup (1 small) chopped onion
1 clove garlic, finely chopped
1 teaspoon curry powder
½ teaspoon salt
⅛ to ¼ teaspoon ground coriander
⅛ teaspoon crushed red pepper
3 cups water
3 MAGGI® Chicken or Vegetarian Vegetable Bouillon Cubes
1¾ cups (15-ounce can) LIBBY'S® Solid Pack Pumpkin
1 cup half-and-half
Sour cream and chopped fresh chives (optional)

MELT butter in large saucepan over medium-high heat. Add onion and garlic; cook for 3 to 5 minutes or until tender. Stir in curry powder, salt, coriander and crushed red pepper; cook for 1 minute. Add water and bouillon; bring to a boil. Reduce heat to low; cook, stirring occasionally, for 15 to 20 minutes to develop flavors. Stir in pumpkin and half-and-half; cook for 5 minutes or until heated through.

TRANSFER mixture to food processor or blender container (in batches, if necessary); cover. Blend until creamy. Serve warm or reheat to desired temperature. Garnish with dollop of sour cream and chives.

Makes 4 to 6 servings

PREPARATION TIP: Soup may be prepared a day ahead. Cool to room temperature after adding pumpkin and half-and-half. Cover and chill. Just before serving, blend then reheat to serving temperature, but do not boil.

215 TOTALLY VEGGIE VEGETARIAN SOUP

10 cups vegetable stock, divided
3 tablespoons CHEF PAUL PRUDHOMME'S Vegetable Magic®
1 large onion, peeled and cut into 8 to 10 wedges
1 large potato, peeled, cut into 1-inch rounds, and quartered
2 large carrots, scrubbed, cut lengthwise in half, then into 1-inch pieces
½ small green cabbage, cut into 4 or 5 wedges
1 large red bell pepper, cut into 1-inch pieces
1 large yellow bell pepper, cut into 1-inch pieces
1 medium-size turnip, scrubbed and cut into 10 wedges
1 medium-size rutabaga, peeled and cut into 10 wedges
4 ribs bok choy, cut into 1-inch diagonal pieces
2 cups apple juice

Place heavy 10-quart stock pot over high heat and add 6 cups stock. Bring to a full boil, then add Vegetable Magic® and one-fourth of each vegetable. Cook until vegetables are tender, about 14 to 16 minutes. Strain cooked vegetables, reserving broth; transfer to food processor. Purée vegetables, adding a little of reserved broth if necessary, until they are liquefied, about 2 to 3 minutes.

Return puréed mixture to stock pot, adding remaining 4 cups stock and apple juice. Mix and bring to a boil. Add remaining vegetables and return mixture to a boil over high heat. Reduce heat to medium; cover and simmer until vegetables are fork-tender, about 25 to 30 minutes.

Makes 20 cups

SIMMERING SAVORY SOUPS

216 LEEK AND FENNEL SOUP

2 leeks
2 fennel bulbs
2 tablespoons FILIPPO BERIO® Olive Oil
1 large onion, chopped
1 clove garlic, minced
3 tablespoons all-purpose flour
2½ cups chicken broth
1 teaspoon lemon juice
    Salt and freshly ground black pepper
    French bread (optional)
    Gruyère or Emmentaler cheese
        (optional)

Cut off root ends and tops of leeks. Split leeks; wash thoroughly and drain. Thinly slice white parts of leeks. Cut off root ends and stalks of fennel. Coarsely chop fennel bulbs. In large saucepan, heat olive oil over medium heat until hot. Add leeks, fennel, onion and garlic; cook and stir 15 minutes. Add flour; stir until mixture is smooth. Cook 1 minute. Gradually whisk in chicken broth; bring mixture to a boil. Cover; reduce heat to low and simmer 20 minutes or until vegetables are tender. Cool slightly.

Process soup in small batches in blender container or food processor until smooth. Return soup to saucepan; stir in lemon juice. Heat through. Season to taste with salt and pepper. Serve hot with French bread and cheese, if desired.   *Makes 6 servings*

217 ZUCCHINI–TOMATO– NOODLE SOUP

3 pounds zucchini, chopped
¾ cup water
½ cup butter
4 cups chopped onions
8 cups tomatoes, cut into eighths
1 can (48 ounces) chicken broth
3 cloves garlic, chopped
1 teaspoon Beau Monde seasoning
1 teaspoon salt
1 teaspoon black pepper
1 pound 100% durum noodles
    Garlic bread (optional)

1. Combine zucchini and water in stockpot; cover. Cook over medium-high heat 10 minutes until partially done, stirring twice.

2. Heat butter in large skillet over medium heat. Add onions; cook and stir in hot butter until tender.

3. Add onion mixture, tomatoes, broth, garlic, seasoning, salt and pepper to zucchini mixture; cover. Simmer 20 to 25 minutes.

4. Meanwhile, cook noodles according to package directions. Drain well.

5. Add noodles to soup; heat through. Serve with garlic bread.   *Makes 8 servings*

SIMMERING SAVORY SOUPS

218 THAI NOODLE SOUP

1 package (3 ounces) ramen noodles
¾ pound chicken tenders
2 cans (about 14 ounces each) chicken broth
¼ cup shredded carrot
¼ cup frozen snow peas
2 tablespoons thinly sliced green onion tops
½ teaspoon bottled minced garlic
¼ teaspoon ground ginger
3 tablespoons chopped cilantro
½ lime, cut into 4 wedges

1. Break noodles into pieces. Cook noodles according to package directions, discarding flavor packet. Drain and set aside.

2. Cut chicken tenders into ½-inch pieces. Combine chicken broth and chicken tenders in large saucepan or Dutch oven; bring to a boil over medium heat. Cook 2 minutes.

3. Add carrot, snow peas, green onion, garlic and ginger. Reduce heat to low; simmer 3 minutes. Add cooked noodles and cilantro; heat through. Serve soup with lime wedges.

Makes 4 servings

For a special touch, garnish soup with green onion curls.

Prep and cook time: 15 minutes

219 CARROT CREAM SOUP

¼ cup butter or margarine
¼ cup chopped onion
¼ teaspoon LAWRY'S® Seasoned Salt
½ teaspoon LAWRY'S® Garlic Powder with Parsley
2 cups chopped carrots
½ cup all-purpose flour
4½ cups chicken broth
¼ cup whipping cream
Chopped fresh parsley for garnish

In large saucepan, melt butter; cook onion over medium-high heat until tender. Add Seasoned Salt, Garlic Powder with Parsley and carrots; cook additional 5 minutes. Stir in flour; mix well. Stirring constantly, add chicken broth; mix well. Bring to a boil over medium-high heat; reduce heat to low and cook, covered, 30 minutes, stirring occasionally. In blender or food processor, purée carrot mixture; return to pan. Stir in cream; heat thoroughly.

Makes 4 servings

SERVING SUGGESTION: Serve warm soup topped with a sprinkling of parsley. Warm French bread or crackers are welcome accompaniments.

HINT: Soup may be prepared in advance. Refrigerate soup until chilled. Purée soup; add cream. In large saucepan, cook soup over medium heat until heated through.

Thai Noodle Soup

SIMMERING SAVORY SOUPS

220 CHILLY ITALIAN TOMATO SOUP

1 cup (14½-ounce can) diced tomatoes, undrained
2 cups tomato juice
½ cup milk
2 tablespoons lemon juice
⅛ teaspoon red pepper flakes (optional)
1 large cucumber, peeled, diced (about 2 cups)
1 medium green bell pepper, diced (about ½ cup)
   Chopped fresh basil (optional)
   Croutons (optional)

In blender container, place tomatoes with juice, tomato juice, milk, lemon juice and red pepper flakes; blend until smooth. Pour into large bowl or soup tureen; stir in cucumber and bell pepper. Sprinkle with basil and croutons just before serving.

Makes 6 cups

221 MIDDLE EASTERN LENTIL SOUP

1 cup dried lentils
2 tablespoons olive oil
1 onion, chopped
1 red bell pepper, chopped
½ teaspoon ground cumin
1 teaspoon fennel seed
¼ teaspoon ground red pepper
4 cups water
½ teaspoon salt
1 tablespoon lemon juice
   Fresh parsley
½ cup plain yogurt

1. Rinse lentils, discarding any debris or blemished lentils; drain.

2. Heat oil in large saucepan over medium-high heat until hot. Add onion and bell pepper; cook and stir 5 minutes or until tender. Add cumin, fennel seed and ground red pepper; cook and stir 1 minute.

3. Add 4 cups water and lentils. Bring to a boil. Reduce heat to low. Cover and simmer 20 minutes. Stir in salt. Simmer 5 to 10 minutes more or until lentils are tender. Refrigerate, covered, overnight or up to 2 days.

4. To complete recipe, reheat soup over medium heat until hot. Stir in lemon juice.

5. While soup is reheating, chop enough parsley to measure 2 tablespoons; stir into yogurt. Serve soup topped with yogurt mixture.   *Makes 4 servings*

For a special touch, top each serving with yellow bell pepper strips.

Make-ahead time: up to 2 days before serving
Final prep time: 10 minutes

Chilly Italian Tomato Soup

SIMMERING SAVORY SOUPS

222 CREAMY CORN BISQUE WITH SPICY RED PEPPER CREAM

RED PEPPER CREAM
- 1 jar (7 ounces) roasted red peppers, drained and patted dry
- 3 tablespoons sour cream
- 2 tablespoons FRANK'S® Original REDHOT® Cayenne Pepper Sauce

CORN BISQUE
- 1 tablespoon olive oil
- 1 large leek (white portion only), well rinsed and chopped* (1½ cups)
- 2 carrots, diced
- ¾ teaspoon dried thyme leaves
- ½ teaspoon dried basil leaves
- 1 can (14½ ounces) reduced-sodium chicken broth
- ¾ pound potatoes, peeled and cut into ½-inch pieces (2 cups)
- 1 can (10¾ ounces) condensed cream of corn soup
- 1 cup half 'n' half
- 1 cup frozen corn
- ¼ teaspoon salt
- 1 tablespoon FRANK'S® Original REDHOT® Cayenne Pepper Sauce

You may substitute 6 small green onions (white portion only), chopped.

1. Combine roasted peppers, sour cream and 2 tablespoons RedHot® sauce in blender or food processor. Cover; process until puréed. Set aside.

2. Heat oil in large saucepan. Add leek and carrots; cook over medium heat 4 minutes until just tender. Add thyme and basil; cook 1 minute. Stir in chicken broth and potatoes. Bring to a boil. Reduce heat to low; cook, covered, 5 minutes or until potatoes are just tender. Stir in corn soup, 1 cup water, half 'n' half, corn and salt. Bring just to a boil. Reduce heat to low; cook 3 minutes, stirring. Stir in 1 tablespoon RedHot® sauce.

3. Ladle soup into bowls. Top with dollop of reserved red pepper cream; swirl into soup. Garnish with chives, if desired.

Makes 6 servings
(7 cups soup, 1 cup pepper cream)

Prep Time: 30 minutes
Cook Time: about 15 minutes

Creamy Corn Bisque with
Spicy Red Pepper Cream

SIMMERING SAVORY SOUPS

223 CARROT & CORIANDER SOUP

4 tablespoons butter or margarine
4 cups grated carrots (about 1 pound)
1 cup finely chopped onion
3 cups chicken broth
2 tablespoons fresh lemon juice
1½ teaspoons ground coriander
1½ teaspoons ground cumin
1 clove garlic, finely chopped
2 tablespoons finely chopped fresh coriander (cilantro)
Salt and pepper

Heat butter in medium saucepan over medium-high heat until melted and bubbly. Cook and stir carrots and onion in hot butter 5 minutes or until onion begins to soften. Add broth, lemon juice, ground coriander, cumin and garlic. Bring to a boil over high heat. Reduce heat to low. Cover; simmer 25 to 30 minutes until vegetables are soft.

Process soup in batches in food processor or blender until smooth. Stir in fresh coriander. Season to taste with salt and pepper. Serve immediately or cool and store up to 1 week in refrigerator. Reheat before serving. *Makes 4 to 6 servings*

224 SOUTH–OF–THE–BORDER CORN AND ONION SOUP

2 cans (13¾ ounces each) chicken broth
1 package (16 ounces) frozen whole kernel corn
1 cup mild taco sauce
1⅓ cups (2.8-ounce can) FRENCH'S® French Fried Onions, divided
1 tablespoon FRANK'S® Original REDHOT® Cayenne Pepper Sauce
½ teaspoon ground cumin
1 cup (4 ounces) shredded Cheddar or Monterey Jack cheese with jalapeño pepper
1 can (4 ounces) chopped green chilies, drained
1 cup low-fat sour cream

Combine chicken broth, corn, taco sauce, ⅔ cup French Fried Onions, RedHot® sauce and cumin in large saucepan. Bring to a boil over high heat, stirring often. Reduce heat to low. Simmer, uncovered, 10 minutes, stirring occasionally.

Pour one third of the soup into blender or food processor. Cover tightly; process until puréed. Transfer to large bowl. Repeat with remaining soup, processing in batches. Return all puréed mixture to saucepan.

Add cheese; whisk until cheese melts and mixture is well blended. Stir in green chilies and sour cream. Cook over low heat until heated through. Do not boil. Ladle soup into individual bowls. Garnish with additional sour cream, if desired. Sprinkle with remaining ⅔ cup onions.
Makes 6 to 8 servings

Prep Time: 30 minutes
Cook Time: 15 minutes

SIMMERING SAVORY SOUPS

225 SPICY SENEGALASE SOUP

1 tablespoon unsalted butter
1 large white onion, chopped
4 cloves garlic, chopped
2 tablespoons all-purpose flour
4 teaspoons curry powder
2 cans (14½ ounces each) chicken broth
½ cup water
1 tart cooking apple, peeled, cored and sliced
1 cup thinly sliced carrots
¼ cup golden raisins
¼ cup FRANK'S® Original REDHOT® Cayenne Pepper Sauce
1 cup half 'n' half

1. Melt butter in large saucepan over medium heat. Add onion and garlic; cook 5 minutes or until tender, stirring occasionally. Add flour and curry powder; cook and stir 1 minute.

2. Gradually blend in broth and water. Add apple, carrots, raisins and RedHot® sauce. Bring to a boil. Reduce heat to low. Cook, covered, 25 minutes or until carrots are tender.

3. Place one-third of the soup in blender or food processor. Cover securely; process on low speed until mixture is puréed. Transfer to large bowl. Repeat with remaining soup. Return puréed mixture to saucepan. Stir in half 'n' half. Cook until heated through.

4. Serve hot or cold. Garnish with chopped apple and dollop of sour cream, if desired.

Makes 6 servings (about 6 cups)

Prep Time: 25 minutes
Cook Time: 30 minutes

226 ONIONY MUSHROOM SOUP

2 cans (10¾ ounces each) condensed golden mushroom soup
1 can (13¾ ounces) reduced-sodium beef broth
1⅓ cups (2.8-ounce can) FRENCH'S® French Fried Onions, divided
½ cup water
⅓ cup dry sherry wine
4 slices French bread, cut ½ inch thick
1 tablespoon olive oil
1 clove garlic, finely minced
1 cup (4 ounces) shredded Swiss cheese

Combine mushroom soup, beef broth, 1 cup French Fried Onions, water and sherry in large saucepan. Bring to a boil over medium-high heat, stirring often. Reduce heat to low. Simmer 15 minutes, stirring occasionally.

Preheat broiler. Place bread on baking sheet. Combine oil and garlic in small bowl. Brush oil over both sides of bread slices. Broil bread until toasted and crisp, turning once.

Ladle soup into 4 broiler-safe bowls. Place 1 slice of bread in each bowl. Sprinkle evenly with cheese and remaining ⅓ cup onions. Place bowls on baking sheet. Place under broiler about 1 minute or until cheese is melted and onions are golden.

Makes 4 servings

TIP: Make all your soups special by topping with French Fried Onions. They'll give your soups a wonderful oniony flavor.

Prep Time: 20 minutes
Cook Time: 18 minutes

SIMMERING SAVORY SOUPS

227 SPLIT PEA SOUP

1 package (16 ounces) dried green or
    yellow split peas
1 pound smoked pork hocks *or* 4 ounces
    smoked sausage link, sliced and
    quartered *or* 1 meaty ham bone
7 cups water
1 medium onion, chopped
2 medium carrots, chopped
¾ teaspoon salt
½ teaspoon dried basil leaves
¼ teaspoon dried oregano leaves
¼ teaspoon black pepper
    Ham and carrot strips for garnish

Rinse peas thoroughly in colander under cold running water, picking out any debris or blemished peas. Place peas, pork hocks and water in 5-quart Dutch oven.

Add onion, carrots, salt, basil, oregano and pepper to Dutch oven. Bring to a boil over high heat. Reduce heat to medium-low; simmer, uncovered, 1 hour 15 minutes or until peas are tender, stirring occasionally. Stir frequently near end of cooking to keep soup from scorching.

Remove pork hocks; cool. Cut meat into bite-size pieces.

Carefully ladle 3 cups hot soup into food processor or blender; cover and process until mixture is smooth.

Return puréed soup and meat to Dutch oven. (If soup is too thick, add a little water until desired consistency is reached.) Heat through. Ladle into bowls. Garnish, if desired. *Makes 6 servings*

228 CREAMY GARLIC AND CHESTNUT SOUP

1 leek
1 tablespoon FILIPPO BERIO® Olive Oil
1 small onion, sliced
4 cloves garlic, peeled
2½ cups chicken broth
2 (8-ounce) cans peeled chestnuts,
    drained
½ cup half-and-half
    Pinch grated nutmeg
    Salt and freshly ground black pepper
    Chopped fresh chives (optional)

Cut off root end and top of leek. Split leek; wash thoroughly and drain. Thinly slice white part of leek. In large saucepan, heat olive oil over medium heat until hot. Add leek, onion and garlic; cook and stir 5 minutes. Add chicken broth and chestnuts. Cover; reduce heat to low and simmer 15 minutes or until vegetables are tender. Cool slightly.

Process soup in small batches in blender container or food processor until smooth. Return soup to saucepan; stir in half-and-half and nutmeg. Heat through. Season to taste with salt and pepper. Garnish with chives, if desired. Serve hot.

Makes 4 servings

Split Pea Soup

SIMMERING SAVORY SOUPS

229 PESTO & TORTELLINI SOUP

1 package (9 ounces) fresh cheese tortellini
3 cans (about 14 ounces each) chicken broth
1 jar (7 ounces) roasted red peppers, drained and slivered
¾ cup frozen green peas
3 to 4 cups fresh spinach, washed and stems removed
1 to 2 tablespoons pesto *or* ¼ cup grated Parmesan cheese

1. Cook tortellini according to package directions; drain.

2. While pasta is cooking, bring broth to a boil over high heat in covered Dutch oven. Add cooked tortellini, peppers and peas; return broth to a boil. Reduce heat to medium and simmer 1 minute.

3. Remove soup from heat; stir in spinach and pesto.   *Makes 6 servings*

KITCHEN HOW–TO: To remove stems from spinach leaves, fold each leaf in half, then pull stem toward top of leaf. Discard stems.

Prep and cook time: 14 minutes

230 CALICO WILD RICE SOUP

4 cups low sodium chicken broth
2 cups cooked wild rice
1 cup frozen corn
½ cup sliced green onions
2 tablespoons chopped red bell pepper
2 tablespoons chopped green bell pepper
1 tablespoon chopped fresh parsley
1 teaspoon dried tarragon leaves, crushed
2 tablespoons cornstarch
2 tablespoons water

Combine broth, rice, corn, green onions, red and green bell pepper, parsley and tarragon in large saucepan; mix well. Cook over medium heat until mixture boils; reduce heat and simmer 5 minutes or until corn is tender. Combine cornstarch and water in small bowl. Stir into broth mixture; cook 5 minutes or until soup thickens slightly, stirring occasionally.

Makes 4 to 6 servings

*Favorite recipe from **Minnesota Cultivated Wild Rice Council***

Pesto & Tortellini Soup

SIMMERING SAVORY SOUPS

231 CLASSIC MATZOH BALL SOUP

1 package cut-up whole chicken (about 3½ pounds)
7 cups plus 2 tablespoons water, divided
3 carrots, cut into 1-inch pieces
3 ribs celery, cut into 1-inch pieces
1 medium onion, unpeeled, quartered
1 large parsnip, cut into 1-inch pieces (optional)
1 head garlic, separated into cloves, unpeeled
3 sprigs parsley
8 to 10 whole black peppercorns
4 eggs
1 cup matzoh meal
¼ cup parve margarine, melted, cooled
1 tablespoon grated onion
½ teaspoon salt
⅛ teaspoon ground white pepper *or* ¼ teaspoon freshly ground black pepper
Chopped fresh parsley, for garnish

Combine chicken and 7 cups water in Dutch oven. Bring to a boil over medium heat. Remove any foam from surface of water with large metal spoon; discard. Add carrots, celery, unpeeled onion, parsnip, garlic, parsley and whole peppercorns. Cover; simmer 3 hours or until chicken is no longer pink in center. Remove from heat; cool 30 minutes. Strain soup; reserve chicken and broth separately. Discard vegetables. Remove skin and bones from chicken; discard.*

Beat eggs in large bowl on medium speed of electric mixer. Add matzoh meal, margarine, remaining 2 tablespoons water, grated onion, salt and ground pepper. Mix at low speed until well blended. Let stand 15 to 30 minutes. With wet hands, form matzoh mixture into 12 (2-inch) balls.

Bring 8 cups water to a boil in Dutch oven. Drop matzoh balls, one at a time, into boiling water. Reduce heat. Cover; simmer 35 to 40 minutes or until matzoh balls are cooked through. Drain well.

Add reserved soup to matzoh balls in Dutch oven. Bring to a boil over high heat. Add salt to taste. Reduce heat; cover. Simmer 5 minutes or until matzoh balls are heated through.

Garnish with parsley, if desired.

Makes 6 servings

* Chicken and broth may be covered and refrigerated up to 3 days or frozen up to 3 months.

232 INDONESIAN CURRIED SOUP

1 can (14 ounces) coconut milk*
1 can (10¾ ounces) condensed tomato soup
¾ cup milk
3 tablespoons FRANK'S® Original REDHOT® Cayenne Pepper Sauce
1½ teaspoons curry powder

* You may substitute 1 cup half 'n' half for coconut milk BUT increase milk to 1½ cups.

1. Combine all ingredients in medium saucepan; stir until smooth.

2. Cook, over low heat, about 5 minutes or until heated through, stirring occasionally.

Makes 6 servings (4 cups)

Prep Time: 5 minutes
Cook Time: 5 minutes

Classic Matzoh Ball Soup

SIMMERING SAVORY SOUPS

233 RED BEAN SOUP

   1 pound dried red kidney beans
   1 sprig thyme
   1 sprig parsley
   2 tablespoons butter or margarine
   1 small onion, finely chopped
   4 carrots, peeled and chopped
   2 ribs celery, chopped
1½ quarts water
   1 pound smoked ham hocks
   1 bay leaf
   3 cloves garlic, finely chopped
   ½ teaspoon salt
   ¼ teaspoon black pepper
   2 tablespoons fresh lemon juice
      Sour cream for garnish
      "Holly" leaf and berry cutouts, made
         from green and red bell peppers
         (optional)

Soak beans in 1 quart water in large bowl 6 hours or overnight. Drain, rinse and set aside. Tie together thyme and parsley sprigs with thread; set aside.

Heat butter in heavy, large stockpot over medium-high heat until melted and bubbly. Cook and stir onion in hot butter 3 minutes or until onion is softened. Add carrots and celery; cook and stir 5 minutes or until browned. Add 1½ quarts water, beans, ham, bay leaf, garlic and reserved thyme and parsley sprigs. Bring to a boil over high heat. Reduce heat to low. Cover; simmer 1¼ to 1½ hours or until beans are softened. Discard bones, thyme and parsley sprigs and bay leaf. Stir in salt and pepper.

Process soup in batches in food processor or blender until smooth. Return to stockpot. Heat to simmering; stir in lemon juice and season to taste with additional salt and pepper. Ladle into bowls. Garnish with dollops of sour cream (or pipe sour cream in decorative design) and green pepper "leaves" and red pepper "berries," if desired.

Makes 6 servings

TIP: For a gift, give this soup in an attractive glass jar accompanied by soup bowls. It can be stored up to 1 week in the refrigerator. Reheat before serving.

BLACK BEAN SOUP: Substitute dried black beans for red kidney beans. Proceed as directed, simmering soup 1½ to 2 hours or until beans are tender. Add 4 to 5 tablespoons dry sherry, to taste, just before serving.

CRANBERRY BEAN SOUP: Substitute dried cranberry beans for red kidney beans. Proceed as directed, simmering soup 2 to 2¼ hours or until beans are tender. (Cranberry beans can be found in specialty food stores. They are the color of cranberries but taste similar to kidney beans.)

SIMMERING SAVORY SOUPS

234 CREAMY ASPARAGUS POTATO SOUP

1 can (14½ ounces) DEL MONTE®
   FreshCut™ Brand Whole New
   Potatoes, drained
1 can (12 ounces) DEL MONTE®
   FreshCut™ Asparagus Spears, drained
½ teaspoon dried thyme, crushed
⅛ teaspoon garlic powder
1 can (14 ounces) chicken broth
1 cup milk or half & half

1. Place potatoes, asparagus, thyme and garlic powder in food processor or blender (in batches, if needed); process until smooth.

2. Pour into medium saucepan; add broth. Bring to boil. Stir in milk; heat through. (Do not boil.) Season with salt and pepper to taste, if desired. Serve hot or cold. Thin with additional milk or water, if desired.

Makes 4 servings

Prep Time: 5 minutes
Cook Time: 5 minutes

235 TOMATO SOUP

1 tablespoon vegetable oil
1 cup chopped onion
2 cloves garlic, coarsely chopped
½ cup chopped carrot
¼ cup chopped celery
2 cans (28 ounces each) crushed tomatoes
   in tomato purée
3½ cups chicken broth*
1 tablespoon Worcestershire sauce
½ to 1 teaspoon salt
½ teaspoon dried thyme
¼ to ½ teaspoon black pepper
2 to 4 drops hot pepper sauce

* Substitute 2 cans (10½ ounces each) condensed chicken broth and 1 cup water for 3½ cups chicken broth.

Heat oil in large Dutch oven over medium-high heat. Add onion and garlic; cook and stir 1 to 2 minutes until onion is soft. Add carrot and celery; cook 7 to 9 minutes until tender, stirring frequently. Stir in tomatoes, broth, Worcestershire sauce, salt, thyme, pepper and pepper sauce. Reduce heat to low. Cover and simmer 20 minutes, stirring frequently.

FOR A SMOOTHER SOUP: Remove from heat. Let cool about 10 minutes. Process soup, in food processor or blender, in small batches until smooth. Return soup to Dutch oven; simmer 3 to 5 minutes until heated through.

Makes 6 servings

SIMMERING SAVORY SOUPS

236 WHITE BEAN SOUP

6 strips (about 6 ounces) bacon, cut into
½-inch pieces
3 cans (15 ounces each) white beans,
drained and rinsed, divided
3 cans (about 14 ounces each) reduced-
sodium chicken broth
1 medium onion, finely chopped
3 cloves garlic, minced
1½ teaspoons dried thyme leaves
1½ teaspoons dried rosemary leaves

1. Cook and stir bacon in Dutch oven over
medium-high heat about 10 minutes or until
crisp.

2. While bacon is cooking, blend 1½ cans
beans and broth in blender or food
processor until smooth.

3. Drain all but 1 tablespoon bacon fat from
Dutch oven. Stir in onion, garlic, thyme and
rosemary. Reduce heat to medium; cover
and cook 3 minutes or until onion is
transparent. Uncover and cook 3 minutes or
until onion is tender, stirring frequently.

4. Add puréed bean mixture and remaining
1½ cans beans to bacon mixture. Cover and
simmer 5 minutes or until heated through.

Makes 4 servings

For a special touch, sprinkle chopped fresh
thyme over soup just before serving.

Prep and cook time: 28 minutes

237 UPSIDE–DOWN ONION SOUP

3 medium onions, thinly sliced
2 tablespoons vegetable oil
1 cup julienne carrot strips, cut 1½ inches
long by ¼ inch thick
1 cup diced zucchini
1 tomato, diced (optional)
6 cups chicken broth
1½ cups water
1 teaspoon salt or to taste
¼ teaspoon ground pepper
2 tablespoons chopped parsley
8 KAVLI® Crispbreads, Thick or Muesli
2 cups shredded JARLSBERG or
NOKKELOST Cheese (or use
combination)

Cook onions in oil in large saucepan or
Dutch oven over medium heat, stirring often,
15 minutes or until tender and just beginning
to brown. Add carrots, zucchini, tomato,
broth, water, salt and pepper. Bring to a boil.
Cover and simmer 15 minutes or until
vegetables are tender. (Soup can be
prepared ahead to this point and reheated
just before serving.) Stir in parsley.

To serve, crumble crispbreads into bite-sized
pieces into each of 8 ovenproof soup bowls
or 12-ounce custard cups. Sprinkle ¼ cup
cheese over each. Just before serving, place
bowls under preheated broiler until cheese
is melted and bubbly. Ladle hot soup into
bowls and serve. *Makes 8 servings*

White Bean Soup

SIMMERING SAVORY SOUPS

238 ONION SOUP WITH CROUTON CRUST

ONION SOUP

1 tablespoon vegetable oil
3 pounds large yellow onions, halved and thinly sliced (about 9 cups)
3 tablespoons all-purpose flour
⅔ cup apple brandy or water
5 cups low sodium beef stock or broth
2⅓ cups low sodium chicken stock or broth
1 tablespoon snipped fresh thyme leaves or 1 teaspoon dried thyme
1 teaspoon freshly ground black pepper
¼ teaspoon salt

CROUTON CRUST

8 slices (½ inch thick) whole wheat or white French bread
¾ cup (3 ounces) shredded ALPINE LACE® Reduced Fat Swiss Cheese

1. To make the Onion Soup: Spray a 6-quart Dutch oven or stockpot with nonstick cooking spray. Add the oil and heat over medium-high heat.

2. Add the onions and cook, stirring occasionally, for about 10 minutes or until browned and caramelized. Stir in the flour, then the brandy. Bring to a boil.

3. Add both of the stocks, the thyme, pepper and salt. Return to a boil, then reduce the heat to low and simmer, uncovered, for 30 minutes.

4. While the soup simmers, make the Crouton Crust: Preheat the broiler. Place the bread slices on a baking sheet and broil until nicely browned on both sides. Remove the bread slices from the baking sheet and set aside.

5. Place 8 ovenproof soup bowls on the baking sheet. Ladle the soup into the bowls and top each with a crouton. Sprinkle crouton and soup with the cheese. Broil 6 inches from the heat for 1 to 2 minutes or until cheese is melted and bubbly.
Makes 8 first-course servings (1 cup each)

239 FRENCH MUSHROOM SOUP

1 pound fresh mushrooms, sliced
1 large onion, thinly sliced
2 tablespoons butter
2 tablespoons all-purpose flour
4 cups beef broth
¾ cup HARVEYS® Bristol Cream®
½ cup shredded Gruyère cheese
6 slices French bread

In 4-quart saucepan, cook mushrooms and onion in butter until onion is soft. Stir in flour. Cook, stirring, 1 to 2 minutes. Add broth. Simmer, covered, 10 minutes. Stir in Harveys® Bristol Cream®. Sprinkle cheese on bread, broil until melted. Place toast on each serving of soup. *Makes 6 servings*

Onion Soup with Crouton Crust

240 GOLDEN TOMATO SOUP

4 teaspoons reduced-calorie margarine
1 cup chopped onion
2 cloves garlic, coarsely chopped
½ cup chopped carrot
¼ cup chopped celery
8 medium Florida tomatoes, blanched, peeled, seeded and chopped
6 cups chicken broth
¼ cup uncooked rice
2 tablespoons tomato paste
1 tablespoon Worcestershire sauce
½ teaspoon dried thyme leaves, crushed
¼ to ½ teaspoon ground black pepper
5 drops hot pepper sauce

Melt margarine in large Dutch oven over medium-high heat. Add onion and garlic; cook and stir 1 to 2 minutes or until onion is tender. Add carrot and celery; cook and stir 7 to 9 minutes or until tender, stirring frequently. Stir in tomatoes, broth, rice, tomato paste, Worcestershire sauce, thyme, black pepper and hot pepper sauce. Reduce heat to low; cook about 30 minutes, stirring frequently.

Remove from heat. Let cool about 10 minutes. In food processor or blender, process soup in small batches until smooth. Return soup to Dutch oven; simmer 3 to 5 minutes or until heated through. Garnish as desired. *Makes 8 servings*

*Favorite recipe from **Florida Tomato Committee***

241 BLACK BEAN SOUP

2 tablespoons vegetable oil
1 large onion, chopped
3 large cloves garlic, minced
4 cans (15 to 19 ounces each) black beans, undrained
2 cans (14½ ounces each) reduced-sodium chicken broth
⅓ cup FRANK'S® Original REDHOT® Cayenne Pepper Sauce
¼ cup minced fresh cilantro
2 teaspoons ground cumin

1. Heat oil in 4- to 5-quart saucepan. Add onion and garlic; cook until tender. Stir in beans with liquid, broth, RedHot® sauce, cilantro and cumin.

2. Bring to a boil. Reduce heat; simmer, partially covered, 30 minutes, stirring often.

3. Remove 1 cup soup. Place in blender; cover securely and process until smooth. Return to saucepan; stir. Serve soup in individual soup bowls. Top with dollop of sour cream, if desired.

Makes 10 servings

This soup freezes well. Freeze leftovers in individual portions. Thaw and reheat in microwave oven.

Prep Time: 10 minutes
Cook Time: 35 minutes

Golden Tomato Soup

SIMMERING SAVORY SOUPS

242 ROASTED WINTER VEGETABLE SOUP

1 small or ½ medium acorn squash, halved
2 medium tomatoes
1 medium onion, unpeeled
1 green bell pepper, halved
1 red bell pepper, halved
2 small red potatoes
3 cloves garlic, unpeeled
1½ cups tomato juice
½ cup water
4 teaspoons vegetable oil
1 tablespoon red wine vinegar
¼ teaspoon ground black pepper
¾ cup chopped fresh cilantro
4 tablespoons nonfat sour cream

1. Preheat oven to 400°F. Spray baking sheet with nonstick cooking spray. Place acorn squash, tomatoes, onion, bell peppers, potatoes and garlic on baking sheet. Bake 40 minutes, removing garlic and tomatoes after 10 minutes. Let stand 15 minutes or until cool enough to handle.

2. Peel vegetables and garlic; discard skins. Coarsely chop vegetables. Combine half of chopped vegetables, tomato juice, water, oil and vinegar in food processor or blender; process until smooth.

3. Combine puréed vegetables, remaining chopped vegetables and black pepper in large saucepan. Bring to a simmer over medium-high heat. Simmer 5 minutes or until heated through, stirring constantly. Top servings evenly with cilantro and sour cream. *Makes 4 servings*

243 MINESTRONE SOUP

½ cup finely chopped leek
3 tablespoons finely chopped onion
1 clove garlic, finely chopped
2 tablespoons vegetable oil
1½ cups chopped zucchini
1½ cups chopped carrots
1½ cups chopped potatoes
½ cup thinly sliced celery
5 cups chicken broth
1 can (28 ounces) whole tomatoes, chopped and undrained
1 can (16 ounces) Great Northern beans
½ teaspoon salt
½ teaspoon dried basil leaves
¼ teaspoon black pepper
1 bay leaf
2 sprigs fresh parsley
1 package (10 ounces) frozen peas
1 cup KELLOGG'S® ALL-BRAN® cereal
3 tablespoons grated Parmesan cheese
Snipped fresh parsley

In 8-quart saucepan, cook and stir leek, onion and garlic in oil. Add zucchini, carrots, potatoes and celery. Cook for 5 minutes, stirring frequently. Add broth, tomatoes with liquid, beans and seasonings. Cover; bring to a boil. Simmer 20 minutes; stir occasionally. Add peas; simmer 10 minutes or until tender.

Remove bay leaf and parsley. Stir in Kellogg's® All-Bran® cereal. Serve hot garnished with Parmesan cheese and snipped fresh parsley.
Makes 9 servings (1½ cups each)

SIMMERING SAVORY SOUPS

244 BUTCH'S BLACK BEAN SOUP

¼ cup olive oil
4 cloves garlic, minced
1 medium onion, diced
4 cups water
2 chicken-flavored bouillon cubes
3 celery stalks, diced
1 medium potato, peeled and diced
2 carrots, diced
1 large can (2 pounds, 8 ounces) black beans, rinsed and drained
2 cups canned corn (15 ounces), undrained
1 cup rice or orzo
¼ cup fresh cilantro, minced
2 (11-ounce) jars NEWMAN'S OWN® Bandito Salsa (medium or hot) *or* 1 (26-ounce) jar NEWMAN'S OWN® Diavolo Spicy Simmer Sauce

Heat oil; cook and stir garlic and onion over high heat until onion is translucent. Add water and bouillon cubes; bring to a boil. Reduce heat to medium; add celery, potato, carrots, beans, corn, rice and cilantro. Stir in Newman's Own® Bandito Salsa and simmer until rice and vegetables are cooked, about 30 minutes.   *Makes 8 servings*

245 GRILLED CORN SOUP

4 ears Grilled Corn-on-the-Cob (recipe follows)
5 green onions
4 cups chicken broth, divided
Salt and black pepper

Cut kernels from cobs to make 2 to 2½ cups. Slice green onions, separating the white part from the green. Place corn, white part of onions and 2 cups chicken broth in blender or food processor; process until mixture is slightly lumpy. Place corn mixture in large saucepan; add remaining chicken broth. Simmer gently 15 minutes. Stir in sliced green onion tops; season to taste with salt and pepper.   *Makes 4 to 6 servings*

GRILLED CORN–ON–THE–COB: Turn back corn husks; do not remove. Remove silks with stiff brush; rinse corn under cold running water. Smooth husks back into position. Grill ears, on a covered grill, over medium-hot KINGSFORD® briquets, about 25 minutes or until tender, turning corn often. Remove husks.

SIMMERING SAVORY SOUPS

246 WILD RICE SOUP

½ cup lentils
3 cups water
1 package (6 ounces) long grain and wild
   rice blend
1 can (14½ ounces) vegetable broth
1 package (10 ounces) frozen mixed
   vegetables
1 cup skim milk
½ cup (2 ounces) reduced-fat processed
   American cheese, cut into pieces

1. Rinse and sort lentils, discarding any debris or blemished lentils. Combine lentils and water in small saucepan. Bring to a boil; reduce heat to low. Simmer, covered, 5 minutes. Let stand, covered, 1 hour. Drain and rinse lentils.

2. Cook rice according to package directions in medium saucepan. Add lentils and remaining ingredients. Bring to a boil; reduce heat to low. Simmer, uncovered, 20 minutes. Garnish as desired.

Makes 6 servings

247 COUNTRY VEGETABLE SOUP

3 cans (13¾ ounces each) chicken broth
1 cup water
1 package (4½ ounces) creamy chicken,
   rice and sauce mix
½ teaspoon dried basil
1 bag (16 ounces) BIRDS EYE® frozen
   Farm Fresh Mixtures Broccoli, Green
   Beans, Pearl Onions and Red Peppers

• Bring broth, water, rice and sauce mix and basil to boil in large saucepan over high heat.

• Reduce heat to medium. Cook, uncovered, 7 minutes.

• Add vegetables; cook 3 minutes or until rice and vegetables are tender.

Makes 4 servings

Prep Time: 5 minutes
Cook Time: 15 minutes

248 CREAMY CHEDDAR CHEESE SOUP

2 cans (10¾ ounces each) condensed
   Cheddar cheese soup
3 cups milk or water
3 cups cooked vegetables, such as
   cauliflower, carrots and asparagus, cut
   into bite-size pieces
2 cups cooked medium shell pasta
1⅓ cups (2.8-ounce can) FRENCH'S® French
   Fried Onions

Combine soup and milk in large saucepan. Stir in vegetables and pasta. Bring to a boil. Reduce heat. Cook until heated through, stirring often.

Place French Fried Onions on microwavable dish. Microwave on HIGH 1 minute or until onions are golden.

Ladle soup into individual bowls. Sprinkle with French Fried Onions.

Makes 6 servings

Prep Time: 10 minutes
Cook Time: 5 minutes

Wild Rice Soup

SIMMERING SAVORY SOUPS

249 VEGETABLE SOUP

2 tablespoons FILIPPO BERIO® Olive Oil
2 medium potatoes, peeled and quartered
2 medium onions, sliced
3 cups beef broth
8 ounces fresh green beans, trimmed and
     cut into 1-inch pieces
3 carrots, peeled and chopped
8 ounces fresh spinach, washed, drained,
     stems removed and chopped
1 green bell pepper, diced
2 tablespoons chopped fresh parsley
1 tablespoon chopped fresh basil *or*
     1 teaspoon dried basil leaves
½ teaspoon ground cumin
1 clove garlic, finely minced
     Salt and freshly ground black pepper

In Dutch oven, heat olive oil over medium-high heat until hot. Add potatoes and onions; cook and stir 5 minutes. Add beef broth, green beans and carrots. Bring mixture to a boil. Cover; reduce heat to low and simmer 10 minutes, stirring occasionally. Add spinach, bell pepper, parsley, basil, cumin and garlic. Cover; simmer an additional 15 to 20 minutes or until potatoes are tender. Season to taste with salt and black pepper. Serve hot.   *Makes 6 to 8 servings*

250 CHILLED ZUCCHINI SOUP

3½ cups low sodium chicken broth
5 medium zucchini, sliced (8 cups)
1 large onion, chopped (1 cup)
1 clove garlic, chopped
1 teaspoon dried basil leaves, crumbled
½ teaspoon salt
½ teaspoon TABASCO® Pepper Sauce
½ tablespoon cornstarch
1 cup low-fat plain yogurt

Combine chicken broth, zucchini, onion, garlic, basil, salt and TABASCO® Sauce in large saucepan. Bring to a boil; reduce heat and simmer 15 minutes or until vegetables are tender. Pour mixture, in several batches, into container of electric blender or food processor; process until smooth. Add cornstarch to yogurt and stir until well blended. Gradually add yogurt to soup mixture, stirring after each addition. Chill before serving.   *Makes about 7 cups*

251 MINESTRONE SOUP

2 (14¼-ounce) cans COLLEGE INN® Beef
     or Chicken Broth
¼ cup uncooked shell macaroni
1 (16-ounce) can mixed vegetables,
     undrained
1 (16-ounce) can stewed tomatoes,
     undrained and coarsely chopped
1 (10½-ounce) can red kidney beans,
     drained
1 teaspoon garlic powder
1 teaspoon dried basil leaves

In large saucepan, over medium-high heat, heat all ingredients to a boil. Reduce heat; simmer 20 minutes or until macaroni is cooked.   *Makes 6 servings*

Vegetable Soup

SIMMERING SAVORY SOUPS

252 DOUBLE PEA SOUP

1 tablespoon vegetable oil
1 large white onion, finely chopped
3 cloves garlic, finely chopped
2 cups water
2 cups dried split peas
1 teaspoon ground mustard
1 bay leaf
1½ cups frozen green peas
1 teaspoon salt
¼ teaspoon ground black pepper
Nonfat sour cream (optional)

1. Heat oil in large saucepan or Dutch oven over medium-high heat until hot. Add onion; cook 5 minutes or until onion is tender, stirring occasionally. Add garlic; cook and stir 2 minutes.

2. Stir water, split peas, mustard and bay leaf into saucepan. Bring to a boil over high heat. Cover; reduce heat to medium-low. Simmer 45 minutes or until split peas are tender, stirring occasionally.

3. Stir green peas, salt and pepper into saucepan; cover. Cook 10 minutes or until green peas are tender. Remove bay leaf; discard. Blend using hand-held blender until smooth or process small batches in blender or food processor until smooth.

4. Top each serving with sour cream before serving. Garnish as desired.

Makes 6 servings

NOTE: If a smoky flavor is desired, a chipotle chili can be added during the last 5 minutes of cooking.

253 CURRIED WILD RICE SOUP

1 medium onion, chopped
¼ cup butter or margarine
2½ cups sliced fresh mushrooms
½ cup chopped celery
½ cup all-purpose flour
6 cups vegetable broth
2 cups cooked California wild rice
2 cups half-and-half
⅔ cup dry sherry
½ teaspoon salt
½ teaspoon white pepper
½ teaspoon curry powder
½ teaspoon dry mustard
½ teaspoon paprika
½ teaspoon dried chervil
Parsley or chives, chopped

Sauté onion in butter in large saucepan until golden brown. Add mushrooms and celery. Cook 2 minutes, stirring constantly. Stir in flour; cook over low heat, stirring until mixture is bubbly. Gradually add broth. Heat to a boil, stirring constantly. Boil and stir 1 minute. Add wild rice, half-and-half, sherry and seasonings; heat to a simmer. Garnish with parsley.

Makes 12 (1-cup) servings

Favorite recipe from California Wild Rice Advisory Board

Double Pea Soup

SIMMERING SAVORY SOUPS

254 CREAM OF ASPARAGUS SOUP

1 pound fresh asparagus
3½ cups chicken broth, divided
¼ cup butter or margarine
¼ cup all-purpose flour
½ cup light cream
½ teaspoon salt
⅛ teaspoon pepper

Trim off coarse ends of asparagus. Cut asparagus into 1-inch pieces. Combine asparagus and 1 cup broth in medium saucepan; cook 12 to 15 minutes or until tender. Melt butter in large saucepan. Remove from heat; stir in flour. Gradually add remaining 2½ cups broth; cook, stirring occasionally, until slightly thickened. Stir in cream, seasonings and cooked asparagus with liquid. Heat thoroughly.

Makes 6 to 8 servings

NOTE: Substitute 3 chicken bouillon cubes and 3½ cups water for 3½ cups chicken broth.

255 MINESTRONE SOUP

1 can (14½ ounces) stewed tomatoes, Italian-style
2 cans (13¾ ounces each) low-sodium chicken broth
½ cup uncooked fine egg noodles or tiny pasta for soup
1 can (15½ ounces) red kidney beans
3 cups BIRDS EYE® frozen Mixed Vegetables
Grated Parmesan cheese

• Drain tomatoes, reserving liquid. Chop tomatoes into bite-size pieces.

• Bring broth, noodles, tomatoes and reserved liquid to boil in large saucepan over high heat. Cook, uncovered, over medium-high heat 6 minutes.

• Add beans and vegetables. Cover and cook 5 minutes or until heated through.

• Sprinkle individual servings with cheese.

Makes 4 servings

Prep Time: 5 minutes
Cook Time: 20 minutes

SIMMERING SAVORY SOUPS

256 QUICK AND ZESTY VEGETABLE SOUP

1 pound lean ground beef
½ cup chopped onion
    Salt and pepper
2 cans (14½ ounces each) DEL MONTE® Italian Recipe Stewed Tomatoes
2 cans (14 ounces each) beef broth
1 can (14½ ounces) DEL MONTE® Mixed Vegetables
½ cup uncooked medium egg noodles
½ teaspoon dried oregano

1. Brown meat with onion in large pot. Cook until onion is tender; drain. Season to taste with salt and pepper.

2. Stir in remaining ingredients. Bring to boil; reduce heat.

3. Cover and simmer 15 minutes or until noodles are tender.   *Makes 8 servings*

Prep Time: 5 minutes
Cook Time: 15 minutes

257 SANTA FE WILD RICE SOUP

2 cups frozen or fresh corn kernels
⅓ cup diced onion
⅓ cup diced carrot
3 (14-ounce) cans chicken broth, divided
2 cups cooked California wild rice
1 (4-ounce) can chopped green chilies
1 teaspoon chili powder
1 teaspoon ground cumin
½ teaspoon dried oregano, crumbled
⅛ teaspoon cayenne pepper (or to taste)
1 tablespoon coarsely chopped cilantro leaves
    Fresh Tomato Salsa (recipe follows)

In large saucepan over medium heat, combine corn, onion, carrot and 1 can broth and bring to a boil. Reduce heat and simmer 10 to 15 minutes or until onion is tender. Stir in remaining 2 cans broth, wild rice, green chilies, chili powder, cumin, oregano and cayenne pepper. Simmer, uncovered, about 5 minutes or until heated through. Sprinkle with cilantro. Top each bowl with heaping tablespoon of Fresh Tomato Salsa.

Makes 4 servings

FRESH TOMATO SALSA
2 medium tomatoes, seeded and diced
⅓ cup chopped green onion
¼ cup chopped cilantro leaves
1 teaspoon lime juice or red wine vinegar
    Salt to taste

Combine all ingredients in medium bowl. Taste to adjust seasonings.

*Favorite recipe from **California Wild Rice Advisory Board***

SIMMERING SAVORY SOUPS

258 TORTILLA SOUP

4 corn tortillas (5 to 6 inches)
  Nonstick cooking spray
2 cans (14½ ounces each) vegetable broth
1 can (14½ ounces) chunky tomatoes, salsa-style or stewed tomatoes, undrained
2 to 3 tablespoons FRANK'S® Original REDHOT® Cayenne Pepper Sauce
1 garlic clove, minced
½ teaspoon ground cumin
¼ teaspoon chili powder
2 large green onions, chopped
¼ cup chopped fresh cilantro
1 tablespoon lime juice

1. Preheat oven to 350°F. Spray 1 side of each tortilla with nonstick cooking spray. Cut tortillas in half. Stack halves; cut crosswise into ¼-inch wide strips. Spread strips on baking sheet. Bake 15 minutes or until golden. Cool.

2. Combine broth, tomatoes with liquid, 1 cup water, RedHot® sauce, garlic, cumin and chili powder in medium saucepan. Bring to a boil. Reduce heat to low; cook, uncovered, 5 minutes. Stir in green onions, cilantro and lime juice.

3. Ladle into individual soup bowls. Sprinkle with tortilla strips. *Makes 6 servings*

TIP: For a tasty variation, add 1 cup shredded cooked chicken or 1 cup cooked corn.

Prep Time: 20 minutes
Cook Time: 20 minutes

259 TOMATO BORSCHT SOUP

1 can (8 ounces) sliced beets, undrained
1 can (10¾ ounces) condensed tomato soup
1 tablespoon packed light brown sugar
2 teaspoons cider vinegar
⅛ teaspoon ground cloves
⅛ teaspoon ground white pepper
1⅓ cups (2.8-ounce can) FRENCH'S® French Fried Onions, divided
2 tablespoons sour cream
1 tablespoon minced chives

Drain liquid from beets into 2-cup measuring cup, reserving beets. Add enough water to beet liquid to equal 1¼ cups liquid. Pour into medium saucepan. Add tomato soup; stir until smooth.

Cut sliced beets into thin strips; add to saucepan. Stir in sugar, vinegar, cloves and pepper. Bring to a boil, stirring gently.

Place French Fried Onions on microwavable dish. Microwave on HIGH 1 minute. Reserve ⅓ cup French Fried Onions. Finely crush remaining 1 cup onions; stir into soup. Cook until heated through.

Ladle soup into individual bowls. Top with reserved onions, sour cream and chives.
  Makes 4 servings

Prep Time: 10 minutes
Cook Time: 5 minutes

Tortilla Soup

SIMMERING SAVORY SOUPS

260 MULLIGATAWNY SOUP

Nonstick cooking spray
2 cups finely chopped carrots
1 cup chopped green bell pepper
2 ribs celery, thinly sliced
½ cup finely chopped onion
3 cloves garlic, minced
¼ cup all-purpose flour
1 to 2 teaspoons curry powder
¼ teaspoon ground nutmeg
3 cups fat-free reduced-sodium chicken broth
1 cup 2% low-fat milk
1 pound boneless skinless chicken breasts, cooked and cut into ½-inch pieces
1 cup chopped seeded tomato
1 medium apple, cored, sliced and peeled
¼ cup uncooked converted rice
½ teaspoon salt
⅛ teaspoon ground black pepper

1. Spray large nonstick saucepan with cooking spray; heat over medium heat until hot. Add carrots, bell pepper, celery, onion and garlic; cook and stir 5 minutes. Sprinkle with flour, curry powder and nutmeg; cook and stir 1 to 2 minutes.

2. Add chicken broth, milk, chicken, tomato, apple, rice, salt and black pepper; heat to a boil. Reduce heat to low and simmer, covered, 20 minutes or until rice is tender.

Makes 8 servings

261 CHILLED CARROT SOUP

2 tablespoons vegetable oil
1 cup chopped onion (1 large)
1½ teaspoons curry powder
3½ cups low sodium chicken broth
1 pound carrots, sliced (4 cups)
2 stalks celery, sliced (1 cup)
1 bay leaf
½ teaspoon ground cumin
½ teaspoon TABASCO® Pepper Sauce
1 tablespoon cornstarch
2 cups yogurt

Heat oil in large saucepan over medium-high heat; cook and stir onion and curry powder over medium heat 3 to 5 minutes or until onion is translucent. Reduce heat to low. Add chicken broth, carrots, celery, bay leaf, cumin and TABASCO® Sauce; mix well. Bring to a boil over high heat; reduce heat to low and simmer 25 minutes or until vegetables are tender. Remove bay leaf. Spoon mixture, in several batches, into container of electric blender or food processor; process until smooth. Add cornstarch to yogurt and stir until well blended. Gradually add yogurt to soup mixture, stirring after each addition. Chill before serving. Serve with additional TABASCO® Sauce, if desired.

Makes about 7 cups

Mulligatawny Soup

SIMMERING SAVORY SOUPS

262 CREAMY TOMATILLO SOUP

1 cup finely chopped onion
1 cup finely chopped celery
2 cloves garlic, minced
1 tablespoon soft margarine
¼ cup all-purpose flour
1 can (14.5 ounces) low sodium chicken broth, defatted
2 cups skim milk
1 jar (11.5 ounces) GUILTLESS GOURMET® Green Tomatillo Salsa
  Tomatillo slices and red chili pepper strips (optional)
¾ cup crushed GUILTLESS GOURMET® Unsalted Baked Tortilla Chips

MICROWAVE DIRECTIONS: Combine onion, celery, garlic and margarine in 2-quart glass measure or microwave-safe casserole. Cover with vented plastic wrap or lid; microwave on HIGH (100% power) 5 to 6 minutes or until vegetables are crisp-tender. Stir in flour. Gradually stir in broth and milk until well blended. Microwave on HIGH 10 minutes more or until slightly thickened, stirring every 3 minutes. Blend in tomatillo salsa; microwave on HIGH 1 minute more or until heated through. Garnish each serving with with tomatillo and pepper, if desired. Top each with 2 tablespoons tortilla chips.

Makes 6 servings

STOVE–TOP DIRECTIONS: Heat margarine in 2-quart saucepan over medium-high heat until bubbly. Add onion, celery and garlic; cook and stir until vegetables are crisp-tender. Remove from heat; stir in flour. Gradually stir in broth and milk until blended. Bring to a boil over medium heat. Reduce heat to low; simmer until slightly thickened. Blend in tomatillo salsa; simmer 1 minute more or until heated through.

263 PAPPA AL POMODORO ALLA PAPA NEWMAN (BREAD AND TOMATO SOUP)

¾ cup olive oil plus extra for drizzling on soup, divided
3 large cloves garlic, smashed
1 teaspoon dried sage
12 ounces stale Italian or French bread, thinly sliced, crusts removed (about 30 slices), divided
1 jar NEWMAN'S OWN® Bombolina Sauce (about 3 cups)
4 cups chicken broth
½ teaspoon hot red pepper flakes
½ teaspoon freshly ground black pepper
  Freshly grated Parmesan cheese

1. In large skillet, heat ¼ cup of the oil over medium heat. Add garlic and sage and cook, stirring frequently, 1 to 2 minutes. Remove garlic from oil. Add ⅓ of the bread slices and cook, turning once, until golden brown on both sides, 2 to 3 minutes per side. Remove from heat; repeat with remaining oil and bread.

2. In large heavy saucepan, heat Newman's Own® Bombolina Sauce and chicken broth over medium-high heat to boiling. Reduce heat to low. Add red pepper flakes, black pepper and bread; simmer, covered, 30 minutes. Remove from heat and let stand 30 minutes to 1 hour. Ladle into soup bowls. Drizzle lightly with olive oil and sprinkle with Parmesan cheese.

Makes 6 to 8 servings

Creamy Tomatillo Soup

SIMMERING SAVORY SOUPS

264 GREEK LEMON AND RICE SOUP

1 to 2 fresh lemons
2 tablespoons butter
⅓ cup minced green onions with tops
6 cups canned chicken broth
⅔ cup uncooked long grain white rice
4 eggs
⅛ teaspoon white pepper (optional)

1. To juice lemon, cut lemon in half on cutting board with utility knife. With tip of knife, remove any visible seeds; discard. Using citrus reamer or squeezing tightly with hand, squeeze juice from lemon into small bowl. Discard any remaining seeds from bowl; set aside.

2. Melt butter in 3-quart saucepan over medium heat. Add green onions. Cook and stir about 3 minutes or until green onions are tender.

3. Stir in chicken broth and rice. Bring to a boil over medium-high heat. Reduce heat to low; simmer, covered, 20 to 25 minutes until rice is tender.

4. Beat eggs in medium bowl with wire whisk until well beaten.

5. Add lemon juice and ½ cup broth mixture to bowl. Gradually return lemon juice mixture to broth mixture in saucepan, stirring constantly. Cook and stir over low heat 2 to 3 minutes until broth mixture thickens enough to lightly coat spoon. Do not boil.

6. Stir in pepper, if desired. Garnish with fresh mint and lemon peel, if desired.

Makes 6 to 8 servings

265 CREAMY GROUNDNUT SOUP

1 jar (18 ounces) creamy or chunky peanut butter
2 cups milk
1 can (about 14 ounces) chicken broth
2 teaspoons bottled minced garlic
1½ teaspoons ground cumin
¼ teaspoon black pepper
¼ teaspoon ground red pepper
1 cup uncooked white rice

1. Combine peanut butter, milk, chicken broth, garlic, cumin, black pepper and red pepper in medium saucepan. Cook over low heat about 10 minutes, stirring frequently to blend. At this point, soup may be chilled up to 2 days.

2. To complete recipe, bring 2 cups water to a boil in small saucepan. Add rice; cover and simmer about 18 minutes or until rice is tender and water is absorbed.

3. While rice is cooking, heat soup in microwave on HIGH about 6 minutes or until hot, stirring occasionally. Top each bowl of soup with scoop of hot cooked rice.

Makes 6 servings

For a special touch, top each serving with shredded carrot and thin mango slices.

Make-ahead time: up to 2 days before serving
Final prep and cook time: 25 minutes

Greek Lemon and Rice Soup

SIMMERING SAVORY SOUPS

266 MINESTRONE SOUP

¾ cup small shell pasta
2 cans (about 14 ounces each) vegetable broth
1 can (28 ounces) crushed tomatoes in tomato purée
1 can (15 ounces) white beans, drained and rinsed
1 package (16 ounces) frozen vegetable medley, such as broccoli, green beans, carrots and red peppers
4 to 6 teaspoons prepared pesto

1. Bring 4 cups water to a boil in large saucepan over high heat. Stir in pasta; cook 8 to 10 minutes or until tender. Drain.

2. While pasta is cooking, combine broth, tomatoes and beans in Dutch oven. Cover and bring to a boil over high heat. Reduce heat to low; simmer 3 to 5 minutes.

3. Add vegetables to broth mixture and return to a boil over high heat. Stir in pasta. Ladle soup into bowls; spoon about 1 teaspoon pesto in center of each serving.
Makes 4 to 6 servings

267 EGGPLANT & ORZO SOUP WITH ROASTED RED PEPPER SALSA

2 medium eggplants (1 pound each)
1½ cups finely chopped onions
2 cloves garlic, minced
2 cans (14.5 ounces each) low sodium chicken broth, defatted
1 jar (11.5 ounces) GUILTLESS GOURMET® Roasted Red Pepper Salsa
1 teaspoon coarsely ground black pepper
¾ cup uncooked orzo, cooked according to package directions
6 sprigs fresh thyme (optional)

Preheat oven to 425°F. Coat baking sheet with nonstick cooking spray. Halve eggplants lengthwise and place cut sides down on baking sheet. Bake about 15 to 20 minutes or until skins are wrinkled and slightly charred. Allow eggplants to cool until safe enough to handle. Peel eggplants; carefully remove and discard seeds. Finely chop eggplants; set aside.

Combine onions and garlic in 2-quart microwave-safe casserole. Cover with vented plastic wrap or lid; microwave on HIGH (100% power) 5 to 6 minutes or until onions are tender. Add eggplants, broth, salsa and pepper; cover. Microwave on HIGH 6 to 8 minutes more or until soup bubbles. To serve, place ⅓ cup orzo into each of 6 individual soup bowls. Ladle 1 cup soup over orzo in each bowl. Garnish with thyme, if desired. *Makes 6 servings*

STOVE–TOP DIRECTIONS: Prepare eggplants as directed. Bring ¼ cup broth to a boil in 2-quart saucepan over medium-high heat. Add onions and garlic; cook and stir until onions are tender. Add eggplants, remaining broth, salsa and pepper. Return to a boil. Serve as directed.

Minestrone Soup

SIMMERING SAVORY SOUPS

268 FRENCH ONION SOUP

2 tablespoons unsalted butter
3 medium onions, thinly sliced and
    separated into rings
1 package (1 ounce) LAWRY'S® Au Jus
    Gravy Mix
3 cups water
4 thin slices sourdough French bread
4 slices Swiss or Gruyère cheese

In large skillet, melt butter; cook onions over medium-high heat until tender. In small bowl, combine Au Jus Gravy Mix and water; add to onions. Bring to a boil over medium-high heat. Reduce heat to low and cook, covered, 15 minutes, stirring occasionally. Broil bread until lightly toasted on both sides. Top toasted bread with cheese; broil until cheese melts.   *Makes 4 servings*

SERVING SUGGESTION: To serve, pour soup into tureen or individual bowls. Top each serving with toast.

HINT: If using individual, ovenproof bowls, pour soup into bowls; top each with a slice of untoasted bread. Top with cheese. Place under broiler just until cheese is melted.

269 POTATO & CHEDDAR SOUP

2 cups water
2 cups red potatoes, peeled and cut into
    cubes
3 tablespoons butter or margarine
1 small onion, finely chopped
3 tablespoons all-purpose flour
    Red and black pepper to taste
3 cups milk
½ teaspoon sugar
1 cup shredded Cheddar cheese
1 cup cubed cooked ham

Bring water to a boil in large saucepan. Add potatoes and cook until tender. Drain, reserving liquid. Measure 1 cup, adding water if necessary. Melt butter in saucepan over medium heat. Add onion; cook and stir until tender but not brown. Add flour; season with red and black pepper. Cook 3 to 4 minutes. Gradually add potatoes, reserved liquid, milk and sugar to onion mixture; stir well. Add cheese and ham. Simmer over low heat 30 minutes, stirring frequently.
          Makes 12 servings

French Onion Soup

SIMMERING SAVORY SOUPS

270 CHILLED MINTED PEA SOUP

1 cup uncooked dried split green peas
1 carrot
2 tablespoons butter
½ cup chopped onion
½ cup chopped celery
4 cups canned chicken broth
2 teaspoons dried mint leaves *or*
    2 tablespoons chopped fresh mint,
    divided
1 teaspoon sugar
⅛ teaspoon white pepper
1 cup heavy cream

1. Rinse peas thoroughly in fine strainer under cold running water, picking out debris and any blemished peas; set aside.

2. Wash and peel carrot. Cut carrot lengthwise in half with utility knife. Place carrot halves, cut sides down, on cutting board. Make ¼-inch diagonal slices, beginning at large end of carrot; set aside.

3. Heat butter in medium saucepan over medium heat. Add carrot, onion and celery. Cook and stir 5 minutes or until vegetables are tender.

4. Stir in chicken broth, peas and 1 teaspoon dried mint. Bring to a boil over medium-high heat. Reduce heat to low; simmer, covered, 1 hour or until peas are very tender.

5. Transfer soup to food processor. Add remaining teaspoon dried mint, sugar and pepper. Process until smooth, scraping side of bowl occasionally.

6. Place soup in medium bowl; stir in cream. Cover tightly with plastic wrap. Refrigerate 3 to 4 hours until well chilled. Garnish with sour cream and mint leaves, if desired.

Makes 4 to 6 servings

271 HOT & SOUR SOUP

1 can (10½ ounces) condensed chicken
    broth
2 soup cans water
1 can (4 ounces) sliced mushrooms
2 tablespoons cornstarch
2 tablespoons KIKKOMAN® Soy Sauce
2 tablespoons distilled white vinegar
½ teaspoon TABASCO® pepper sauce
1 egg, beaten
2 green onions and tops, chopped

Combine chicken broth, water, mushrooms, cornstarch, soy sauce, vinegar and pepper sauce in medium saucepan. Bring to boil over high heat, stirring constantly, until slightly thickened. Gradually pour egg into boiling soup, stirring constantly in 1 direction. Remove from heat; stir in green onions. Garnish with additional chopped green onions or cilantro, as desired. Serve immediately. *Makes about 5 cups*

Chilled Minted Pea Soup

SIMMERING SAVORY SOUPS

272 POTATO–BACON SOUP

2 cans (about 14 ounces each) chicken broth
3 russet potatoes (1¾ to 2 pounds), peeled and cut into ½-inch cubes
1 medium onion, finely chopped
1 teaspoon dried thyme leaves
4 to 6 strips bacon (4 to 6 ounces), chopped
½ cup (2 ounces) shredded Cheddar cheese

1. Combine broth, potatoes, onion and thyme in Dutch oven; bring to a boil over high heat. Reduce heat to medium-high and boil 10 minutes or until potatoes are tender.

2. While potatoes are cooking, place bacon in microwavable container. Cover with paper towels and cook on HIGH 6 to 7 minutes or until bacon is crisp, stirring after 3 minutes. Break up bacon.

3. Immediately transfer bacon to broth mixture with slotted spoon; simmer 3 to 5 minutes. Season to taste with salt and pepper. Ladle into bowls and sprinkle with cheese. *Makes 4 servings*

CUTTING CORNERS: Instead of using a knife to chop the bacon, try snipping it with a pair of scissors while it is partially frozen—you'll find this method quicker and easier.

Prep and cook time: 27 minutes

273 SPICED CARROT, LENTIL AND CORIANDER SOUP

3 tablespoons FILIPPO BERIO® Olive Oil
1 large onion, sliced
1 pound carrots, sliced
8 ounces dried red or brown lentils (about 1¼ cups), rinsed and drained
2 teaspoons ground coriander
2 teaspoons ground cumin
6 cups chicken broth
2 cups milk
   Salt and freshly ground black pepper
   Fresh cilantro sprigs (optional)

In large saucepan, heat olive oil over medium heat until hot. Add onion and carrots; cook and stir 5 minutes. Add lentils, coriander and cumin; cook and stir 1 minute. Stir in chicken broth; bring to a boil. Cover; reduce heat to low and simmer 30 minutes or until lentils and carrots are tender. Cool slightly.

Process soup in small batches in blender container or food processor until smooth. Return soup to saucepan; stir in milk. Heat through. Season to taste with salt and pepper. Garnish with cilantro, if desired. Serve hot. *Makes 6 to 8 servings*

Potato-Bacon Soup

SIMMERING SAVORY SOUPS

274 ONION SOUP WITH BEL PAESE®

1 to 1½ pounds onions, sliced
  Vegetable oil for frying
1 teaspoon all-purpose flour
4 cups beef broth or beef bouillon,
  prepared
¼ teaspoon salt
⅛ teaspoon black pepper
4 slices Italian bread, toasted
4 ounces BEL PAESE® Cheese,* cut into
  4 slices
½ cup CLASSICA™ Grated Parmesan
  Cheese (about 1 ounce)

Remove wax coating and moist, white crust from cheese.

Preheat oven to 350°F. In large saucepan, cook and stir onions in oil until golden. Sprinkle with flour and cook an additional 5 minutes. Add broth, salt and pepper. Reduce heat and simmer for 30 minutes.

In each of 4 small ovenproof crocks, place 1 slice toast. Top with 1 slice Bel Paese® Cheese and 2 tablespoons Classica™ Grated Parmesan Cheese. Ladle onion soup into crocks. Bake for 10 minutes. Serve hot.

Makes 4 servings

275 FRESH TOMATO PASTA SOUP

1 tablespoon olive oil
½ cup chopped onion
1 clove garlic, minced
3 pounds fresh tomatoes, coarsely
  chopped
3 cups ⅓-less-salt chicken broth
1 tablespoon minced fresh basil
1 tablespoon minced fresh marjoram
1 tablespoon minced fresh oregano
1 teaspoon fennel seed
½ teaspoon ground black pepper
¾ cup uncooked rosamarina or other small
  pasta
½ cup (2 ounces) shredded part-skim
  mozzarella cheese

1. Heat oil in large saucepan over medium heat. Add onion and garlic; cook and stir until onion is tender. Add tomatoes, broth, basil, marjoram, oregano, fennel seed and black pepper.

2. Bring to a boil; reduce heat. Cover; simmer 25 minutes. Remove from heat; cool slightly.

3. Purée tomato mixture in food processor or blender in batches. Return to saucepan; bring to a boil. Add pasta; cook 7 to 9 minutes or until tender. Transfer to serving bowls. Sprinkle with mozzarella. Garnish with marjoram sprigs, if desired.

Makes 8 (¾-cup) servings

Onion Soup with Bel Paese®

SIMMERING SAVORY SOUPS

276 MINESTRONE

1 tablespoon extra virgin olive oil
1 cup chopped red onion
2 teaspoons minced garlic
5 cups low sodium chicken broth
1 cup water
1 can (16 ounces) low sodium whole
    tomatoes, chopped and juices
    reserved
1 bay leaf
½ teaspoon salt or to taste
¼ teaspoon freshly ground black pepper
¾ cup uncooked ditalini pasta (mini
    macaroni)
2 packages (10 ounces each) frozen Italian
    vegetables
1 can (16 ounces) cannellini beans, rinsed
    and drained
⅓ cup slivered fresh basil leaves
1 cup (4 ounces) shredded ALPINE LACE®
    Fat Free Pasteurized Process Skim
    Milk Cheese Product—For Parmesan
    Lovers

1. In an 8-quart Dutch oven, heat the oil over medium-high heat. Add the onion and garlic and sauté for 5 minutes or until the onion is soft.

2. Stir in the broth, water, tomatoes and their juices, the bay leaf, salt and pepper. Bring to a rolling boil, add the pasta and return to a rolling boil. Cook, uncovered, for 10 minutes or until the pasta is almost tender.

3. Stir in the vegetables and beans. Return to a boil. Reduce the heat to low and simmer 5 minutes longer or until the vegetables are tender. Remove the bay leaf and discard. Stir in the basil, sprinkle with the cheese and serve immediately.

*Makes 10 first-course servings
(1 cup each) or 5 main-dish servings
(2 cups each)*

277 HOT 'N' CHILLY MANGO MELON SOUP

1 medium cantaloupe, seeded and cut into
    2-inch pieces (4 cups)
2 mangos, seeded and cut into 2-inch
    pieces (2 cups)
1 cup plain yogurt
¼ cup honey
2 to 3 tablespoons FRANK'S® Original
    REDHOT® Cayenne Pepper Sauce
1 tablespoon grated peeled fresh ginger
1 can (12 ounces) cold ginger ale

1. Combine cantaloupe and mangos in blender or food processor. Cover; process until very smooth. (Process in batches if necessary.) Transfer to large bowl. Stir in yogurt, honey, RedHot® sauce and ginger. Cover; refrigerate at least 3 hours or overnight.

2. Stir in ginger ale just before serving. Garnish with mint, if desired.

Makes 6 cups

Prep Time: 15 minutes
Chill Time: 3 hours

Minestrone

Robust Stews & Chilies

278 CARIBBEAN PORK STEW

¼ cup all-purpose flour
½ to ¾ teaspoon ground red pepper
½ teaspoon salt
½ teaspoon paprika
1½ pounds lean boneless pork, cubed
3 tablespoons vegetable oil
1 medium onion, coarsely chopped
2 cloves garlic, minced
1 can (16 ounces) crushed tomatoes, undrained
¼ cup water
2 tablespoons white wine
½ teaspoon ground ginger
½ teaspoon ground allspice
¼ teaspoon ground nutmeg
1 cup sliced fresh mushrooms
1 green bell pepper, coarsely chopped
1 red bell pepper, coarsely chopped
Sage leaves and tomato curls for garnish

1. Combine flour, ground red pepper, salt and paprika in resealable plastic food storage bag; add meat. Seal bag; shake to coat meat.

2. Heat oil in 5-quart Dutch oven over medium-high heat. Add meat; brown, stirring frequently. Add onion and garlic. Cook and stir 4 minutes or until onion is soft.

3. Add tomatoes, water, wine, ginger, allspice and nutmeg; bring to a boil over high heat. Reduce heat; simmer, uncovered, 30 minutes, stirring occasionally.

4. Add mushrooms and bell peppers. Simmer, uncovered, 12 minutes or until peppers are tender. Garnish, if desired.

Makes 6 servings

Caribbean Pork Stew

ROBUST STEWS & CHILIES

279 QUICK AND EASY SAUSAGE STEW

1 package (12 ounces) HEBREW NATIONAL® Beef Polish Sausage, cut into 1-inch slices
1 large onion, chopped
2 cloves garlic, minced
1 red bell pepper, seeded, cut into 1-inch pieces
1 green bell pepper, seeded, cut into 1-inch pieces
1 medium zucchini, cut into ½-inch slices
8 ounces fresh mushrooms, thickly sliced
2 cans (14½ ounces each) stewed tomatoes, undrained
1 teaspoon dried basil leaves
¼ teaspoon crushed red pepper
¼ teaspoon salt

Cook sausage, onion and garlic in large deep nonstick skillet over medium-high heat 3 minutes. Add bell peppers, zucchini and mushrooms; cook 5 minutes, stirring occasionally.

Add stewed tomatoes with liquid, basil, crushed pepper and salt. Bring to a boil. Reduce heat. Cover; simmer 25 minutes, stirring occasionally.   *Makes 6 servings*

280 CIDER STEW

2 pounds stew beef, cut into 1-inch cubes
2 tablespoons margarine
¼ cup all-purpose flour
2 cups water
1 cup apple cider
½ cup A.1.® Steak Sauce
2 teaspoons dried thyme leaves
½ teaspoon ground black pepper
1 bay leaf
3 medium potatoes, peeled and cut into 1-inch cubes
3 medium carrots, sliced
1 medium onion, chopped
1 (10-ounce) package frozen cut green beans

In large heavy saucepan, over medium-high heat, brown beef in margarine. Stir in flour. Gradually stir in water, cider and steak sauce. Bring to a boil over high heat; stir in thyme, pepper and bay leaf. Reduce heat to low; cover and simmer 2 hours.

Add potatoes, carrots, onion and beans. Cover and cook 30 minutes or until vegetables are tender. Discard bay leaf before serving.   *Makes 6 to 8 servings*

Quick and Easy Sausage Stew

ROBUST STEWS & CHILIES

281 FRENCH BEEF STEW

1½ pounds stew beef, cut into 1-inch cubes
¼ cup all-purpose flour
2 tablespoons vegetable oil
2 cans (14½ ounces each) DEL MONTE®
     FreshCut™ Brand Diced Tomatoes
     with Garlic & Onion
1 can (14 ounces) beef broth
4 medium carrots, peeled and cut into
     1-inch chunks
2 medium potatoes, peeled and cut into
     1-inch chunks
¾ teaspoon dried thyme, crushed
2 tablespoons Dijon mustard (optional)

1. Combine meat and flour in large plastic food storage bag; toss to coat evenly.

2. Brown meat in hot oil in 6-quart saucepan. Season with salt and pepper, if desired.

3. Add all remaining ingredients except mustard. Bring to boil; reduce heat to medium-low. Cover; simmer 1 hour or until beef is tender.

4. Blend in mustard. Garnish and serve with warm crusty French bread, if desired.

Makes 6 to 8 servings

Prep Time: 10 minutes
Cook Time: 1 hour

282 SHRIMP & SAUSAGE GUMBO

1 tablespoon vegetable oil
1 large onion, chopped
2 ribs celery, chopped
2 cloves garlic, minced
½ pound sweet Italian sausage, casings
     removed
1 can (14½ ounces) tomatoes, cut up,
     undrained
3 tablespoons FRANK'S® Original
     REDHOT® Cayenne Pepper Sauce
2 teaspoons minced fresh thyme *or*
     1 teaspoon dried thyme leaves
1 bay leaf
1 package (10 ounces) frozen cut okra,
     thawed and drained
½ pound raw large shrimp, shelled and
     deveined
Cooked white rice (optional)

1. Heat oil in large nonstick skillet over medium-high heat. Add onion, celery and garlic; cook until tender. Add sausage; cook until no longer pink, stirring to separate meat. Drain well.

2. Add tomatoes with liquid, RedHot® sauce, thyme and bay leaf. Bring to a boil. Reduce heat to low; cook, covered, 10 minutes.

3. Stir in okra and shrimp; cook, covered, 3 minutes or until okra is tender and shrimp turn pink. Remove and discard bay leaf. Serve over rice, if desired.

Makes 4 servings

Prep Time: 20 minutes
Cook Time: 23 minutes

French Beef Stew

ROBUST STEWS & CHILIES

283 SAVORY BEAN STEW

1 tablespoon olive or vegetable oil
1 cup frozen vegetable seasoning blend (onions, celery, red and green bell peppers)
1 can (15½ ounces) chick-peas, rinsed and drained
1 can (15 ounces) pinto beans, rinsed and drained
1 can (15 ounces) black beans, rinsed and drained
1 can (14½ ounces) diced tomatoes with roasted garlic, undrained
¾ teaspoon dried thyme leaves
¾ teaspoon dried sage leaves
½ to ¾ teaspoon dried oregano leaves
¾ cup vegetable broth or chicken broth, divided
1 tablespoon all-purpose flour

POLENTA
¾ cup yellow cornmeal
¾ teaspoon salt

1. Heat oil in large saucepan over medium-heat until hot. Add vegetable seasoning blend; cook and stir 5 minutes. Stir in beans, tomatoes and herbs. Mix ½ cup vegetable broth and flour. Stir into bean mixture; bring to a boil. Boil, stirring constantly, 1 minute. Reduce heat to low; simmer, covered, 10 minutes. Add remaining ¼ cup broth to stew; season to taste with salt and pepper.

2. While stew is simmering, prepare Polenta. Bring 3 cups water to a boil. Reduce heat to medium; gradually stir in cornmeal and salt. Cook 5 to 8 minutes or until cornmeal thickens and holds its shape, but is still soft. Season to taste with pepper. Spread Polenta over plate and top with stew.

Makes 6 (1-cup) servings

Prep and Cook Time: 30 minutes

284 IRISH STEW IN BREAD

1½ pounds lean, boned American lamb shoulder, cut into 1-inch cubes
¼ cup all-purpose flour
2 tablespoons vegetable oil
2 cloves garlic, crushed
2 cups water
¼ cup Burgundy wine
5 medium carrots, chopped
3 medium potatoes, peeled and sliced
2 large onions, peeled and chopped
2 celery ribs, sliced
¾ teaspoon black pepper
1 beef bouillon cube, crushed
1 cup frozen peas
¼ pound fresh sliced mushrooms
  Round bread, unsliced*

* Stew may be served individually or in one large loaf. Slice bread crosswise near top to form lid. Hollow larger piece, leaving 1-inch border. Fill "bowl" with hot stew; cover with "lid." Serve immediately.

Coat lamb with flour while heating oil over low heat in Dutch oven. Add lamb and garlic; cook and stir until brown. Add water, wine, carrots, potatoes, onions, celery, pepper and bouillon. Cover; simmer 30 to 35 minutes.

Add peas and mushrooms. Cover; simmer 10 minutes. Bring to a boil; correct seasonings, if necessary. Serve in bread.

Makes 6 to 8 servings

*Favorite recipe from **American Lamb Council***

Savory Bean Stew

ROBUST STEWS & CHILIES

285 BEEF BOURGUIGNONNE

1 boneless beef sirloin steak, ½ inch thick, trimmed, cut into ½-inch pieces (about 3 pounds)
½ cup all-purpose flour
4 slices bacon, diced
3 cups Burgundy wine or beef broth
2 medium carrots, diced
1 teaspoon dried marjoram leaves, crushed
½ teaspoon dried thyme leaves, crushed
½ teaspoon salt
Pepper to taste
1 bay leaf
2 tablespoons vegetable oil
20 to 24 fresh pearl onions
8 small new red potatoes, cut into quarters
8 to 10 mushrooms, sliced
3 cloves garlic, minced

Coat beef with flour, shaking off excess. Set aside.

Cook and stir bacon in 5-quart Dutch oven over medium-high heat until partially cooked. Brown half of beef with bacon in Dutch oven over medium-high heat. Remove with slotted spoon; set aside. Brown remaining beef. Pour off drippings. Return beef and bacon to Dutch oven.

Stir in wine, carrots, marjoram, thyme, salt, pepper and bay leaf. Bring to a boil over high heat. Reduce heat to low. Cover and simmer 10 minutes.

Meanwhile, heat oil in large saucepan over medium-high heat. Cook and stir onions, potatoes, mushrooms and garlic about 10 minutes. Add to Dutch oven. Cover and simmer 50 minutes or until meat is fork-tender. Discard bay leaf before serving.

Makes 10 to 12 servings

286 SOUTHWESTERN PUMPKIN STEW

1 tablespoon vegetable oil
1 pound boneless, skinless chicken breast meat, cut into 1-inch pieces
1 cup (1 small) chopped onion
½ cup (1 small) sliced carrot
1 cup (2 large stalks) sliced celery
½ cup chopped red bell pepper
1¾ cups (15-ounce can) LIBBY'S® Solid Pack Pumpkin
1¾ cups (14½-ounce can) chicken broth
1¼ cups (15-ounce can) hominy
½ cup sour cream
3 tablespoons chopped fresh cilantro
½ teaspoon salt
½ teaspoon ground black pepper
½ teaspoon dried oregano leaves, crushed
½ teaspoon ground cumin
⅛ teaspoon ground nutmeg

HEAT oil in large saucepan over medium-high. Add chicken, onion and carrot; cook, stirring frequently, for 3 to 4 minutes or until chicken is no longer pink. Add celery and bell pepper; cook, stirring frequently, for 3 to 4 minutes or until vegetables are crisp-tender.

STIR in pumpkin, broth, hominy, sour cream, cilantro, salt, pepper, oregano, cumin and nutmeg. Reduce heat to low; cook, stirring occasionally, for 10 to 15 minutes or until flavors are blended.

Makes 6 to 8 servings

Beef Bourguignonne

ROBUST STEWS & CHILIES

287 FRUITED LAMB STEW

1 pound boneless lamb
2 tablespoons all-purpose flour
½ teaspoon salt
   Dash ground red pepper
2 tablespoons vegetable oil
3 cups chicken broth
1 small leek, sliced
½ teaspoon grated fresh ginger
8 ounces peeled baby carrots
¾ cup cut-up mixed dried fruit
      (½ of 8-ounce package)
½ cup frozen peas
   Black pepper
1⅓ cups hot cooked couscous
   Fresh chervil for garnish

Preheat oven to 350°F. Cut lamb into ¾-inch cubes.

In medium bowl, combine flour, salt and red pepper. Toss meat with flour mixture.

Heat oil in 5-quart ovenproof Dutch oven over medium-high heat. Add lamb; brown, stirring frequently. Add chicken broth, leek, and ginger to Dutch oven. Bring to a boil over high heat. Cover; cook 45 minutes.

Remove from Dutch oven; stir in carrots. Cover and cook in oven 30 minutes more or until meat and carrots are almost tender.

Stir fruit and peas into stew. Cover and cook 10 minutes. If necessary, skim off fat with large spoon. Season with pepper to taste. Serve stew in bowls; top with couscous. Garnish, if desired.   *Makes 4 servings*

288 HUNGARIAN BEEF STEW

¼ cup vegetable oil
1 medium onion, chopped
1 cup sliced mushrooms
2 teaspoons paprika
1 boneless beef sirloin steak, ½ inch thick, trimmed, cut into ½-inch pieces (about 2 pounds)
½ cup beef broth
½ teaspoon caraway seeds
   Salt and pepper to taste
2 tablespoons all-purpose flour
1 cup sour cream
   Hot buttered noodles (optional)
   Chopped parsley for garnish

Heat oil in 5-quart Dutch oven over medium-high heat. Cook and stir onion and mushrooms in oil until onion is soft. Stir in paprika. Remove with slotted spoon; set aside.

Brown half of beef in Dutch oven over medium-high heat. Remove with slotted spoon; set aside. Brown remaining beef. Pour off drippings. Return beef, onion and mushrooms to Dutch oven. Stir in broth, caraway seeds, salt and pepper. Bring to a boil over high heat. Reduce heat to low. Cover and simmer 45 minutes or until beef is fork-tender.

Whisk flour into sour cream in small bowl. Whisk into stew. Stir until slightly thickened. Do not boil. Serve over noodles. Garnish with parsley.   *Makes 6 to 8 servings*

Fruited Lamb Stew

ROBUST STEWS & CHILIES

289 POZOLE

1 large onion, thinly sliced
1 tablespoon olive oil
2 teaspoons dried oregano leaves
1 clove garlic, minced
½ teaspoon ground cumin
2 cans (about 14 ounces each) chicken
  broth
1 package (10 ounces) frozen whole
  kernel corn
1 to 2 cans (4 ounces each) chopped
  green chilies, undrained
1 can (2¼ ounces) sliced ripe olives,
  drained
¾ pound boneless skinless chicken breasts

1. Combine onion, oil, oregano, garlic and cumin in Dutch oven. Cover and cook over medium heat about 6 minutes or until onion is tender, stirring occasionally.

2. Stir broth, corn, chilies and olives into onion mixture. Cover and bring to a boil over high heat.

3. While soup is cooking, cut chicken into thin strips. Add to soup. Reduce heat to medium-low; cover and cook 3 to 4 minutes or until chicken is cooked through.
Makes 6 servings

For a special touch, sprinkle Pozole with chopped fresh cilantro before serving.

Prep and cook time: 20 minutes

290 PECOS "RED" STEW

2 pounds boneless pork shoulder or
  sirloin, cut into 1½-inch cubes
2 tablespoons vegetable oil
2 cups chopped onions
1 cup chopped green bell pepper
2 cloves garlic, minced
¼ cup chopped fresh cilantro
3 to 4 tablespoons chili powder
2 teaspoons dried oregano leaves
1 teaspoon salt
½ teaspoon crushed red pepper
2 cans (14½ ounces) chicken broth
3 cups cubed, peeled potatoes, cut in
  1-inch pieces
2 cups fresh or frozen whole kernel corn
1 can (16 ounces) garbanzo beans,
  drained

Heat oil in Dutch oven. Brown pork over medium-high heat. Stir in onions, bell pepper, garlic, cilantro, chili powder, oregano, salt, red pepper and chicken broth. Cover; cook over medium-low heat 45 to 55 minutes or until pork is tender. Add potatoes, corn and beans. Cover; cook 15 to 20 minutes longer. *Makes 8 servings*

Prep Time: 20 minutes
Cook Time: 60 minutes

*Favorite recipe from **National Pork Producers Council***

Pozole

ROBUST STEWS & CHILIES

291 CORDERO STEW WITH CORNMEAL DUMPLINGS

2 pounds lean lamb stew meat with bones, cut into 2-inch pieces *or* 1½ pounds lean boneless lamb, cut into 1½-inch cubes
1 teaspoon salt
½ teaspoon black pepper
2½ tablespoons vegetable oil, divided
1 large onion, chopped
1 clove garlic, minced
2 tablespoons tomato paste
2 teaspoons chili powder
1 teaspoon ground coriander
4 cups water
3 small potatoes, cut into 1½-inch chunks
2 large carrots, cut into 1-inch pieces
1 package (10 ounces) frozen whole kernel corn
⅓ cup coarsely chopped celery leaves
½ cup yellow cornmeal
½ cup all-purpose flour
1 teaspoon baking powder
¼ teaspoon salt
2½ tablespoons cold butter or margarine
½ cup milk
Whole celery leaves for garnish

Sprinkle meat with salt and pepper. Heat 2 tablespoons oil in 5-quart Dutch oven over medium-high heat. Add meat, a few pieces at a time, and cook until browned on all sides. Transfer meat to medium bowl. Heat remaining ½ tablespoon oil over medium heat in same Dutch oven. Add onion and garlic; cook until onion is tender. Stir in tomato paste, chili powder, coriander and water. Return meat to Dutch oven. Add potatoes, carrots, corn and chopped celery leaves. Bring to a boil. Cover; reduce heat and simmer 1 hour and 15 minutes or until meat is tender.

During last 15 minutes of cooking, prepare Cornmeal Dumplings. Drop dough onto stew, making six dumplings. Cover and simmer an additional 18 minutes or until dumplings are firm to the touch and wooden toothpick inserted in center comes out clean. To serve, spoon stew onto individual plates; serve with dumplings. Garnish with whole celery leaves. *Makes 6 servings*

CORNMEAL DUMPLINGS: Combine cornmeal, flour, baking powder and salt in medium bowl. Cut in butter with fingers, pastry blender or two knives until mixture resembles coarse crumbs. Make well in center; add milk all at once and stir with fork until mixture forms dough.

Cordero Stew with Cornmeal Dumplings

ROBUST STEWS & CHILIES

292 CHICKEN STEW WITH DUMPLINGS

2 tablespoons vegetable oil
2 cups sliced carrots
1 cup chopped onion
1 large green bell pepper, sliced
½ cup sliced celery
2 cans (about 14 ounces each) fat-free
reduced-sodium chicken broth
¼ cup plus 2 tablespoons all-purpose flour
2 pounds boneless skinless chicken
breasts, cut into 1-inch pieces
3 medium potatoes, unpeeled and cut into
1-inch pieces
6 ounces mushrooms, halved
¾ cup frozen peas
1 teaspoon dried basil leaves
¾ teaspoon dried rosemary
¼ teaspoon dried tarragon
¾ to 1 teaspoon salt
¼ teaspoon black pepper

HERB DUMPLINGS
2 cups biscuit mix
½ teaspoon dried basil leaves
½ teaspoon dried rosemary
¼ teaspoon dried tarragon
⅔ cup 2% milk

1. Heat oil in 4-quart Dutch oven over
medium heat until hot. Add carrots, onion,
green bell pepper and celery; cook and stir 5
minutes or until onion is tender. Stir in
chicken broth, reserving ½ cup; bring to a
boil. Mix reserved ½ cup broth and flour; stir
into boiling mixture. Boil, stirring constantly,
1 minute or until thickened. Stir chicken,
potatoes, mushrooms, peas and herbs into
mixture. Reduce heat to low; simmer,
covered, 18 to 20 minutes or until vegetables
are almost tender and chicken is no longer
pink in center. Add salt and pepper; cool
completely. Refrigerate, covered, up to 2
days.

2. To complete recipe, bring stew just to a
boil in large saucepan over medium heat.
For Herb Dumplings, combine biscuit mix
and herbs in small bowl; stir in milk to form
soft dough. Spoon dumpling mixture on top
of stew in 8 large spoonfuls. Reduce heat to
low. Cook, uncovered, 10 minutes. Cover
and cook 10 minutes or until biscuits are
tender and toothpick inserted in center
comes out clean. Serve in shallow bowls.
Makes 8 (1¼-cup) servings

293 SHRIMP AND FISH GUMBO

8 ounces fresh or frozen orange roughy or
other fish fillets
6 ounces deveined shelled raw shrimp
3¾ cups water, divided
1 cup chopped onion
½ cup chopped green bell pepper
2 cloves garlic, minced
½ teaspoon chicken or fish bouillon
granules
2 cans (14½ ounces each) no-salt-added
stewed tomatoes, undrained
1½ cups frozen okra, thawed
1 teaspoon dried thyme leaves
1 teaspoon dried savory leaves
¼ teaspoon ground red pepper
⅛ teaspoon black pepper
2 tablespoons cornstarch
2 tablespoons finely chopped low-sodium
ham
2 cups hot cooked brown rice

Remove and discard skin from fish; cut fish
into 1-inch pieces. Bring 3 cups water to a
boil in medium saucepan over high heat.
Add fish and shrimp; cook 3 to 4 minutes or
until fish flakes easily when tested with fork
and shrimp are opaque. Drain; set aside.

ROBUST STEWS & CHILIES

Combine onion, bell pepper, additional ½ cup water, garlic and bouillon granules in large saucepan. Bring to a boil over medium-high heat; reduce to medium-low. Cover and simmer 2 to 3 minutes or until vegetables are crisp-tender.

Stir in stewed tomatoes with liquid, okra, thyme, savory, red pepper and black pepper. Return to a boil; reduce heat. Simmer, uncovered, 3 to 5 minutes or until okra is tender. Combine remaining ¼ cup water and cornstarch in small bowl. Stir into mixture in saucepan. Cook and stir over medium heat until mixture boils and thickens. Cook and stir 2 minutes more. Add fish, shrimp and ham; heat through. Serve over rice.

Makes 4 servings

294 SPICY VEGETABLE STEW

 1 tablespoon vegetable oil
 2 carrots, chopped
 ½ onion, chopped
 2 cloves garlic, minced
 1 teaspoon ground cumin
 1 teaspoon paprika
 ¾ teaspoon ground cinnamon
 ½ teaspoon salt
 ½ teaspoon ground ginger
 ½ teaspoon black pepper
 1 can (14½ ounces) diced tomatoes
 1 can (about 14 ounces) vegetable broth
 1 cup frozen hash brown potatoes
 1 cup frozen green beans
 2 tablespoons tomato paste
 ¼ to ½ teaspoon hot pepper sauce
 1⅓ cups uncooked couscous

1. Heat oil in large saucepan over medium-high heat until hot. Add carrots, onion, garlic, cumin, paprika, cinnamon, salt, ginger and black pepper; cook and stir about 5 minutes or until vegetables are tender.

2. Stir in tomatoes, broth, potatoes, green beans, tomato paste and hot pepper sauce; bring to a boil. Reduce heat to low and simmer, uncovered, 10 minutes.

3. While stew is simmering, prepare couscous. Bring 1⅓ cups water to a boil in small saucepan over high heat. Stir in couscous. Cover and remove saucepan from heat; let stand 5 minutes.

4. Fluff couscous with fork. Serve vegetable stew over couscous. *Makes 4 servings*

For a special touch, garnish with fresh Italian parsley.

Prep and cook time: 23 minutes

ROBUST STEWS & CHILIES

295 FRENCH–STYLE PORK STEW

1 package (6.2 ounces) long grain and
   wild rice
1 tablespoon vegetable oil
1 pork tenderloin (16 ounces), cut into
   ¾- to 1-inch cubes
1 medium onion, coarsely chopped
1 rib celery, sliced
2 tablespoons all-purpose flour
1½ cups chicken broth
½ package (16 ounces) frozen mixed
   vegetables (carrots, potatoes and
   peas)
1 jar (4.5 ounces) sliced mushrooms,
   drained
½ teaspoon dried basil leaves
¼ teaspoon dried rosemary leaves
¼ teaspoon dried oregano leaves
2 teaspoons lemon juice
⅛ teaspoon ground nutmeg

1. Prepare rice according to package directions, discarding spice packet, if desired.

2. While rice is cooking, heat oil in large saucepan over medium-high heat until hot. Add pork, onion and celery; cook 5 minutes or until pork is browned. Stir flour into chicken broth until dissolved; add to pork mixture. Cook over medium heat 1 minute, stirring constantly.

3. Stir in frozen vegetables, mushrooms, basil, rosemary and oregano; bring to a boil. Reduce heat to low; simmer, covered, 6 to 8 minutes or until pork is tender and barely pink in center. Stir in lemon juice, nutmeg and salt and pepper to taste. Serve stew over rice. *Makes 4 (1-cup) servings*

Prep and Cook Time: 20 minutes

296 SANTA FE STEW OLÉ

1 tablespoon vegetable oil
1½ pounds beef stew meat, cut into bite-
   size pieces
1 can (28 ounces) stewed tomatoes
2 medium carrots, cut into ¼-inch slices
1 medium onion, coarsely chopped
1 package (1.0 ounce) LAWRY'S® Taco
   Spices & Seasonings
2 tablespoons diced green chiles
½ teaspoon LAWRY'S® Seasoned Salt
¼ cup water
2 tablespoons all-purpose flour
1 can (15 ounces) pinto beans, drained

In Dutch oven, heat oil. Brown stew meat over medium-high heat. Add tomatoes, carrots, onion, Taco Spices & Seasonings, green chiles and Seasoned Salt; mix well. Bring to a boil over medium-high heat; reduce heat to low and cook, covered, 40 minutes. In small bowl, combine water and flour; mix well. Stir into stew mixture. Add pinto beans; cook over low heat additional 15 minutes. *Makes 4 servings*

SERVING SUGGESTION: Serve with warm corn and flour tortillas.

French-Style Pork Stew

ROBUST STEWS & CHILIES

297 HEARTY VEGETABLE GUMBO

½ cup chopped onion
½ cup chopped green bell pepper
¼ cup chopped celery
2 cloves garlic, minced
2 cans (about 14 ounces each) no-salt-added stewed tomatoes, undrained
2 cups no-salt-added tomato juice
1 can (15 ounces) red beans, drained and rinsed
1 tablespoon chopped fresh parsley
¼ teaspoon dried oregano leaves
¼ teaspoon hot pepper sauce
2 bay leaves
1½ cups quick-cooking brown rice
1 package (10 ounces) frozen chopped okra, thawed

1. Spray 4-quart Dutch oven with nonstick cooking spray; heat over medium heat until hot. Add onion, bell pepper, celery and garlic. Cook and stir 3 minutes or until crisp-tender.

2. Add stewed tomatoes, juice, beans, parsley, oregano, pepper sauce and bay leaves. Bring to a boil over high heat. Add rice. Reduce heat to medium-low. Simmer, covered, 15 minutes or until rice is tender.

3. Add okra; simmer, covered, 5 minutes more or until okra is tender. Remove bay leaves; discard. Garnish as desired.

Makes 4 (2-cup) servings

298 ITALIAN SAUSAGE AND VEGETABLE STEW

1 pound hot or mild Italian sausage, cut into 1-inch pieces
1 package (16 ounces) frozen mixed vegetables (onions and green, red and yellow peppers)
2 medium zucchini, sliced
4 cloves garlic, minced
1 can (14½ ounces) diced Italian-style tomatoes, undrained
1 jar (4½ ounces) sliced mushrooms, drained

1. Cook sausage in large saucepan, covered, over medium to medium-high heat 5 minutes or until browned; pour off drippings.

2. Add frozen vegetables, zucchini, garlic, tomatoes with juice and mushrooms; bring to a boil. Reduce heat to low; simmer, covered, 10 minutes. Cook uncovered 5 to 10 minutes or until juices have thickened slightly. *Makes 6 (1-cup) servings*

SERVING SUGGESTION: Italian Sausage and Vegetable Stew is excellent served with garlic bread.

Prep and cook time: 30 minutes

Hearty Vegetable Gumbo

ROBUST STEWS & CHILIES

299 BRUNSWICK STEW

12 ounces smoked ham or cooked chicken
    breast, cut into ¾- to 1-inch cubes
1 cup sliced onion
4½ teaspoons all-purpose flour
1 can (14½ ounces) stewed tomatoes,
    undrained
2 cups frozen mixed vegetables for soup
    (such as okra, lima beans, potatoes,
    celery, corn, carrots, green beans and
    onions)
1 cup chicken broth

1. Spray large saucepan with nonstick cooking spray; heat over medium heat until hot. Add ham and onion; cook 5 minutes or until ham is browned. Stir in flour; cook over medium to medium-low heat 1 minute, stirring constantly.

2. Stir in remaining ingredients; bring to a boil. Reduce heat to low; simmer, covered, 5 to 8 minutes or until vegetables are tender. Simmer, uncovered, 5 to 8 minutes or until slightly thickened. Season to taste with salt and pepper.   *Makes 4 (1-cup) servings*

SERVING SUGGESTION: Brunswick Stew is excellent served over rice or squares of cornbread.

COOK'S NOTES: In 1828, Brunswick County, Virginia, was the birthplace of Brunswick stew, originally made of squirrel meat and onion.

Prep and cook time: 30 minutes

300 FISHERMAN'S STEW

2 cups water
1 pound fish fillets (scrod, halibut,
    monkfish or cod), cut into 2-inch
    pieces
1 clove garlic, minced
1 tablespoon FILIPPO BERIO® Olive Oil
1 medium onion, chopped
¼ cup chopped almonds
¼ cup seasoned dry bread crumbs
2 cups vegetable broth or bouillon
2 medium tomatoes, diced
¼ teaspoon paprika
¼ teaspoon freshly ground black pepper
    Salt

In large saucepan or Dutch oven, bring water to a boil over high heat. Add fish and garlic. Cover; reduce heat to low and simmer 15 minutes or until fish is opaque and flakes easily when tested with fork. Remove fish with slotted spoon; set aside. Reserve stock (about 2 cups).

Meanwhile, in small nonstick skillet, heat olive oil over medium heat until hot. Add onion; cook and stir 5 minutes or until softened. Add almonds and bread crumbs; cook and stir 3 to 5 minutes or until lightly browned. Add to reserved fish stock along with vegetable broth, tomatoes, paprika and pepper. Add fish; cover and cook until fish is heated through. Season to taste with salt. Serve hot.   *Makes 4 to 6 servings*

Brunswick Stew

ROBUST STEWS & CHILIES

301 SANTA FE TACO STEW

1 tablespoon vegetable oil
½ cup diced onion
½ teaspoon LAWRY'S® Garlic Powder with Parsley
1 package (1.0 ounce) LAWRY'S® Taco Spices & Seasonings
1 can (28 ounces) diced tomatoes, undrained
1 can (15 ounces) pinto beans, drained
1 can (8¾ ounces) whole kernel corn, drained
1 can (4 ounces) diced green chilies, drained
1 cup beef broth
½ teaspoon cornstarch
1 pound pork butt or beef chuck, cooked and shredded
    Dairy sour cream (garnish)
    Tortilla chips (garnish)
    Fresh cilantro (garnish)

In Dutch oven or large saucepan, heat oil. Add onion and Garlic Powder with Parsley; cook over medium-high heat 2 to 3 minutes until onion is tender. Add Taco Spices & Seasonings, tomatoes, beans, corn and chilies; mix well. In small bowl, gradually combine broth and cornstarch using wire whisk. Stir into stew. Add cooked meat. Bring to a boil over medium-high heat, stirring frequently. Reduce heat to low; cook, uncovered, 30 minutes, stirring occasionally. (Or, cook over low heat longer for a thicker stew.)   *Makes 8 servings*

SERVING SUGGESTION: Garnish each serving with sour cream, tortilla chips and fresh cilantro, if desired.

HINT: Substitute 3 cups cooked, shredded chicken for pork or beef.

302 GREEK PORK STEW

¼ cup olive oil
1 pork tenderloin, cut into ½-inch cubes (about 2½ pounds)
½ pound small white onions, cut into halves
3 cloves garlic, chopped
1¼ cups dry red wine
1 can (6 ounces) tomato paste
1 can (14½ ounces) ready-to-serve beef broth
2 tablespoons balsamic vinegar or red wine vinegar
2 bay leaves
1½ teaspoons ground cinnamon
⅛ teaspoon ground coriander
    Hot cooked rice (optional)

Heat oil in 5-quart Dutch oven over medium-high heat. Brown half of pork in Dutch oven. Remove with slotted spoon; set aside. Brown remaining pork. Remove with slotted spoon; set aside.

Add onions and garlic to Dutch oven. Cook and stir about 5 minutes or until onion is soft. Return pork to Dutch oven.

Combine wine and tomato paste in small bowl until blended; add to pork. Stir in broth, vinegar, bay leaves, cinnamon and coriander. Bring to a boil over high heat. Reduce heat to low. Cover and simmer 45 minutes or until pork is fork-tender. Remove bay leaves before serving. Serve with rice.   *Makes 6 to 8 servings*

Santa Fe Taco Stew

ROBUST STEWS & CHILIES

303 TUSCAN VEGETABLE STEW

2 tablespoons olive oil
2 teaspoons bottled minced garlic
2 packages (4 ounces each) sliced mixed exotic mushrooms *or* 1 package (8 ounces) sliced button mushrooms
¼ cup sliced shallots or chopped sweet onion
1 jar (7 ounces) roasted red peppers
1 can (14½ ounces) Italian-style stewed tomatoes, undrained
1 can (19 ounces) cannellini beans, drained
1 bunch fresh basil*
1 tablespoon balsamic vinegar
Grated Romano, Parmesan or Asiago cheese

If fresh basil is not available, add 2 teaspoons dried basil leaves to stew with tomatoes.

1. Heat oil and garlic in large deep skillet over medium heat. Add mushrooms and shallots; cook 5 minutes, stirring occasionally.

2. While mushroom mixture is cooking, drain and rinse peppers; cut into 1-inch pieces. Snip tomatoes in can into small pieces with scissors.

3. Add peppers, tomatoes and beans to skillet; bring to a boil. Reduce heat to medium-low. Cover and simmer 10 minutes, stirring once.

4. While stew is simmering, cut basil leaves into thin strips to measure ¼ cup packed. Stir basil and vinegar into stew; add salt and pepper to taste. Sprinkle each serving with cheese.   *Makes 4 servings*

Prep and cook time: 18 minutes

304 SKILLET SAUSAGE AND BEAN STEW

1 pound spicy Italian sausage, casing removed and sliced ½ inch thick
½ onion, chopped
2 cups frozen O'Brien-style potatoes with onions and peppers
1 can (15 ounces) pinto beans, undrained
¾ cup water
1 teaspoon beef bouillon granules *or* 1 beef bouillon cube
1 teaspoon dried oregano leaves
⅛ teaspoon ground red pepper

1. Combine sausage slices and onion in large nonstick skillet; cook and stir over medium-high heat 5 to 7 minutes or until meat is no longer pink. Drain drippings.

2. Stir in potatoes, beans, water, bouillon, oregano and red pepper; reduce heat to medium. Cover and simmer 15 minutes, stirring occasionally.   *Makes 4 servings*

LIGHTEN UP: You can reduce the calories and fat content of this dish by substituting turkey sausage for Italian sausage. Add hot pepper sauce to taste if you prefer a spicier stew.

Prep and cook time: 30 minutes

Tuscan Vegetable Stew

ROBUST STEWS & CHILIES

305 JAMAICAN BLACK BEAN STEW

2 cups uncooked brown rice
2 pounds sweet potatoes
3 pounds butternut squash
1 can (about 14 ounces) vegetable broth
1 large onion, coarsely chopped
3 cloves garlic, minced
1 tablespoon curry powder
1½ teaspoons ground allspice
½ teaspoon ground red pepper
¼ teaspoon salt
2 cans (15 ounces each) black beans, rinsed and drained
½ cup raisins
3 tablespoons fresh lime juice
1 cup diced tomato
1 cup diced, peeled cucumber

1. Prepare rice according to package directions; set aside. Peel sweet potatoes; cut into ¾-inch chunks to measure 4 cups. Peel squash; remove seeds. Cut into ¾-inch cubes to measure 5 cups.

2. Combine potatoes, squash, broth, onion, garlic, curry powder, allspice, pepper and salt in Dutch oven. Bring to a boil; reduce heat to low. Simmer, covered, 5 minutes. Add beans and raisins. Simmer 5 minutes or just until sweet potatoes and squash are tender and beans are hot. Remove from heat; stir in lime juice.

3. Serve stew over brown rice; top with tomato and cucumber. Garnish with lime peel. *Makes 8 servings*

306 CHICKEN STEW À LA MOROCCO

¼ cup olive oil
½ pound eggplant, peeled and cubed
1 large onion, sliced
2 to 3 cloves garlic, chopped
2 tablespoons lemon juice
2 teaspoons ground coriander
1 teaspoon ground turmeric
¼ teaspoon crushed red pepper flakes
5 boneless skinless chicken breast halves (about 1½ pounds)
10 boneless skinless chicken thighs (about 1½ pounds)
1 cup chicken broth
¼ cup golden raisins
½ cup sliced pimiento-stuffed green olives
Peel of 1 lemon, coarsely chopped
Hot cooked couscous or rice (optional)
Chopped mint for garnish

Heat oil in 5-quart Dutch oven over medium-high heat. Cook and stir eggplant, onion and garlic in oil until soft. Stir in lemon juice, seasonings and red pepper flakes; move vegetables to side of pan.

Brown chicken, in batches, in Dutch oven 10 minutes. Remove with slotted spoon; reserve chicken. Repeat until all remaining chicken is browned. Return chicken to Dutch oven.

Add broth and raisins. Bring to boil over high heat. Reduce heat to low. Cover and simmer 25 minutes. Stir in olives and lemon peel. Cover and simmer 25 minutes more or until chicken is fork-tender and no longer pink in center. Serve over couscous. Garnish with mint. *Makes 8 to 10 servings*

Jamaican Black Bean Stew

307 CURRIED TURKEY STEW WITH DUMPLINGS

2 pounds turkey thighs
1 medium onion, chopped
4¾ cups cold water, divided
1 teaspoon salt
1 teaspoon dried thyme leaves
⅛ teaspoon black pepper
¼ cup cornstarch
1 teaspoon curry powder
2 cups frozen mixed broccoli, cauliflower and carrots
1 large tart apple, peeled, cored, coarsely chopped
¾ cup all-purpose flour
1 tablespoon chopped fresh parsley
1¼ teaspoons baking powder
¼ teaspoon onion salt
2 tablespoons shortening
¼ cup milk
   Paprika
¼ cup chopped peanuts
   Fresh herb sprig for garnish

Rinse turkey. Place onion, turkey, 4 cups water, salt, thyme and pepper in 5-quart Dutch oven. Bring to a boil over high heat. Reduce heat to medium-low; simmer, uncovered, 1 hour 45 minutes or until turkey is tender.

Remove turkey from soup and let cool slightly. Remove fat from soup by using large spoon, skimming off as much fat as possible. (Or, refrigerate soup several hours and remove fat that rises to surface. Refrigerate turkey if chilling soup to remove fat.)

Remove turkey meat from bones; discard skin and bones. Cut turkey into bite-size pieces.

Stir together remaining ¾ cup cold water, cornstarch and curry powder in small bowl until smooth. Stir into broth. Cook and stir over medium heat until mixture comes to a boil and thickens.

Stir in frozen vegetables, turkey pieces and apple. Bring to a boil over high heat, stirring occasionally.

For dumplings, stir together flour, parsley, baking powder and onion salt. Cut in shortening until mixture forms pea-sized pieces. Stir in milk until just combined.

Drop dough into six mounds on stew.

Cover and simmer over medium-low heat about 15 minutes or until wooden toothpick inserted in center of dumplings comes out clean.

Sprinkle dumplings with paprika. Spoon stew into bowls, placing dumpling on top of each serving; sprinkle with peanuts. Garnish, if desired. *Makes 6 servings*

Curried Turkey Stew with Dumplings

ROBUST STEWS & CHILIES

308 PORK AND VEGETABLE STEW WITH NOODLES

1 pound lean boneless pork
2 tablespoons vegetable oil
3 cups beef broth
3 tablespoons chopped fresh parsley, divided
1 can (14½ ounces) stewed tomatoes
1 large carrot, sliced
3 green onions, sliced
2 teaspoons Dijon mustard
¼ teaspoon rubbed sage
⅛ teaspoon black pepper
3 cups uncooked noodles
1 teaspoon butter or margarine
2 tablespoons all-purpose flour
⅓ cup cold water
   Apples and parsley for garnish

Cut pork into ¾-inch cubes. Heat oil in large saucepan over medium-high heat. Add meat; brown, stirring frequently. Carefully add beef broth. Stir in 1 tablespoon chopped parsley, tomatoes, carrot, onions, mustard, sage and pepper. Bring to a boil over high heat. Reduce heat to medium-low; simmer, uncovered, 30 minutes.

Meanwhile, cook noodles according to package directions; drain. Add reserved 2 tablespoons chopped parsley and butter; toss lightly. Keep warm until ready to serve.

Stir flour into cold water in cup until smooth. Stir into stew. Cook and stir over medium heat until slightly thickened. To serve, spoon noodles onto each plate. Ladle stew over noodles. Garnish, if desired.

Makes 4 servings

309 BEEF BURGUNDY STEW

1 (1-pound) boneless beef sirloin steak, cut into 1½-inch cubes
3 tablespoons all-purpose flour
6 slices bacon, cut into 1-inch pieces (about ¼ pound)
1 large onion, cut into wedges (about 1½ cups)
3 carrots, peeled, cut into ½-inch pieces (about 1½ cups)
12 small fresh mushrooms
2 cloves garlic, minced
1 cup Burgundy or other dry red wine
½ cup A.1.® Original or A.1.® Bold & Spicy Steak Sauce

Coat beef with flour, shaking off excess; set aside.

In 6-quart pot, over medium heat, cook bacon until crisp; remove with slotted spoon. Set aside.

In same pot, brown beef, a few pieces at a time, in drippings. Return cooked beef and bacon to pot; stir in onion, carrots, mushrooms, garlic, wine and steak sauce. Cover; simmer 40 minutes or until carrots are tender, stirring occasionally. Serve immediately.   *Makes 6 servings*

Pork and Vegetable Stew with Noodles

ROBUST STEWS & CHILIES

310 PESCADO VIEJO (FISH STEW)

1 tablespoon vegetable oil
2 medium onions, chopped
1 green bell pepper, finely chopped
2 cans (14½ ounces each) whole peeled tomatoes, undrained and cut up
1 large red potato, cubed
1 can (13¾ ounces) beef broth
⅓ cup red wine
1 bay leaf
1 package (1.5 ounces) LAWRY'S® Original Style Spaghetti Sauce Spices & Seasonings
¾ teaspoon LAWRY'S® Garlic Powder with Parsley
½ teaspoon LAWRY'S® Seasoned Salt
½ teaspoon celery seed
1 pound halibut or swordfish steaks, rinsed and cubed

In Dutch oven, heat oil. Cook onions and bell pepper over medium-high heat until tender. Stir in remaining ingredients except fish. Bring to a boil over medium-high heat; reduce heat to low and cook, covered, 20 minutes. Add fish. Cook over low heat 10 to 15 minutes longer or until fish flakes easily with fork. Remove bay leaf before serving.

Makes 10 servings

SERVING SUGGESTION: Serve with thick, crusty bread sticks.

311 BRUNSWICK STEW

1 (14½-ounce) can peeled tomatoes, undrained
1 (17-ounce) can green lima beans, undrained
1 (2½-pound) chicken, cut up
1 (14¼-ounce) can COLLEGE INN® Chicken Broth
2 (6-ounce) cans tomato paste
2 tablespoons red wine vinegar
2 tablespoons Worcestershire sauce
¼ teaspoon ground red pepper
2 cups cubed cooked pork

Drain tomatoes and lima beans, reserving liquid; coarsely chop tomatoes. In large heavy saucepan, over medium-high heat, combine chicken, chicken broth, tomato paste, reserved tomato liquid, reserved lima bean liquid, red wine vinegar, Worcestershire sauce and pepper; heat to a boil. Reduce heat; cover and simmer 20 minutes. Add tomatoes, lima beans and pork; cover. Simmer 20 to 25 minutes more or until chicken is done.

Makes 6 servings

MICROWAVE DIRECTIONS: In 5-quart microwavable casserole, combine chicken, broth, tomato paste, reserved tomato liquid, reserved bean liquid, vinegar, Worcestershire sauce and pepper as above. Cover with waxed paper. Microwave on MEDIUM (50% power) for 28 to 30 minutes, stirring twice during cooking time. Add tomatoes, lima beans and pork; cover. Microwave on LOW (30% power) for 18 to 20 minutes. Let stand, covered, 10 minutes before serving.

Pescado Viejo (Fish Stew)

ROBUST STEWS & CHILIES

312 SPICY SICHUAN PORK STEW

2 pounds boneless pork shoulder (Boston butt)
¼ cup all-purpose flour
2 tablespoons vegetable oil
1¾ cups water, divided
¼ cup KIKKOMAN® Soy Sauce
3 tablespoons dry sherry
2 cloves garlic, pressed
1 teaspoon minced fresh ginger root
½ teaspoon crushed red pepper
¼ teaspoon fennel seed, crushed
8 green onions and tops, cut into 1-inch lengths, separating whites from tops
2 large carrots, cut into chunks
Hot cooked rice

Cut pork into 1-inch cubes. Coat in flour; reserve 2 tablespoons remaining flour. Heat oil in Dutch oven or large pan over medium-high heat; brown pork on all sides in hot oil. Add 1½ cups water, soy sauce, sherry, garlic, ginger, red pepper, fennel and white parts of green onions. Cover pan; bring to boil. Reduce heat and simmer 30 minutes. Add carrots; simmer, covered, 30 minutes longer, or until pork and carrots are tender. Meanwhile, combine reserved flour and remaining ¼ cup water; set aside. Stir green onion tops into pork mixture; simmer 1 minute. Add flour mixture; bring to boil. Cook and stir until mixture is slightly thickened. Serve over rice.

Makes 6 servings

313 BROWN RICE AND LENTIL STEW

¾ cup uncooked brown rice
½ cup dry lentils, rinsed
½ cup chopped onion
½ cup sliced celery
½ cup sliced carrots
¼ cup chopped parsley
1 teaspoon Italian herb seasonings
1 clove garlic, minced
1 bay leaf
2½ cups chicken broth
2 cups water
1 can (14½ ounces) tomatoes, chopped, undrained
1 tablespoon cider vinegar

Combine rice, lentils, onion, celery, carrots, parsley, seasonings, garlic, bay leaf, broth, water, tomatoes and vinegar in Dutch oven. Bring to a boil over high heat. Reduce heat to low. Simmer, uncovered, about 1 hour or until rice is tender, stirring occasionally. Remove bay leaf before serving.

Makes 4 servings

*Favorite recipe from **USA Rice Federation***

Spicy Sichuan Pork Stew

ROBUST STEWS & CHILIES

314 NEW ORLEANS PORK GUMBO

1 pound pork loin roast
  Nonstick cooking spray
1 tablespoon margarine
2 tablespoons all-purpose flour
1 cup water
1 can (16 ounces) stewed tomatoes,
  undrained
1 package (10 ounces) frozen cut okra
1 package (10 ounces) frozen succotash
1 beef bouillon cube
1 teaspoon hot pepper sauce
1 teaspoon coarsely ground black pepper
1 bay leaf

1. Cut pork into ½-inch cubes. Spray large Dutch oven with cooking spray. Heat over medium heat until hot. Add pork; cook and stir 4 minutes or until pork is browned. Remove pork from Dutch oven.

2. Add margarine to Dutch oven. Stir in flour. Cook and stir until roux is browned. Whisk in water. Add pork and remaining ingredients. Bring to a boil. Reduce heat to low and simmer 15 minutes. Remove bay leaf. *Makes 4 servings*

315 KIELBASA AND LENTIL STEW

1 pound kielbasa sausages or smoked
  Polish sausages
1 tablespoon olive oil
2 cups shredded cabbage
1 large onion, chopped
1 cup shredded carrots
2 cloves garlic, minced
½ pound dried lentils, rinsed and sorted
2 cans (14½ ounces each) beef broth
1 can (14½ ounces) tomatoes, cut up,
  undrained
3 tablespoons FRANK'S® Original
  REDHOT® Cayenne Pepper Sauce
  Cooked white rice (optional)

1. Cut sausages lengthwise into halves. Cut halves into ¼-inch-thick slices. Heat oil in 5-quart saucepan or Dutch oven over medium-high heat. Add sausage; cook and stir 3 minutes or until lightly browned. Transfer to platter; set aside. Drain off all but 1 tablespoon fat.

2. Add cabbage, onion, carrots and garlic to saucepan. Cook and stir 3 to 5 minutes or until tender. Return sausage to saucepan; add lentils, broth, tomatoes with liquid, ½ cup water and RedHot® sauce. Bring to a boil. Reduce heat to low; cook, partially covered, 40 minutes or until lentils are tender.

3. Ladle into soup bowls. Serve over cooked rice, if desired.

Makes 6 servings (8 cups)

Prep Time: 20 minutes
Cook Time: 50 minutes

New Orleans Pork Gumbo

ROBUST STEWS & CHILIES

316 PASTA E FAGIOLI

2 tablespoons olive oil
1 cup chopped onion
3 cloves garlic, minced
2 cans (14½ ounces each) Italian-style
    stewed tomatoes, undrained
3 cups fat-free reduced-sodium chicken
    broth
1 can (about 15 ounces) cannellini beans
    (white kidney beans), undrained*
¼ cup chopped fresh Italian parsley
1 teaspoon dried basil leaves
¼ teaspoon black pepper
4 ounces uncooked small shell pasta

*One can (about 15 ounces) Great Northern beans,
undrained, may be substituted for cannellini beans.*

1. Heat oil in 4-quart Dutch oven over
medium heat until hot; add onion and garlic.
Cook and stir 5 minutes or until onion is
tender.

2. Stir tomatoes with liquid, chicken broth,
beans with liquid, parsley, basil and pepper
into Dutch oven; bring to a boil over high
heat, stirring occasionally. Reduce heat to
low. Simmer, covered, 10 minutes.

3. Add pasta to Dutch oven. Simmer,
covered, 10 to 12 minutes or until pasta is
just tender. Serve immediately. Garnish as
desired.   *Makes 8 servings*

317 CANTON PORK STEW

1½ pounds boneless lean pork shoulder or
    pork loin roast, cut into 1-inch pieces
1 teaspoon ground ginger
¼ teaspoon ground cinnamon
¼ teaspoon ground red pepper
1 tablespoon peanut or vegetable oil
1 large onion, coarsely chopped
3 cloves garlic, minced
1 can (about 14 ounces) chicken broth
¼ cup dry sherry
1 package (about 10 ounces) frozen baby
    carrots, thawed
1 large green bell pepper, cut into 1-inch
    pieces
3 tablespoons soy sauce
1½ tablespoons cornstarch
    Cilantro for garnish

Sprinkle pork with ginger, cinnamon and
ground red pepper; toss well. Heat large
saucepan or Dutch oven over medium-high
heat. Add oil; heat until hot.

Add pork to saucepan; brown on all sides.
Add onion and garlic; cook 2 minutes,
stirring frequently. Add broth and sherry.
Bring to a boil over high heat. Reduce heat
to medium-low. Cover and simmer 40
minutes.

Stir in carrots and green pepper; cover and
simmer 10 minutes or until pork is fork-
tender. Blend soy sauce into cornstarch in
cup until smooth. Stir into stew. Cook and
stir 1 minute or until stew boils and
thickens. Ladle into soup bowls. Garnish
with cilantro.   *Makes 6 servings*

Pasta e Fagioli

ROBUST STEWS & CHILIES

318 SOUTHWEST CHILI

1 large onion, chopped
1 tablespoon olive oil
2 large tomatoes, chopped
1 (4-ounce) can chopped green chilies, undrained
1 tablespoon chili powder
1 teaspoon ground cumin
1 (15-ounce) can red kidney beans, undrained
1 (15-ounce) can Great Northern beans, undrained
¼ cup cilantro leaves, chopped (optional)

Cook and stir onion in oil in large saucepan over medium heat until onion is soft. Stir in tomatoes, chilies, chili powder and cumin. Bring to a boil. Add beans with liquid. Reduce heat to low. Cover and simmer 15 minutes, stirring occasionally. Sprinkle individual servings with cilantro.

Makes 4 servings

319 OLIVE–BEAN CHILI

3 tablespoons molasses
1½ teaspoons dry mustard
1½ teaspoons soy sauce
2 teaspoons olive oil
2 medium carrots, cut diagonally into ¼-inch slices
1 large onion, chopped
1 tablespoon chili powder
3 large tomatoes (1½ pounds), chopped
1 (15-ounce) can pinto beans, drained
1 (15-ounce) can kidney beans, drained
¾ cup California ripe olives, sliced
½ cup plain nonfat yogurt
Crushed red pepper flakes

Combine molasses, mustard and soy sauce; set aside. Heat oil in large skillet; add carrots, onion, chili powder and ¼ cup water. Cook, covered, about 4 minutes or until carrots are almost tender. Uncover and cook, stirring, until liquid has evaporated. Add molasses mixture with tomatoes, pinto beans, kidney beans and olives. Cook, stirring gently, about 5 minutes or until mixture is hot and tomatoes are soft. Ladle chili into bowls; top with yogurt. Sprinkle with pepper flakes to taste.

Makes 4 servings

Prep Time: about 15 minutes
Cook Time: about 10 minutes

*Favorite recipe from **California Olive Industry***

Southwest Chili

ROBUST STEWS & CHILIES

320 ARIZONA PORK CHILI

1 tablespoon vegetable oil
1½ pounds boneless pork, cut into ¼-inch cubes
   Salt and black pepper (optional)
1 can (15 ounces) black, pinto or kidney beans, drained
1 can (14½ ounces) DEL MONTE® FreshCut™ Brand Diced Tomatoes with Garlic & Onion, undrained
1 can (4 ounces) diced green chilies, drained
1 teaspoon ground cumin
   Tortillas and sour cream (optional)

1. Heat oil in large skillet over medium-high heat. Add pork; cook until browned. Season with salt and pepper to taste, if desired.

2. Add beans, tomatoes, chilies and cumin. Simmer 10 minutes, stirring occasionally. Serve with tortillas and sour cream, if desired. *Makes 6 servings*

Prep Time: 10 minutes
Cook Time: 25 minutes

321 CHILI CON QUESO CON SURIMI

1 cup chopped onion
2 tablespoons olive or vegetable oil
1 can (16 ounces) tomatoes, coarsely chopped
1 can (4 ounces) diced green chilies
8 ounces (2 cups) shredded low fat or regular Monterey Jack cheese
8 ounces (2 cups) shredded low-fat Cheddar cheese
1 tablespoon cornstarch
8 ounces surimi seafood, flake-style or chunk-style, coarsely chopped

Cook onion in oil in large saucepan over medium heat until tender but not brown, stirring occasionally. Add tomatoes and chilies; bring to a simmer and cook 5 minutes. Meanwhile, toss cheeses with cornstarch; gradually add to tomato mixture and stir until melted. Stir in surimi seafood. Transfer to top of chafing dish or fondue pot (over hot water or alcohol or candle burner) to keep warm. Serve with corn chips, crackers and raw vegetables for dipping. *Makes 4½ cups*

*Favorite recipe from **National Fisheries Institute***

Arizona Pork Chili

ROBUST STEWS & CHILIES

322 CHUNKY VEGETABLE CHILI

2 tablespoons vegetable oil
1 medium onion, chopped
2 ribs celery, diced
1 carrot, diced
3 cloves garlic, minced
2 cans (about 15 ounces each) Great Northern beans, rinsed and drained
1½ cups water
1 cup frozen corn
1 can (6 ounces) tomato paste
1 can (4 ounces) diced mild green chilies, undrained
1 tablespoon chili powder
2 teaspoons dried oregano leaves
1 teaspoon salt

1. Heat oil in large skillet over medium-high heat until hot. Add onion, celery, carrot and garlic; cook 5 minutes or until vegetables are tender, stirring occasionally.

2. Stir beans, water, corn, tomato paste, chilies, chili powder, oregano and salt into skillet. Reduce heat to medium-low. Simmer 20 minutes, stirring occasionally. Garnish with cilantro, if desired.

Makes 8 servings

323 HEAD-'EM-OFF-AT-THE-PASS WHITE CHILI

1 tablespoon olive oil
½ cup chopped onion
2 cans (15 ounces each) cannellini beans, undrained
1 jar (11 ounces) NEWMAN'S OWN® Bandito Salsa, divided
1½ cups chopped cooked chicken
½ cup chicken broth
1 teaspoon oregano leaves
½ teaspoon celery salt
1½ cups (6 ounces) shredded mozzarella cheese, divided

Heat oil in 2-quart saucepan; add onion and cook and stir until tender. Stir in beans, ½ cup of Newman's Own® Bandito Salsa, chicken, chicken broth, oregano and celery salt. Cover; simmer over medium heat 10 minutes, stirring occasionally. Just before serving, stir in 1 cup of mozzarella cheese. Divide chili evenly among serving bowls. Top each with a portion of remaining mozzarella and salsa. *Makes 4 servings*

Chunky Vegetable Chili

ROBUST STEWS & CHILIES

324 SPICY TOMATO CHILI WITH RED BEANS

1 tablespoon olive oil
1 cup chopped onion
1 cup chopped green bell pepper
1 cup sliced celery
1 clove garlic, minced
1 can (15 ounces) diced tomatoes, undrained
1 can (15 ounces) red beans, drained and rinsed
1 can (10 ounces) diced tomatoes with green chilies
1 can (8 ounces) low-sodium tomato sauce
8 (6-inch) corn tortillas

1. Preheat oven to 400°F.

2. Heat oil in large saucepan over medium heat until hot. Add onion, bell pepper, celery and garlic. Cook and stir 5 minutes or until onion is translucent.

3. Add remaining ingredients except tortillas. Bring to a boil; reduce heat to low. Simmer, uncovered, 15 minutes.

4. Cut each tortilla into 8 wedges. Place on baking sheet; bake 8 minutes or until crisp. Crush about half of tortilla wedges; place in bottom of soup bowls. Spoon chili over tortillas. Serve with remaining tortilla wedges.
Makes 4 servings

325 BULGUR CHILI

1 cup chopped onion
½ cup chopped celery
4 teaspoons sugar
2 tablespoons chili powder
1 tablespoon dried oregano
1 teaspoon ground cumin
1 teaspoon black pepper
2 teaspoons vegetable oil
⅔ cup uncooked bulgur
1½ cups water
1 can (28 ounces) tomatoes, crushed or stewed
1 can (14 ounces) black beans, rinsed and drained *or* 2 cups cooked beans
1 can (14 ounces) cannellini or navy beans, rinsed and drained *or* 2 cups cooked beans

In 3- to 4-quart saucepan, sauté onion, celery, sugar and spices in oil 5 minutes. Stir in bulgur and water. Simmer, covered, over low heat 10 minutes, stirring occasionally. Add tomatoes and beans. Simmer, covered, over low heat 15 to 20 minutes, stirring occasionally. Serve in warmed bowls.
Makes 4 servings

*Favorite recipe from **The Sugar Association, Inc.***

Spicy Tomato Chili with Red Beans

ROBUST STEWS & CHILIES

326 TURKEY CHILI WITH BLACK BEANS

1 pound ground turkey breast
1 can (about 14½ ounces) fat-free reduced-sodium chicken broth
1 large onion, finely chopped
1 green bell pepper, seeded and diced
2 teaspoons chili powder
½ teaspoon ground allspice
¼ teaspoon ground cinnamon
¼ teaspoon paprika
1 can (15 ounces) black beans, rinsed and drained
1 can (14 ounces) crushed tomatoes in tomato purée, undrained
2 teaspoons apple cider vinegar

1. Heat large nonstick skillet over high heat. Add turkey, chicken broth, onion and bell pepper. Cook and stir, breaking up turkey. Cook until turkey is no longer pink.

2. Add chili powder, allspice, cinnamon and paprika. Reduce heat to medium-low; simmer 10 minutes. Add black beans, tomatoes and vinegar; bring to a boil.

3. Reduce heat to low; simmer 20 to 25 minutes or until thickened to desired consistency. Garnish as desired.

Makes 4 servings

327 SPICY CHILI WITH CORNMEAL DUMPLINGS

1½ pounds ground beef
1¼ cups finely chopped green bell peppers
½ cup chopped onion
1 clove garlic, minced
½ cup A.1.® Original or A.1.® Bold & Spicy Steak Sauce
3 large tomatoes, chopped (about 3½ cups)
1 (1¼-ounce) package taco seasoning mix
¼ teaspoon ground cumin
½ teaspoon crushed red pepper flakes
1 (6.5-ounce) package corn muffin mix
⅓ cup milk
1 egg
½ cup shredded Cheddar cheese (2 ounces)
¼ cup sliced green onions

In large skillet, over medium-high heat, cook beef, green peppers, onion and garlic until beef is browned, stirring occasionally to break up beef. Stir in steak sauce, tomatoes, seasoning mix, cumin and pepper flakes. Heat to a boil; reduce heat. Cover; simmer 10 to 15 minutes to blend flavors.

Meanwhile, mix corn muffin mix according to package directions, using milk and egg. Drop batter into 6 mounds on chili mixture. Cover; simmer 10 to 12 minutes. (Do not lift cover.) Sprinkle with cheese and green onions. Serve immediately.

Makes 6 servings

Turkey Chili with Black Beans

328 SOUTHWEST BEAN CHILI

1 cup uncooked dried garbanzo beans
¾ cup uncooked dried red kidney beans
¾ cup uncooked dried black beans
5½ cups canned reduced-sodium, fat-free chicken broth
4 cloves garlic, minced
3 ears fresh corn, husks and silk removed
2 medium green bell peppers, seeded and chopped
1 can (16 ounces) tomato sauce
1 can (14½ ounces) Mexican-style stewed tomatoes, undrained
3 tablespoons chili powder
1 tablespoon cocoa powder
1 teaspoon ground cumin
½ teaspoon salt
  Hot cooked rice
  Shredded cheese, ripe olive, avocado and green onion slices (optional)

1. Rinse beans thoroughly in colander under cold running water, picking out debris and any blemished beans. Soak beans overnight according to package directions.

2. Drain beans. Combine beans, chicken broth and garlic in heavy, large saucepan. Bring to a boil over high heat. Reduce heat to low; simmer, covered, 1 hour.

3. Cut down sides of cob with paring knife, releasing kernels without cutting into cob.

4. Press down cob to release any remaining corn and liquid with dull edge of utility knife; discard cob. Repeat with remaining ears.

5. Add corn, bell peppers, tomato sauce, tomatoes and juice, chili powder, cocoa powder, cumin and salt to bean mixture. Cover partially; simmer 45 minutes or until beans are tender and mixture is thick.

6. Spoon rice into bowls; top with chili. Serve with cheese, olives, avocado and onions, if desired.

Makes 8 to 10 servings

Southwest Bean Chili

ROBUST STEWS & CHILIES

329 KAHLÚA® TURKEY CHILI VERDE

3½ pounds turkey thighs
¼ cup olive oil
2 medium onions, chopped
12 large cloves garlic, peeled and chopped
1 large green bell pepper, chopped
2 tablespoons all-purpose flour
1 (28-ounce) can Italian tomatoes, drained and chopped
1 (14½-ounce) can chicken broth
1 (13-ounce) can tomatillos,* drained and mashed
1½ cups chopped cilantro
4 (7-ounce) cans diced mild green chilies
½ cup KAHLÚA® Liqueur
2 jalapeño chilies, diced
5 teaspoons dried oregano leaves
2 teaspoons ground coriander seeds
2 teaspoons ground cumin
Salt, freshly ground black pepper and fresh lime juice

Tomatillos (Mexican green tomatoes) can be found in the ethnic section of large supermarkets.

In large skillet, brown turkey thighs in olive oil over high heat, turning occasionally, about 15 minutes. Transfer to large roasting pan. Set aside. Discard all but ¼ cup drippings in skillet. Add onions, garlic and bell pepper; cook over medium heat until soft, about 10 minutes, stirring frequently. Add flour; cook and stir 3 to 4 minutes. Stir in tomatoes, chicken broth, tomatillos, cilantro, green chilies, Kahlúa®, jalapeño chilies, oregano, coriander and cumin. Bring to boil. Pour over turkey thighs in roasting pan. Cover tightly with heavy foil; bake at 350°F, 1 hour.

Remove from oven; loosen foil. Set aside to cool. When cool enough to handle, remove skin and bones from turkey. Cut meat into ½-inch cubes and place in large saucepan with sauce. Cook over medium heat until heated through. Season to taste with salt, pepper and lime juice. Serve hot; garnish as desired.   *Makes about 16 servings*

ROBUST STEWS & CHILIES

330 CHILI SOUP JARLSBERG

2 tablespoons vegetable oil
1 pound beef round steak, cubed
2 cans (14½ ounces each) beef broth
1 can (15 ounces) dark red kidney beans, rinsed and drained
1 can (14½ ounces) tomatoes, chopped, undrained
1 medium green bell pepper, chopped
1 medium red bell pepper, chopped
1 large onion, chopped
1 large clove garlic, minced
3¼ teaspoons chili powder, divided
¼ teaspoon ground cumin
1½ cups (6 ounces) shredded JARLSBERG or JARLSBERG Lite™ Cheese, divided
¼ cup butter or margarine, softened
1 small clove garlic, minced
12 KAVLI® Norwegian Thick-Style Crispbreads

Heat oil in large, deep saucepan over medium-high heat. Add beef and cook until browned. Add beef broth; bring to a boil over high heat. Reduce heat to low. Cover and simmer 1 hour. Add beans, tomatoes, peppers, onion, large garlic clove, 3 teaspoons chili powder and cumin. Simmer, covered, 30 minutes. Gradually blend in ½ cup cheese. Heat just until cheese is melted.

Blend butter, small garlic clove and remaining ¼ teaspoon chili powder in small bowl. Spread on crispbreads; arrange on cookie sheet. Bake in preheated 375°F oven about 3 to 5 minutes or until butter is melted. Sprinkle with ½ cup cheese. Bake just until cheese is melted.

Ladle soup into bowls. Garnish with remaining ½ cup cheese. Serve with crispbreads. *Makes 6 servings*

331 TURKEY CHILI

1 tablespoon vegetable oil
1 medium onion, chopped
1 pound ground turkey*
1 can (15 ounces) pinto beans, drained
1 can (14½ ounces) whole tomatoes, chopped, undrained
1 green bell pepper, chopped
½ cup water
1 package (1.48 ounces) LAWRY'S® Spices & Seasonings for Chili
½ teaspoon LAWRY'S® Garlic Powder with Parsley

3 cups chopped cooked turkey may be substituted for ground turkey. Omit browning step for turkey. Add cooked turkey with remaining ingredients.

In large saucepan, heat oil. Cook onion over high heat until tender. Add turkey and cook until no longer pink. Drain fat. Add remaining ingredients. Bring to a boil over medium-high heat; reduce heat to low and cook, uncovered, 10 minutes, stirring occasionally. *Makes 5½ cups*

SERVING SUGGESTION: Serve with additional chopped bell pepper and onion for garnish.

ROBUST STEWS & CHILIES

332 VEGETARIAN CHILI

1 tablespoon vegetable oil
2 cloves garlic, finely chopped
1½ cups thinly sliced mushrooms
⅔ cup chopped red onion
⅔ cup chopped red bell pepper
2 teaspoons chili powder
¼ teaspoon ground cumin
⅛ teaspoon ground red pepper
⅛ teaspoon dried oregano leaves
1 can (28 ounces) peeled whole tomatoes
⅔ cup frozen baby lima beans
½ cup canned Great Northern beans, rinsed and drained
3 tablespoons nonfat sour cream
3 tablespoons shredded reduced-fat Cheddar cheese

1. Heat oil in large nonstick saucepan over medium-high heat until hot. Add garlic. Cook and stir 3 minutes. Add mushrooms, onion and bell pepper. Cook 5 minutes, stirring occasionally. Add chili powder, cumin, ground red pepper and oregano. Cook and stir 1 minute. Add tomatoes and beans. Reduce heat to medium-low. Simmer 15 minutes, stirring occasionally.

2. Top servings evenly with sour cream and cheese.   *Makes 4 servings*

333 WHITE CHILI

1 pound ground turkey
2 cloves garlic, finely chopped
2 cans (15 ounces each) white kidney beans, undrained
2 cans (4 ounces each) chopped green chilies, undrained
1⅓ cups (2.8-ounce can) FRENCH'S® French Fried Onions, divided
1 cup frozen whole kernel corn
¼ cup chopped fresh cilantro
3 tablespoons lime juice
1 tablespoon ground cumin
¼ teaspoon ground white pepper
1 large tomato, chopped
¼ cup low-fat sour cream

Heat large nonstick skillet or Dutch oven over medium heat. Add turkey and garlic; cook and stir about 5 minutes or until turkey is no longer pink.

Stir in beans, green chilies, ⅔ cup French Fried Onions, corn, cilantro, lime juice, cumin and white pepper. Bring to a boil over high heat. Reduce heat to low; simmer 5 minutes, stirring often.

Stir in tomato and sour cream; cook until hot and bubbly, stirring often. Sprinkle with remaining ⅔ cup onions.

Makes 4 to 6 servings

Prep Time: 15 minutes
Cook Time: 20 minutes

Vegetarian Chili

ROBUST STEWS & CHILIES

334 SCRUMPTIOUS SPAM™ SPRING CHILI

Nonstick cooking spray
4 cloves garlic, minced
2 green bell peppers, cut into strips
1 cup sliced green onions
3 (4.25-ounce) jars CHI-CHI'S® Diced
   Green Chilies
2 jalapeño peppers, seeded and minced
2 teaspoons dried oregano leaves
2 teaspoons ground cumin
2 (15-ounce) cans cannellini beans or
   kidney beans
2 (10¾-ounce) cans condensed chicken
   broth, undiluted
1 (12-ounce) can SPAM® Luncheon Meat,
   cubed

In large saucepan coated with cooking spray, sauté garlic over medium heat 1 minute. Add bell peppers, green onions, chilies, jalapeños, oregano and cumin; sauté 5 minutes. Stir in beans and broth. Bring to a boil. Cover. Reduce heat and simmer 10 minutes. Stir in Spam®. Simmer 2 minutes.

Makes 4 to 6 servings

335 TURKEY WILD RICE CHILI

1 tablespoon oil
1 medium onion, chopped
1 garlic clove, minced
1¼ pounds turkey breast slices, cut into
   ½-inch pieces
2 cups cooked wild rice
1 can (15 ounces) Great Northern beans,
   drained
1 can (11 ounces) white corn
2 cans (4 ounces each) diced green chilies
1 can (14½ ounces) low sodium chicken
   broth
1 teaspoon ground cumin
   Hot pepper sauce (optional)
4 ounces low-fat Monterey Jack Cheese,
   shredded
   Parsley (optional)

Heat oil in large skillet over medium heat; add onion and garlic. Cook and stir until onion is tender. Add turkey, wild rice, beans, corn, chilies, broth and cumin. Cover and simmer over low heat 30 minutes or until turkey is tender. Stir in hot pepper sauce to taste. Serve with shredded cheese. Garnish with parsley, if desired.

Makes 8 servings

*Favorite recipe from **Minnesota Cultivated Wild Rice Council***

Scrumptious Spam™ Spring Chili

336 TEXAS REDHOT CHILI

4 tablespoons vegetable oil, divided
2 large onions, chopped
3 large cloves garlic, minced
2 pounds boneless sirloin or round steak, cut into ½-inch cubes
1 pound ground beef
2 cans (16 ounces each) tomatoes in purée
1 can (15 to 19 ounces) red kidney beans, undrained
⅓ cup FRANK'S® Original REDHOT® Cayenne Pepper Sauce
¼ cup chili powder
2 tablespoons ground cumin
1 tablespoon dried oregano leaves
½ teaspoon ground black pepper

1. Heat 1 tablespoon oil in 5-quart saucepan or Dutch oven. Add onions and garlic; cook 5 minutes or until tender. Transfer to small bowl; set aside.

2. Heat remaining 3 tablespoons oil in saucepan. Add sirloin and ground beef in batches; cook about 15 minutes or until well browned. Drain off fat.

3. Stir in remaining ingredients. Bring to a boil over medium-high heat. Return onions and garlic to saucepan. Simmer, partially covered, 1 hour or until meat is tender. Garnish with shredded Cheddar cheese and chopped green onion, if desired.

Makes 10 servings

Prep Time: 15 minutes
Cook Time: 1 hour 20 minutes

337 JALAPEÑO TWO–BEAN CHILI

1 tablespoon vegetable oil
1 medium onion, chopped
1 green bell pepper, seeded and chopped
2 cloves garlic, minced
1 can (16 ounces) pinto beans, rinsed and drained
1 can (16 ounces) black beans, rinsed and drained
1 can (14½ ounces) stewed tomatoes or Mexican-style stewed tomatoes, undrained
1 can (10½ ounces) kosher condensed beef or chicken broth
½ cup water
2 teaspoons chili powder
2 teaspoons ground cumin
1 to 2 teaspoons chopped bottled or fresh jalapeño peppers
1 package (12 ounces) HEBREW NATIONAL® Beef Hot Sausage
Chopped cilantro (optional)
Diced avocado (optional)

Heat oil in large saucepan over medium heat. Add onion, bell pepper and garlic; cook 8 minutes, stirring occasionally. Add pinto and black beans, tomatoes with liquid, broth, water, chili powder, cumin and jalapeño peppers; bring to a boil. Cut sausage into ½-inch slices. Cut slices into quarters. Stir in sausage; reduce heat to medium-low. Simmer, uncovered, 15 minutes, stirring occasionally. Ladle into shallow bowls; top with cilantro and avocado, if desired. *Makes 6 servings*

Texas Redhot Chili

ROBUST STEWS & CHILIES

338 CHUNKY VEGETARIAN CHILI

1 tablespoon vegetable oil
1 medium green bell pepper, chopped
1 medium onion, chopped
3 cloves garlic, minced
2 cans (14½ ounces each) Mexican-style tomatoes, undrained
1 can (15 ounces) kidney beans, rinsed, drained
1 can (15 ounces) pinto beans, rinsed, drained
1 can (11 ounces) whole-kernel corn, drained
2½ cups water
1 cup uncooked rice
2 tablespoons chili powder
1½ teaspoons ground cumin
   Sour cream (optional)

Heat oil in 3-quart saucepan or Dutch oven over medium-high heat. Add bell pepper, onion and garlic; cook and stir 5 minutes or until tender. Add tomatoes, beans, corn, water, rice, chili powder and cumin; stir well. Bring to a boil. Reduce heat; cover. Simmer 30 minutes, stirring occasionally. To serve, top with sour cream, if desired.

Makes 6 servings

Favorite recipe from **USA Rice Federation**

339 TURKEY CHILI

1 tablespoon vegetable oil
1 pound ground turkey
1 large onion, chopped
1 large green bell pepper, chopped
1 can (14 ounces) chunky tomatoes, salsa style
1 can (8 ounces) no-salt-added tomato sauce
¾ cup HOLLAND HOUSE® Red Cooking Wine
1 package (1¼ ounces) chili seasoning mix
1 can (15 ounces) kidney beans, drained (optional)

In large saucepan, heat oil. Add turkey, onion and bell pepper. Cook until onion is tender. Stir in tomatoes, tomato sauce, red cooking wine and chili seasoning mix. Bring to a boil and simmer, partially covered, 10 minutes. Stir in beans and heat through.

Serve, if desired, with rice, shredded cheese and chopped onion.

Makes about 4 servings

NOTE: Serve this healthy chili with a crisp green salad and cornbread for a delicious meal.

Chunky Vegetarian Chili

ROBUST STEWS & CHILIES

340 THREE–BEAN CARIBBEAN CHILI

1 tablespoon olive oil
1 large onion, chopped
2 cloves garlic, minced
1 jalapeño chili, minced*
2 large red or green bell peppers, seeded and diced
1 tablespoon plus 2 teaspoons sweet paprika
1 tablespoon plus 2 teaspoons chili powder
2 teaspoons ground cumin
¼ teaspoon ground cloves
2 teaspoons sugar
½ teaspoon salt
1 can (6 ounces) tomato paste
3 cups water
1 can (15 ounces) red kidney beans, drained
1 can (15 ounces) cannellini beans, drained
1 can (15 ounces) black beans, drained
1 tablespoon balsamic vinegar
Mango Salsa (recipe follows)
Hot cooked brown rice
Fresh cilantro for garnish

Chilies can sting and irritate the skin; wear rubber gloves when handling and do not touch your eyes. Wash your hands after handling chilies.

1. Heat oil in large saucepan over medium heat until hot. Add onion and garlic; cook and stir 4 minutes. Add jalapeño and bell peppers; cook and stir 5 minutes or until tender.

2. Add paprika, chili powder, cumin, cloves, sugar and salt; cook and stir 1 minute.

3. Stir in tomato paste and water until blended. Bring to a boil over high heat. Reduce heat to low. Cover and simmer 15 minutes. Stir in beans and vinegar; partially cover and simmer 15 minutes or until hot.

4. Meanwhile, prepare Mango Salsa.

5. Serve chili over rice. Top with Mango Salsa. Garnish, if desired.

Makes 6 (1-cup) servings

MANGO SALSA

1 large mango, peeled and cut into ¾-inch cubes
1 small, firm, ripe banana, peeled and cubed
3 tablespoons minced fresh cilantro
1 tablespoon thawed frozen orange juice concentrate
1 teaspoon balsamic vinegar

Combine mango, banana and cilantro in medium bowl. Stir together juice concentrate and vinegar. Pour over fruit; toss.

Makes 1¼ cups

Three-Bean Caribbean Chili

ROBUST STEWS & CHILIES

341 VEGETABLE–BEEF CHILI

1 (1-pound) beef top round or chuck steak, cut into ¼-inch cubes
1 tablespoon vegetable oil
1 cup coarsely chopped green bell pepper
½ cup coarsely chopped onion
1 clove garlic, minced
3 to 4 tablespoons chili powder
¾ cup A.1.® Original or A.1.® Bold & Spicy Steak Sauce
2 (16-ounce) cans tomatoes, undrained, coarsely chopped
1 (15-ounce) can kidney beans, drained
1 (17-ounce) can corn, drained

In 6-quart pot, over medium-high heat, brown steak in oil; drain if necessary. Reduce heat to medium; add pepper, onion and garlic. Cook and stir until vegetables are tender, about 3 minutes. Mix in chili powder; cook and stir 1 minute. Add steak sauce and tomatoes with liquid; heat to a boil. Reduce heat. Cover; simmer 45 minutes, stirring occasionally. Add beans and corn; simmer 15 minutes more or until steak is tender. Serve immediately. Garnish as desired.

Makes 6 servings

342 CHUNKY CHILI CON CARNE

2 pounds ground beef
1 cup chopped onions
1 tablespoon minced fresh garlic
1 (14½-ounce) can HUNT'S® Whole Peeled Tomatoes
1 (14½-ounce) can beef broth
1 (6-ounce) can HUNT'S® Tomato Paste
3 tablespoons GEBHARDT® Chili Powder
1 teaspoon ground cumin
½ teaspoon dried oregano
½ teaspoon cayenne pepper
1 teaspoon salt
1 (30-ounce) can HUNT'S® Chili Beans

In large pot, brown meat with onion and garlic over medium heat; drain. Stir in tomatoes, broth, tomato paste, chili powder, cumin, oregano, cayenne pepper and salt; reduce heat to low and simmer 20 minutes. Stir in beans and simmer additional 10 minutes.

Makes 6 to 8 servings

Vegetable-Beef Chili

343 CHILI CON CARNE WINCHESTER

  2 tablespoons vegetable oil
⅓ cup chopped onion
⅓ cup chopped green bell pepper
  1 pound ground beef
  1 clove garlic, minced
  2 (15-ounce) cans kidney beans, drained
  1 (1-pound) can stewed tomatoes
  1 (15-ounce) can VEG-ALL® Mixed
      Vegetables, with liquid

1. Heat oil in 3-quart stockpot over medium-high heat. Add onion and pepper; cook and stir until soft.

2. Add ground beef, garlic, kidney beans and stewed tomatoes. Bring to a boil; cover. Reduce heat and simmer 30 minutes.

3. Stir in Veg-All® vegetables and cook 10 minutes longer. Serve hot.

Makes 6 servings

344 TEXAS FAJITA CHILI

1¼ cups chopped onions
  1 cup chopped green bell pepper
  1 tablespoon vegetable oil
  2 cans (15¼ ounces each) kidney beans,
      drained
  1 pound shredded cooked pork or beef
  1 can (14½ ounces) whole peeled
      tomatoes, undrained and cut up
  1 cup LAWRY'S® Fajitas Skillet Sauce
  1 can (7 ounces) whole kernel corn,
      drained
  ½ cup tomato juice or beer
1½ teaspoons chili powder

In large skillet, sauté onions and bell pepper in oil 10 minutes or until tender. Stir in kidney beans, shredded meat, tomatoes, Fajitas Skillet Sauce, corn, tomato juice and chili powder. Bring mixture to a boil; reduce heat, cover and simmer 20 minutes.

Makes 6 servings

PRESENTATION: Serve in individual bowls topped with shredded Monterey Jack cheese or sour cream. If desired, serve with dash of hot pepper sauce.

Chili con Carne Winchester

ROBUST STEWS & CHILIES

345 FIVE–WAY CINCINNATI CHILI

1 pound uncooked spaghetti, broken in half
1 pound ground chuck
2 cans (10 ounces each) tomatoes with green chilies, undrained
1 can (10½ ounces) condensed French onion soup
1 can (15 ounces) red kidney beans, drained
1¼ cups water
1 tablespoon chili powder
1 teaspoon sugar
½ teaspoon salt
¼ teaspoon ground cinnamon
½ cup (2 ounces) shredded Cheddar cheese
½ cup chopped onion

1. Cook pasta according to package directions; drain.

2. While pasta is cooking, cook and stir beef in large saucepan over medium-high heat until browned; drain. Return meat to saucepan with tomatoes, soup, beans, 1¼ cups water, chili powder, sugar, salt and cinnamon; bring to a boil. Reduce heat to low. Simmer, uncovered, 10 minutes, stirring occasionally. Serve chili over spaghetti; sprinkle with cheese and onion.

Makes 6 servings

COOK'S NOTES: Serve this traditional chili your way or one of the ways Cincinnatians do—two-way over spaghetti, three-way with cheese, four-way with cheese and chopped onion or five-way with beans added to the chili.

Prep and cook time: 20 minutes

346 BLACK AND WHITE CHILI

1 pound chicken tenders, cut into ¾-inch pieces
1 cup coarsely chopped onion
1 can (15½ ounces) Great Northern beans, drained
1 can (15 ounces) black beans, drained
1 can (14½ ounces) Mexican-style stewed tomatoes, undrained
2 tablespoons Texas-style chili powder seasoning mix

1. Spray large saucepan with nonstick cooking spray; heat over medium heat until hot. Add chicken and onion; cook and stir over medium to medium-high heat 5 to 8 minutes or until chicken is browned.

2. Stir remaining ingredients into saucepan; bring to a boil. Reduce heat to low; simmer, uncovered, 10 minutes.

Makes 6 (1-cup) servings

SERVING SUGGESTION: For a change of pace, this delicious chili is excellent served over cooked rice or pasta.

Prep and cook time: 30 minutes

Five-Way Cincinnati Chili

ROBUST STEWS & CHILIES

347 CALIFORNIA TURKEY CHILI

1¼ cups chopped onion
1 cup chopped green bell pepper
2 cloves garlic, minced
3 tablespoons vegetable oil
1 can (28 ounces) kidney beans, drained
1 can (28 ounces) stewed tomatoes, undrained
1 cup red wine or water
3 cups cubed cooked California-grown turkey
1 tablespoon chili powder
1 tablespoon chopped cilantro *or*
    1 teaspoon dried coriander
1 teaspoon crushed red pepper
½ teaspoon salt
    Shredded Cheddar cheese (optional)
    Additional chopped onion (optional)
    Chopped cilantro (optional)

Cook and stir onion, green pepper, garlic and oil in large saucepan over high heat until tender. Add beans, tomatoes with liquid, wine, turkey, chili powder, cilantro, red pepper and salt. Cover; simmer 25 minutes or until heated through. Top with cheese, onion or cilantro, if desired.

Makes 6 servings

Favorite recipe from **California Poultry Industry Federation**

348 30–MINUTE CHILI OLÉ

1 cup chopped onion
2 cloves garlic, minced
1 tablespoon vegetable oil
2 pounds ground beef
1 (15-ounce) can tomato sauce
1 (14½-ounce) can stewed tomatoes
¾ cup A.1.® Steak Sauce
1 tablespoon chili powder
1 teaspoon ground cumin
1 (16-ounce) can black beans, rinsed and drained
1 (11-ounce) can corn, drained
    Shredded cheese, sour cream and chopped tomato, for garnish

In 6-quart heavy pot, over medium-high heat, sauté onion and garlic in oil until tender. Add beef; cook and stir until brown. Drain; stir in tomato sauce, stewed tomatoes, steak sauce, chili powder and cumin. Heat to a boil; reduce heat to low. Cover; simmer for 10 minutes, stirring occasionally. Stir in beans and corn; simmer, uncovered, for 10 minutes. Serve hot, garnished with cheese, sour cream and tomatoes.

Makes 8 servings

California Turkey Chili

ROBUST STEWS & CHILIES

349 EASY CHILI CON CARNE

½ medium onion, chopped
1 stalk celery, sliced
1 teaspoon chili powder
1 can (15¼ ounces) kidney beans, drained
1 can (14½ ounces) DEL MONTE® Chili Style Chunky Tomatoes
1 cup cooked cubed beef

MICROWAVE DIRECTIONS: In 2-quart microwavable dish, combine first 3 ingredients. Add 1 tablespoon water. Cover; microwave on HIGH 3 to 4 minutes. Add remaining ingredients. Cover; microwave on HIGH 6 to 8 minutes or until heated, stirring halfway through cooking time. For a spicier chili, serve with hot pepper sauce.

Makes 4 servings

Prep Time: 8 minutes
Microwave Cook Time: 12 minutes

350 CAJUN CHILI

6 ounces spicy sausage links, sliced
4 boneless chicken thighs, skinned and cut into cubes
1 medium onion, chopped
⅛ teaspoon cayenne pepper
1 can (15 ounces) black-eyed peas or kidney beans, drained
1 can (14½ ounces) DEL MONTE® *FreshCut*™ Brand Diced Tomatoes with Garlic & Onion
1 medium green bell pepper, chopped

1. Lightly brown sausage in large skillet over medium-high heat. Add chicken, onion and cayenne pepper; cook until browned. Drain.

2. Stir in remaining ingredients. Cook 5 minutes, stirring occasionally.

Makes 4 servings

Prep & Cook Time: 20 minutes

Cajun Chili

ROBUST STEWS & CHILIES

351 COUNTRY CHICKEN CHOWDER

1 pound chicken tenders
2 tablespoons margarine or butter
1 small onion, chopped
1 rib celery, sliced
1 small carrot, sliced
1 can (10¾ ounces) cream of potato soup
1 cup milk
1 cup frozen corn
½ teaspoon dried dill weed

1. Cut chicken tenders into ½-inch pieces.

2. Melt margarine in large saucepan or Dutch oven over medium-high heat. Add chicken; cook and stir 5 minutes.

3. Add onion, celery and carrot; cook and stir 3 minutes. Stir in soup, milk, corn and dill; reduce heat to low. Cook about 8 minutes or until corn is tender and chowder is heated through. Add salt and pepper to taste.   *Makes 4 servings*

For a special touch, garnish soup with croutons and fresh dill.

SERVING SUGGESTION: For a hearty winter meal, serve the chowder in hollowed-out toasted French rolls or small round sourdough loaves.

Prep and cook time: 27 minutes

352 CORN AND ONION CHOWDER

¼ pound uncooked bacon, chopped
2 medium potatoes (¾ pound), peeled and cut into ¼-inch cubes
1⅓ cups (2.8-ounce can) FRENCH'S® French Fried Onions, divided
½ cup chopped celery
1 tablespoon fresh thyme *or* ¾ teaspoon dried thyme leaves
1 bay leaf
1½ cups water
2 cans (15 ounces each) cream-style corn, undrained
1½ cups milk
½ teaspoon salt
¼ teaspoon ground white or black pepper

Cook and stir bacon in large saucepan over medium-high heat until crisp and browned. Remove with slotted spoon to paper towel. Pour off all but 1 tablespoon drippings.

Add potatoes, ⅔ cup French Fried Onions, celery, thyme and bay leaf to saucepan. Stir in water. Bring to a boil over medium-high heat. Reduce heat to low. Cover; simmer 10 to 12 minutes or until potatoes are fork-tender, stirring occasionally.

Stir in corn, milk, salt, pepper and reserved bacon. Cook until heated through. Do not boil. Discard bay leaf. Ladle into individual soup bowls. Sprinkle with remaining ⅔ cup onions.   *Makes 6 to 8 servings*

Prep Time: 20 minutes
Cook Time: 20 minutes

Country Chicken Chowder

353 TURKEY CHOWDER IN EDIBLE BREAD BOWLS

Edible Bread Bowls (recipe follows)
2 tablespoons butter or margarine
½ cup chopped carrot
½ cup chopped celery
½ cup chopped onion
⅓ cup uncooked long-grain white rice
⅓ cup barley
2 cans (14.5 ounces each) chicken broth
½ teaspoon dried thyme leaves
2 cups chopped cooked turkey
1 package (10 ounces) frozen corn, thawed
½ cup half-and-half
Salt and pepper

1. Prepare Edible Bread Bowls. While bread bowls are baking, melt butter in large saucepan. Add carrot, celery and onion; cook and stir until tender. Stir in rice and barley; cook 2 minutes. Add broth and thyme; bring to a boil. Reduce heat to low; simmer 20 to 25 minutes or until rice and barley are tender. Add turkey and corn; cook 5 minutes or until heated through. Add half-and-half; heat, but do not boil. Season with salt and pepper to taste.

2. Place bread bowls on rimmed plates or in shallow bowls. Ladle chowder into bread bowls. Garnish, if desired.

Makes 5 servings

EDIBLE BREAD BOWLS

1 package (16 ounces) hot roll mix, plus ingredients to prepare mix
3 tablespoons grated Parmesan cheese
2 egg yolks
1 tablespoon cold water

1. Prepare hot roll mix according to package directions. Stir in cheese. Place dough on lightly floured surface; knead until smooth, about 5 minutes. Place in large greased bowl. Cover loosely; let stand 15 minutes.

2. Divide dough into 5 equal pieces. From each piece, remove and set aside about ¼ of the dough. Place 1 of the larger dough pieces on lightly floured surface. With rolling pin, roll dough into 8-inch round; repeat with the remaining 4 larger pieces of dough. Divide each of the 5 remaining smaller dough pieces in half; roll each half into 20-inch rope.

3. Grease 2 baking sheets and outsides of custard cups. Place inverted cups on prepared baking sheets. Press dough rounds onto outsides of custard cups; trim edges of dough if necessary. Braid 2 dough ropes together. Attach to base of dough-covered bowl; pinch dough together to seal. Repeat with remaining ropes and bowls. Cover loosely; let rise in warm place until doubled in size, about 30 minutes.

4. Preheat oven to 375°F. Beat together egg yolks and water with fork; brush onto dough. Bake 20 to 25 minutes or until golden brown. Remove to wire rack. Remove bread bowls from cups. Serve warm or at room temperature. *Makes 5 bread bowls*

Turkey Chowder in Edible Bread Bowls

ROBUST STEWS & CHILIES

354 ALBACORE CORN CHOWDER

2 tablespoons butter or margarine
½ cup sliced celery
½ cup chopped onion
¾ cup chopped carrot
2 to 3 tablespoons flour
1 teaspoon dried thyme or Italian
    seasoning
1 can (17 ounces) cream-style corn
2 cups milk
1 can (12 ounces) STARKIST® Solid White
    Tuna, drained and flaked
1 cup water
1 teaspoon chicken flavor instant bouillon

In medium saucepan, melt butter over
medium heat; sauté celery, onion and carrot
about 3 minutes. Add flour and thyme; blend
well. Cook 3 more minutes. Add corn, milk,
tuna, water and bouillon, stirring to blend.
Cover and simmer (do not boil) 5 minutes to
heat through, stirring occasionally.

Makes 4 servings

Prep Time: 20 minutes

355 VEGETABLE–BEAN CHOWDER

½ cup chopped onion
½ cup chopped celery
2 cups water
½ teaspoon salt
2 cups cubed peeled potatoes
1 cup carrot slices
1 can (15 ounces) cream-style corn
1 can (15 ounces) cannellini beans, rinsed
    and drained
¼ teaspoon dried tarragon leaves
¼ teaspoon ground black pepper
2 cups 1% low-fat milk
2 tablespoons cornstarch

1. Spray 4-quart Dutch oven or large
saucepan with nonstick cooking spray; heat
over medium heat until hot. Add onion and
celery. Cook and stir 3 minutes or until crisp-
tender.

2. Add water and salt. Bring to a boil over
high heat. Add potatoes and carrot. Reduce
heat to medium-low. Simmer, covered, 10
minutes or until potatoes and carrot are
tender. Stir in corn, beans, tarragon and
pepper. Simmer, covered, 10 minutes or until
heated through.

3. Stir milk into cornstarch in medium bowl
until smooth. Stir into vegetable mixture.
Simmer, uncovered, until thickened. Garnish
as desired.   *Makes 5 (1½-cup) servings*

Albacore Corn Chowder

356 VEGETABLE AND SHRIMP CHOWDER

1½ cups diced Spanish onions
½ cup sliced carrots
½ cup diced celery
2 tablespoons margarine or butter
2 cups peeled and diced baking potatoes
1 (10-ounce) package frozen corn
5 cups COLLEGE INN® Chicken Broth or Lower Sodium Chicken Broth
½ pound small shrimp, peeled and deveined
⅓ cup GREY POUPON® Dijon Mustard
¼ cup chopped parsley

In large saucepan, over medium heat, cook onions, carrots and celery in margarine or butter for 3 to 4 minutes or until tender. Add potatoes, corn and chicken broth; heat to a boil. Reduce heat; simmer for 20 to 25 minutes or until potatoes are tender. Add shrimp, mustard and parsley; cook for 5 minutes more or until shrimp are cooked. Garnish as desired. Serve warm.

Makes 8 servings

357 CREAMY LEEK CHOWDER

1 package (1.8 ounces) leek soup mix
2¼ cups water
1½ cups milk
1 can (14.5 ounces) whole new potatoes, drained and cut into small cubes
1⅓ cups (2.8-ounce can) FRENCH'S® French Fried Onions, divided
2 teaspoons chopped fresh thyme *or* ½ teaspoon dried thyme leaves
¼ teaspoon ground black pepper
Sour cream
Chopped parsley

Combine soup mix, water and milk in large saucepan; whisk until well blended. Stir in potatoes, 1 cup French Fried Onions, thyme and pepper. Bring to a boil over medium-high heat. Reduce heat to low. Simmer, uncovered, 10 minutes, stirring occasionally.

Ladle into individual bowls. Top with sour cream, parsley and remaining ⅓ cup onions.

Makes 4 servings

TIP: To crisp and brown French Fried Onions, place on paper towels and microwave on HIGH 1 minute.

Prep Time: 10 minutes
Cook Time: 10 minutes

Vegetable and Shrimp Chowder

ROBUST STEWS & CHILIES

358 HEARTY PASTA AND CHICK–PEA CHOWDER

6 ounces uncooked rotini pasta
2 tablespoons olive oil
¾ cup chopped onion
½ cup chopped celery
½ cup thinly sliced carrot
2 cloves garlic, minced
¼ cup all-purpose flour
1½ teaspoons Italian seasoning
⅛ teaspoon crushed red pepper
⅛ teaspoon black pepper
2 cans (13¾ ounces each) chicken broth
1 can (19 ounces) chick-peas, rinsed and drained
1 can (14½ ounces) Italian-style stewed tomatoes, undrained
6 slices bacon

1. Cook rotini according to package directions. Rinse, drain and set aside.

2. Meanwhile, heat oil in 4-quart Dutch oven over medium-high heat until hot. Add onion, celery, carrot and garlic. Reduce heat to medium; cook and stir 5 to 6 minutes or until vegetables are crisp-tender.

3. Remove from heat. Stir in flour, Italian seasoning, crushed red pepper and black pepper until well blended. Gradually stir in broth. Return to heat and bring to a boil, stirring frequently. Boil, stirring constantly, 1 minute. Reduce heat to medium. Stir in cooked pasta, chick-peas and tomatoes. Cook 5 minutes or until heated through.

4. Meanwhile, place bacon between double layer of paper towels on paper plate. Microwave on HIGH 5 to 6 minutes or until bacon is crisp. Drain and crumble.

5. Sprinkle each serving with bacon. Serve immediately.

Makes 6 servings (about 7 cups)

SERVING SUGGESTION: Top with grated Parmesan cheese and serve with crusty bread, salad greens tossed with Italian dressing and fruit cobbler.

Prep and cook time: 30 minutes

359 SPAM™ CORN CHOWDER

1 cup chopped onion
1 tablespoon butter or margarine
1½ cups diced peeled potatoes
½ cup chopped green bell pepper
2 (17-ounce) cans cream-style corn
2 cups milk
1 (12-ounce) can SPAM® Luncheon Meat, cubed

In 3-quart saucepan over medium heat, sauté onion in butter 5 to 10 minutes or until golden. Add potatoes and bell pepper. Cook and stir 2 minutes. Add corn and milk. Bring to a boil. Reduce heat and simmer 15 minutes or until potatoes are tender, stirring occasionally. Stir in Spam®. Simmer 2 minutes. *Makes 6 to 8 servings*

ROBUST STEWS & CHILIES

360 BAJA CORN CHOWDER

¼ **cup butter or margarine**
3 **cans (17 ounces each) whole kernel corn, drained, divided**
1 **medium red bell pepper, diced**
2 **cups chicken broth**
1 **quart half-and-half**
1 **can (7 ounces) diced green chilies, drained**
1 **package (1.27 ounces) LAWRY'S® Spices & Seasonings for Fajitas**
2 **cups (8 ounces) shredded Monterey jack cheese**
½ **teaspoon LAWRY'S® Seasoned Pepper**
Hot pepper sauce to taste

In Dutch oven or large saucepan, melt butter. Add one can of corn and bell pepper; cook over medium-high heat 5 minutes, stirring occasionally. Remove from heat. In food processor or blender, place remaining two cans of corn and chicken broth; process until smooth. Add to Dutch oven with half-and-half, chilies and Spices & Seasonings for Fajitas. Return to heat. Bring just to a boil over medium-high heat, stirring constantly. Remove from heat; blend in cheese, Seasoned Pepper and hot pepper sauce.

Makes 4 to 6 servings

SERVING SUGGESTION: Serve with warmed corn tortillas and honey butter.

361 VEG–ALL® CHEESY CHOWDER

¼ **cup butter**
1 **medium onion, chopped**
⅓ **cup all-purpose flour**
2 **cups milk**
1 **(10¾-ounce) can chicken broth**
1 **package (8 ounces) pasteurized process cheese spread, cubed**
¼ **teaspoon hot pepper sauce**
¼ **teaspoon white pepper**
1 **(15-ounce) can VEG-ALL® Mixed Vegetables, drained**
2 **tablespoons chopped parsley**

Melt butter in large saucepan. Add onion; cook until tender. Add flour, whisking until smooth. Cook 1 minute over low heat, stirring constantly. Gradually add milk and chicken broth; cook over medium heat, stirring constantly until thickened and bubbly. Add cheese and seasonings, stirring until cheese is melted. Add Veg-All® and parsley. Reduce heat and cook until thoroughly heated. Do not boil.

Makes 6 servings

ROBUST STEWS & CHILIES

362 KALEIDOSCOPE CHOWDER

3 cups water
3 large potatoes, peeled and diced
1 (26-ounce) jar NEWMAN'S OWN®
    Diavolo Sauce
2 large carrots, peeled and thinly sliced
1½ to 2 pounds assorted seafood, such as
    fish fillets, bay scallops, shrimp or
    clams
½ cup dry white wine
2 cups shredded fresh spinach leaves
1 yellow bell pepper, seeded and diced
    Freshly grated Parmesan cheese

In large stockpot, bring water to a boil. Add potatoes; cook 5 minutes. Stir in Newman's Own® Diavolo Sauce and carrots. Bring to a boil; reduce heat and simmer 5 minutes.

Cut fish fillets into bite-size pieces. Peel and devein shrimp. Add seafood and wine to soup. Cook over medium-high heat, stirring often, until fish is opaque, 3 to 4 minutes. Add spinach and pepper; cover. Remove from heat and let stand until spinach and pepper are heated through, about 2 minutes. Serve with Parmesan cheese.

Makes 4 servings

TIP: This chowder is also excellent with diced cooked chicken breast.

363 TUNA CORN CHOWDER

2 strips bacon
1 small onion
2 ribs celery, chopped
1½ tablespoons all-purpose flour
2 cups 2% milk
½ teaspoon dried thyme leaves
¼ teaspoon salt
¼ teaspoon black pepper
1 cup frozen whole kernel corn
1 can (6 ounces) tuna packed in water,
    drained

1. Cook bacon in large saucepan over medium-high heat until browned and crisp, turning once. Drain on paper towels, reserving drippings in saucepan.

2. Add onion and celery to pan drippings; cook and stir over medium-high heat 3 minutes or until softened.

3. Add flour, stirring until well blended; cook 1 minute. Stir in milk, thyme, salt and pepper. Cook, stirring frequently, until thickened.

4. Stir in corn and tuna; cook over medium heat 5 minutes or until corn is tender, stirring frequently.

5. Crumble bacon. Serve chowder sprinkled with bacon. *Makes 2 servings*

For a special touch, top chowder with red bell pepper strips or popped popcorn.

Prep and cook time: 25 minutes

Kaleidoscope Chowder

ROBUST STEWS & CHILIES

364 CORN AND TOMATO CHOWDER

1½ cups plum tomatoes, peeled and diced
¾ teaspoon salt, divided
2 ears corn, husks removed
1 tablespoon margarine
½ cup finely chopped shallots
1 clove garlic, minced
1 can (12 ounces) evaporated skimmed milk
1 cup chicken broth
1 tablespoon finely chopped fresh sage *or* 1 teaspoon rubbed sage
¼ teaspoon black pepper
1 tablespoon cornstarch
2 tablespoons cold water

1. Place tomatoes in nonmetal colander over bowl. Sprinkle ½ teaspoon salt on top; toss to mix well. Allow tomatoes to drain at least 1 hour.

2. Meanwhile, cut corn kernels off the cobs into small bowl. Scrape cobs with dull side of knife to extract liquid from cobs into same bowl; set aside. Discard 1 cob; break remaining cob in half.

3. Heat margarine in heavy medium saucepan over medium-high heat until melted and bubbly. Add shallots and garlic; reduce heat to low. Cover and cook about 5 minutes or until shallots are soft and translucent. Add milk, broth, sage, pepper and reserved corn cob halves. Bring to a boil over high heat. Reduce heat to low; simmer, uncovered, 10 minutes. Remove and discard cob halves.

4. Add corn with liquid; return to a boil over medium-high heat. Reduce heat to low; simmer, uncovered, 15 minutes more. Dissolve cornstarch in water; add to chowder, mixing well. Stir until thickened. Remove from heat; stir in drained tomatoes and remaining ¼ teaspoon salt. Spoon into bowls. Garnish with additional fresh sage, if desired. *Makes 6 appetizer servings*

365 HUNT'S® HEARTY MANHATTAN CLAM CHOWDER

2 slices bacon, cut into ½-inch pieces
½ cup chopped onion
½ cup chopped celery
1 (14½-ounce) can HUNT'S® Whole Peeled Tomatoes, undrained and crushed
1 (14½-ounce) can whole new potatoes, drained and cubed
1 (8-ounce) bottle clam juice
1 (6½-ounce) can chopped clams, drained and rinsed
2 tablespoons chopped fresh parsley
¼ teaspoon thyme
⅛ teaspoon pepper
⅛ teaspoon garlic powder

In large saucepan, fry bacon until crisp. Add onion and celery; sauté until tender. Stir in tomatoes, potatoes, clam juice, clams, parsley, thyme, pepper and garlic powder. Simmer, uncovered, 15 minutes, stirring occasionally. *Makes 4 servings*

Corn and Tomato Chowder

ACKNOWLEDGMENTS

The publisher would like to thank the companies and organizations listed below for the use of their recipes and photographs in this publication.

A.1.® Steak Sauce

Alpine Lace Brands, Inc.

American Lamb Council

Birds Eye®

California Olive Industry

California Poultry Industry Federation

California Wild Rice Advisory Board

Chef Paul Prudhomme's Magic Seasoning Blends®

COLLEGE INN® Broth

Corte & Co.

Cucina Classica Italiana, Inc.

Del Monte Corporation

Delmarva Poultry Industry, Inc.

Filippo Berio Olive Oil

FLEISCHMANN'S® Original Spread

Florida Tomato Committee

GREY POUPON® Mustard

Guiltless Gourmet®

Harveys® Bristol Cream®

Hormel Foods Corporation

Hunt-Wesson, Inc.

Kahlúa® Liqueur

Kellogg Company

Kikkoman International Inc.

Kraft Foods, Inc.

Lawry's ® Foods, Inc.

McIlhenny Company (Tabasco® pepper sauce)

Minnesota Cultivated Wild Rice Council

MOTT'S® Inc., a division of Cadbury Beverages Inc.

Nabisco Biscuit Company

National Fisheries Institute

National Foods

National Pork Producers Council

National Turkey Federation

Nestlé USA, Inc.

Newman's Own, Inc.®

Norseland, Inc.

Perdue Farms Incorporated

Reckitt & Colman Inc.

The Rival Company Crock-Pot® is a registered Trademark of the Rival Company

Riviana Foods Inc.

StarKist® Seafood Company

The Sugar Association, Inc.

USA Rice Federation

Veg-All®

Wisconsin Milk Marketing Board

INDEX

INDEX

INDEX

INDEX

INDEX

METRIC CONVERSION CHART

VOLUME MEASUREMENTS (dry)

¹/₈ teaspoon = 0.5 mL
¹/₄ teaspoon = 1 mL
¹/₂ teaspoon = 2 mL
³/₄ teaspoon = 4 mL
1 teaspoon = 5 mL
1 tablespoon = 15 mL
2 tablespoons = 30 mL
¹/₄ cup = 60 mL
¹/₃ cup = 75 mL
¹/₂ cup = 125 mL
²/₃ cup = 150 mL
³/₄ cup = 175 mL
1 cup = 250 mL
2 cups = 1 pint = 500 mL
3 cups = 750 mL
4 cups = 1 quart = 1 L

VOLUME MEASUREMENTS (fluid)

1 fluid ounce (2 tablespoons) = 30 mL
4 fluid ounces (¹/₂ cup) = 125 mL
8 fluid ounces (1 cup) = 250 mL
12 fluid ounces (1¹/₂ cups) = 375 mL
16 fluid ounces (2 cups) = 500 mL

WEIGHTS (mass)

¹/₂ ounce = 15 g
1 ounce = 30 g
3 ounces = 90 g
4 ounces = 120 g
8 ounces = 225 g
10 ounces = 285 g
12 ounces = 360 g
16 ounces = 1 pound = 450 g

DIMENSIONS

¹/₁₆ inch = 2 mm
¹/₈ inch = 3 mm
¹/₄ inch = 6 mm
¹/₂ inch = 1.5 cm
³/₄ inch = 2 cm
1 inch = 2.5 cm

OVEN TEMPERATURES

250°F = 120°C
275°F = 140°C
300°F = 150°C
325°F = 160°C
350°F = 180°C
375°F = 190°C
400°F = 200°C
425°F = 220°C
450°F = 230°C

BAKING PAN SIZES

Utensil	Size in Inches/Quarts	Metric Volume	Size in Centimeters
Baking or	8×8×2	2 L	20×20×5
Cake Pan	9×9×2	2.5 L	23×23×5
(square or	12×8×2	3 L	30×20×5
rectangular)	13×9×2	3.5 L	33×23×5
Loaf Pan	8×4×3	1.5 L	20×10×7
	9×5×3	2 L	23×13×7
Round Layer	8×1½	1.2 L	20×4
Cake Pan	9×1½	1.5 L	23×4
Pie Plate	8×1¼	750 mL	20×3
	9×1¼	1 L	23×3
Baking Dish	1 quart	1 L	—
or Casserole	1½ quart	1.5 L	—
	2 quart	2 L	—